# THE PRE-WRATH RAPTURE OF THE CHURCH

# THE PRE-WRATH RAPTURE OF THE CHURCH

Marvin Rosenthal

THOMAS NELSON PUBLISHERS
*Nashville*

Published in Nashville, Tennessee, by Thomas Nelson, Inc., and distributed in Canada by Lawson Falle, Ltd., Cambridge, Ontario.

Printed in the United States of America.



**Library of Congress Cataloging-in-Publication Data**

Rosenthal, Marvin J.
The prewrath rapture of the church / Marvin J. Rosenthal.
Includes bibliographical references.
ISBN 0-8407-3160-4
1. Rapture (Christian eschatology) I. Title.
BT887.R67 1990
236′.9—dc20 89-78174
CIP

During the writing of this book, more than two thousand believers called or wrote me to offer encouragement. These "citizens of Heaven" included students, homemakers, businessmen, pastors, missionaries, seminary professors, and college presidents. Their views concerning the timing of Christ's return to rapture the Church were varied, but they almost unanimously shared these thoughts in common:

> First, the conviction that the timing of the Rapture (not the fact of it) should not be a divisive issue among those redeemed through the blood of the Lamb.
>
> Second, an eagerness to see *The Prewrath Rapture of the Church* published, with the promise that they will read the manuscript with a pure heart and an open mind.

To such fair-minded men and women who heeded the inspired penman's warning, "He that answereth a matter before he heareth it, it is folly and shame unto him" (Prov. 18:13), it is only fitting that this book be warmly dedicated. God knows them, each one.

# CONTENTS

## PART I: JESUS IS COMING



## PART II: THE DAY OF THE LORD



## PART III: THE PREWRATH RAPTURE

# LIST OF ILLUSTRATIONS

# INTRODUCTION

It is important that a word be shared concerning the tone of this book and the importance of prophetic truth. Any consideration of the timing of the Rapture of the church carries with it the potential to stir great emotion. Tragically, on occasion, books on the Rapture have been written with ink dipped in acid; sermons have been preached with little grace and thoughtfulness for others; and lectures have been given that vilify and malign individuals with differing Rapture views than one's own. Of course, such has been done with the conviction that right doctrine has been defended and God's holiness vindicated. But the result has sometimes been splintered ministries, severed friendships, and a reproach on the name of Christ.

In reaction to those potentially unpleasant prospects, some people have relegated the study of prophecy to "the back burner," or worse, taken it "off the stove" altogether. What an indescribably tragic mistake! If prophetic truth is unimportant, then the question of why God included prophecy in His Word must be answered. It has been estimated that as much as one third of the Bible was prophetic at the time it was written. Much was literally fulfilled at Christ's first coming; the rest will be literally fulfilled when He comes the second time.

The importance of understanding still unfulfilled prophecy for contemporary Christian living cannot be overstated. The practicality of prophetic truth is a repeated theme of the inspired New Testament writers. That importance is only heightened and magnified if we are living on the threshold of the end of this age as many competent Bible teachers believe. The twentieth century Bible-believing church simply cannot afford the luxury of neglecting such a God-given treasure as the prophetic Word. If we do so, it will be at our own peril.

The faithful preacher is called upon to proclaim the whole counsel of God. That includes the prophetic Scriptures. Controversy should never be deliberately solicited, but it must never be feared or avoided if it comes as a result of faithful exposition of the Word of God.

Understanding the inherent danger of writing on the timing (the sequence of events, not the time) of the Rapture, I have attempted to address the issue with grace and tact, ever mindful of the frequently cited but not overworked admonition which proclaims that "brethren can disagree without being disagreeable."

I have not written so much as an academician as I have as a preacher; not so much as a scholar who presents a speculative position paper to his peers and inquires "What do you think?" as I have as a servant of the Lord with a crucial message from God's Word. Did I not believe passionately in the thesis of this book, were there any ongoing questioning or lingering hesitancy on my part, I would not have followed the path I now tread. The anguish that accompanies reversing a theological position tenaciously held for more than thirty years can only be fully fathomed by those who have traveled that road and felt its weight upon their shoulders.

In writing *The Prewrath Rapture of the Church,* I have genuinely attempted to show grace toward others—to exhibit love without compromise—without diminishing my own convictions.

If by some, my conviction and force is perceived to be vitriolic, or if for others, the path I have sought under God to forge is offensive, I humbly apologize. But my love for God and His people cannot allow me to write otherwise.

Marvin J. Rosenthal

## ACKNOWLEDGMENTS

Someone has wisely suggested that "saying 'thank you' may be a little thing, but it is never a small thing."

The circumstances surrounding the writing of this book caused the author to lapse into the "red ink" of indebtedness to a number of people and make saying "thank you" an imperative.

"Thank you" Marjorie Hall, for being a faithful friend and loyal secretary for sixteen years, but particularly during that especially tension-filled, final twelve-month period. "Thank you" for reading the manuscript and making helpful suggestions. Perhaps, "thank you" most of all for having confidence in me (by no means, blindly) when it was not a popular thing to do.

"Thank you" Amy Julian, for typing and retyping, checking and rechecking the manuscript, often under the pressure of time restraint and frequently at night or on the weekend. I will never forget that you postponed your surgery to be sure a draft of the manuscript was typed to meet a pressing deadline.

"Thank you" Tom Allen, friend and colleague, for your "sanctified" gift of art and graphics. The early charts, design, and typesetting required so very much work. But for you it was truly a labor of love for the Lord, the more complicated because of the myriad of changes I made. How patient you were with me. I will always remember the through-the-night sessions to get the manuscript completed on time.

"Thank you" David Douglas. You volunteered your (in the best sense) professional editorial skills to make *The Prewrath Rapture of the Church* the best it could be. Your sensitivity and tact in understanding that an author does not want his writing "radically" altered did not go unnoticed.

"Thank you" beloved Pastor Carter, Kathie, and members of

Grace Bible Church of Barrington, New Jersey. My change in conviction concerning the timing of Christ's return put you in a sensitive position. Without infringing on anyone's convictions, you prayed, encouraged, and loved us. You were an example of what a New Testament church should be.

"Thank you" Kevin Howard, young warrior for the faith. You evidenced the two qualities of conviction and courage. Your input into the content of this book has been considerable. Young "Timothy," you have taught me far more than you realize.

"Thank you" Bob VanKampen, for being a very special friend and servant of the Lord. You planted the seed of this book in my heart and mind. Without you, there would have been no book. You gave the impetus which got it started; your persistence kept it going.

"Thank you" David, for defying the generation gap. No father could ask of a son more than I received from you. Your manly courage, concern, and support for your dad will always be a cherished memory.

"Thank you" my darling wife, for traveling beside me during this glorious journey. Your prayers, love, and encouragement were my greatest strength. You were also my toughest critic. Your invaluable suggestions, checking each biblical reference, requests for clarification of the logic, and repeated proofing of each new draft were major contributions to this book.

If God be pleased, may the investment of each who played a part in bringing to fruition *The Prewrath Rapture of the Church* bear eternal dividends.

# PART I

## JESUS IS COMING

# 1

# The Tension and Anguish Surrounding a Consideration of the Timing of the Rapture

Men normally write books because that is what they want to do. I had no desire to write this book. To do so has caused me the most difficult, tension-filled, heart-wrenching two and a half years of my life. Nights of prayer, agonizing, and tears—only God and my wife will ever know how extensive all three were. It is not my desire to be personal, but it will help you to better understand what I have written if you understand how I came to write it.

It began in the year 1986 while at the home of a friend and Christian businessman. He asked me some questions about pretribulation rapturism—the belief that Christ will rapture the church before the tribulation period begins. I answered his questions and thought the issue was settled. How very wrong I was. Several days later the phone rang; it was my friend, and there were some more questions. Once again, I patiently answered his questions. I was certain the difficulties were now resolved. But when the long-distance calls continued almost daily for three months, it became clear that the issue had not yet been put to rest. But by now I knew four things about my friend: He had bulldog tenacity, an unswerving commitment to the great fundamentals of the Christian faith, an amazingly logical mind, and a genuine concern about the timing of the Rapture. To him, any doctrine as important as the Rapture of the church had to be clearly taught in the Word of God itself. The timing of the Rapture could not rest on inference, or a supposedly consistent dispensational approach to Scripture; nor could it rest primarily, as some leading pretribulation rapturists suggest, on the doctrine of ecclesiology with its clear distinction between Israel and the church. He knew that the pretribulation rapture was impossible to prove exegetically. To him the doctrine of the Rapture had to be built primarily on what the Bible specifically says about end-time events.

Then one day my persistent friend called and spoke with more exuberance than usual. The only word that comes to my mind to describe that conversation is *eureka—I found it!* (He had been searching for fifteen years.) "Try this on," he suggested. "The Rapture of the church will occur immediately prior to the Day of the Lord, and the Day of the Lord begins with the opening of the seventh seal" (Rev. 8:1). He went on to share some of the logic behind his conclusion. He was sure he had "found it"—the timing of the Rapture—but I was not quite so optimistic. Good and godly men have been debating when "it" would occur for centuries; and besides, I was a convinced, sincere, unbending, and, in retrospect, to my shame, intolerant pretribulation rapturist for thirty-five years. My pretribulation rapture position was widely known. I had preached it with conviction and sincerity around the world. I had not been hiding it under a bushel. I am both on tape and in print supporting pretribulation rapturism. The Friends of Israel Gospel Ministry is a Bible-believing faith mission which I directed. Upon my recommendation, the board of trustees unanimously approved a doctrinal statement which embraced pretribulation rapturism. I have par-

The timing of the Rapture could not rest on inference, or a supposedly consistent dispensational approach to Scripture.

ticipated in many of the major prophetic conferences in North America, in churches, schools, and Bible conferences—and always as a pretribulation rapturist. I edited and published *Israel My Glory,* a magazine with a circulation of over three hundred thousand subscribers and a readership of almost a million people, and all articles had to be consistent with pretribulation rapturism. The schools I attended, my contemporary heroes of the faith, the overwhelming majority of churches in which I minister, and all of my beloved colleagues in the ministry are pretribulation rapturists. My friend had "found it," but I wasn't at all convinced. I was an uncompromising pretribulationist.

But through many more months of conversation and biblical investigation, something began to happen. I can only describe it by saying that I believe the Spirit of God began to sow a seed of honest inquiry in my heart. Was it possible? Could it be? Notwithstanding my earnestness and sincerity, was I proclaiming a concept which the Bible did not substantiate? Was I prescribing a false hope? Could I be dispensing candy-coated pills that tasted good but did no good? And in the doing, was I keeping from God's children a medicine that would truly help? Was I, however unintentionally, misinterpreting a considerable body of truth, truth that God intended to be a catalyst for holy living at all times and of paramount importance for the generation of believers that will, in fact, move into the seventieth week of the book of Daniel? The very thought troubled me. Of this I was certain: I could not be passive on this question. I would have to go back and reexamine the biblical basis for my pretribulation position and, while I was at it, the mid- and posttribulation positions as well.

(I would encourage those for whom some of these terms are unfamiliar to press on. In due course and proper sequence, terms will be clearly defined and charts provided to illustrate the facts being presented. The content of this book will unfold for you, in an orderly fashion, many of the important prophetic issues over which Bible teachers struggle. Most importantly, these issues have practical implications for your life.)

Although it is never completely possible to be objective, because we are, to a larger degree than perhaps we are willing to admit, a product of our environment and training, I determined to do my best. I had no flag to fly, no hobbyhorse to ride, no point to prove. In the many months that followed, I literally read or did research in hundreds of books of all rapture persuasions. I am committed to the proposition that God has given gifted men to the church—among them teachers from whom I can learn. But I always returned to the Bible as my final authority.

In the blush of those early days, I shared with an esteemed colleague and friend the fact that I had begun my odyssey. His counsel, if heeded, could have saved me a great deal of grief. His words, as I remember them, went like this: "Marv, stay away from it; it's too hot to handle; it will get you into trouble."

Pragmatic counsel, those words. But I am a biblicist. My life has been invested in the preaching of the "whole counsel of God." Whatever other shortcomings I may have in my life—and admittedly there are many—I have never played politics with God's Word. I knew from the beginning, therefore, that I must follow that Word wherever it leads and whatever the personal consequences.

A number of Christian leaders, when they heard that I was pursuing this study, counseled a friend to tell me to "drop it; it would only add confusion to an already confused issue." But my mind reminded my heart that God's Word never tends toward confusion. Jesus' declaration was, for me, greatly encouraging: "Ye shall know the truth, and the truth shall make you free" (John 8:32)—meaning in context, free from the erroneous concept that the Law is a basis for righteousness. But more than that, I knew God's truth emancipates from *all* error.

I began to see the simple but compelling logic of my businessman friend's thinking in Scripture. By now he had purchased two computers, one for himself and one for me. We were on the phone daily, often early in the morning or late at night, sometimes for hours at a time. Rough concepts were put into his computer, discussed, debated, modified, submitted to the platinum yardstick of the Word of God, and often later discarded when seen to be inconsistent with what we viewed as clear biblical truth. We were not trying to defend a system but to allow the Word of God to lead us where it would.

By this time I wanted additional help. I wanted an objective evaluation of where I felt our study was leading us, not verification for an approach that was new, still very much incomplete, and with a multitude of loose ends. I solicited that help from a highly qualified Christian leader. His response was an eighty-eight-page refutation of a rough, preliminary document which my businessman friend had prepared.

I was hoping for nonadversarial counsel—counsel I eagerly sought—but that would not be the case. This experience did enable me to see with greater clarity the emotional implications bound up in the Rapture issue—and the almost reflexive defense posture that is often taken when one's view of the Rapture is questioned. The new position being espoused was not, in my opinion, examined for merit. It was attacked out of fear and intimidation. The reviewer shared the fact that he spent two sleepless weeks contemplating the implications of the position being espoused. If it were right, he was wrong. It was that simple.

I should have understood those facts more fully from the beginning. The Rapture question as popularly presented is, by the very nature of the case, filled with emotion and controversy. Do we get raptured before the Tribulation begins—and thereby escape its horrors? Will we be raptured in the middle of the Tribulation—and escape the worst of it? Or will we be raptured at its end and endure all its terrors before Christ's return? Theologians and Bible teachers, perhaps more than individuals in most other disciplines, are trained to be narrow and dogmatic (in a good sense), to be "set for the defense of the gospel" (Phil. 1:17). But sometimes it is difficult to know where dogma ends and doctrine begins.

Orthodox dogma (that great body of biblical truth that has been held by true believers down through the centuries) is fixed, inviolable, irrescindable, nonnegotiable. Literal creationism, verbal plenary inspiration of the Bible, the virgin birth, the deity of Christ, substitutionary atonement, bodily resurrection, Christ's ascension and enthronement, His second coming, a literal heaven and hell, eternal condemnation of the wicked, eternal bliss for the righteous—these are examples of dogma. Doctrine is somewhat different. We are commanded to "grow in grace, and in the knowledge of our Lord and Saviour Jesus Christ" (2 Pet. 3:18). Growing in "knowledge" of necessity includes learning new truth, examining old truth, and correcting what was erroneously held to be truth. I have never met a pastor who did not wish that he could withdraw some of his sermons, or a Bible professor who didn't lament the content of a lecture that was forever beyond retrieval. The moment we stop learning, examining, or correcting our doctrine, we stop growing.

Doctrines strongly held are not easily released—and that is good. That is as it should be. But sometimes men hold tenaciously to doctrines for many years, preach those doctrines, write about those doctrines, persuade people of those doctrines, and defend those doctrines until the doctrine becomes, in their minds, a dogma. They are no longer willing to submit that doctrine to the searchlight of the Word of God. Anyone who would dare to invade that domain is viewed as hostile—and that is sad and unfortunate. Better the attitude of Charles Haddon Spurgeon who, when asked if he defended the Bible, said, "Yes, the way I would defend a lion. I open the cage and let it out." Christians need not be intimidated by those who legitimately question some area of theology. The Word of God is its own defense.

But now I had a problem. Word would spread quickly that I was rethinking my view of the Rapture. It was, in fact, already spreading from other sources. Distortions would inevitably manifest themselves, as indeed they did. Some thought I had become an amillenarian, others a mid- or posttribulation rapturist. One story spread that I had mental problems, another that the Mission had closed. One Bible teacher, on hearsay alone, suggested to a friend that I had come up with a new doctrine that was "off the wall."

Charles Haddon Spurgeon . . . when asked if he defended the Bible, said, "Yes, the way I would defend a lion. I open the cage and let it out."

I had hoped that during my reevaluation I could avoid unnecessary and distorted rumors. It was quite possible that I would find theological obstacles and drop the whole matter. Now I realized that was impossible.

In less than a week, the board of trustees of the Mission would meet. It was the regularly scheduled annual meeting. All members would be present, and most of their wives. A catered dinner was planned. It was to be a time of rejoicing. The Mission was celebrating its fiftieth anniversary. Only weeks before we had hosted our Jubilee and National Staff Conference. An estimated five thousand people had attended the various functions. Things were further complicated by the fact that three years of planning, work, and expense had brought us to the brink of breaking ground for a new $6,500,000 academic and conference center, a facility that would greatly expand the Mission's ministry for the cause of Christ.

There could be no delay. I picked up the phone and called the chairman of the board and the Mission's lawyer. The latter was also on the board of trustees. My struggle with the timing of the Rapture and its implications for the Mission had to be on the agenda. The scheduling could not have been worse, even if I had planned it. The nights before the meeting were sleepless ones for me. The tension in my soul was excruciating. I had been director of the Mission for almost sixteen years. Under God, the Mission had experienced dramatic growth. Few ministries in history had impacted a greater number of Jewish people with the claims of Christ.

But there was far more involved. Thirty-seven thousand pastors were among the more than three hundred thousand people who regularly received the Mission magazine, *Israel My Glory*. Several hundred thousand cassette tapes were sent out annually; increasingly large numbers of books and tracts were being published and distributed; the number of our field evangelists and missionaries in North America and abroad was rapidly expanding; our exciting and growing Institute of Biblical Studies was entering its third year and was being used to train new missionaries and Christian workers. The opportunity for the Mission to evangelize the lost and provide solid teaching for God's people was virtually unlimited. Then there was Bible scholarship aid to worthy students, financial help to needy believers in Israel and behind the Iron Curtain, and new missionaries who had just settled into new homes.

I knew full well that God did not need me. He alone had raised up the Mission fifty years earlier; He alone had sustained it; and to Him alone belongs all the glory. But reality also forced me to conclude that for almost sixteen years I had been God's choice to direct the Mission. The budget had grown from less than $300,000 in 1972 to more than $5,000,000 in 1988. Eighteen thousand dollars was needed every workday to meet the Mission's needs. And not once in sixteen years did money have to be borrowed for general operating expenses. God had simply provided in an amazing way.

Multitudes of our supporters were personal friends. Would

they feel I had let them down? Worse, that I had betrayed them? Would the thousands of Bible-believing churches (mostly pretribulational in doctrine and whose godly pastors and missions committees had urged them to support the ministry of The Friends of Israel) understand? Would the Mission suffer irreparable harm if I were to stay? On the other hand, would it be worse for the Mission if I left?

These and a myriad of other questions flooded my soul that Thursday afternoon as I met with the board. I would have preferred to have been almost anywhere else in the world. And I would have given almost anything not to have had to share with the board what I felt compelled to share on that occasion.

I blurted it out: "Gentlemen, I am reexamining my view regarding the timing of the Rapture of the church. It will take me until late fall. Unless something surfaces which I have not yet seen, I will not be able to sign the doctrinal statement of the Mission." That comment put me in conflict with my board—to a man, among my dearest friends. My awkwardness only heightened the situation. No presentation of my thinking was shared, only the fact of it. I was dismissed from the meeting and summoned back about two hours later. The board had reconfirmed its pretribulational position and called for all board members to sign the doctrinal statement. They asked that I sign it with an asterisk noting that I was reevaluating my position. I acknowledged that I would. I volunteered that when the rough written draft of my study was completed, I would provide a copy for each board member and a number of nationally known theologians for evaluation and comment. If my growing conviction were fatally flawed, I would be grateful for evidence of that before I was in print. I strongly hoped that these men would evaluate with a measure of objectivity without feeling intimidated. While the board did not commit to any formal consideration of my emerging position, they did ask that I proceed and keep them informed. The dinner that followed the meeting was intended to be a joyous occasion, a glorious celebration. Instead, it turned into a strained affair not far removed from the atmosphere of a wake.

In the days that followed, I was very low. For a person who is normally almost never down, I was emotionally drained. I found myself weeping far more than I would like my masculinity to admit. How could I cause so much hurt to so many people? But how could I also abandon truth which I believed was more strongly substantiated by Scripture than the position I had previously held for thirty-five years?

The board wisely chose to inform the Mission administrators, and a general statement was given to the field staff alerting them to a possible problem. In the office, everyone knew there was a problem, although few were aware of the details. It was most difficult for the administrators. They knew more of what was involved. Most were formally trained theologians, each his own man, each with strong personal convictions, each committed to pretribulation rapturism—each and every one not simply a colleague but a close personal friend. They were caught in the painful vice of friendship and loyalty to me and a greater loyalty to God and their spiritual convictions. Each one was, in his own way, agonizing over the future of the Mission. I prayed for them each night and wished that I could do more. Without solicitation on their part, my action had placed a cloud of uncertainty over their own ministries and the future of the Mission. I wondered, what would the board do? If the doctrinal statement were broadened to accommodate my emerging position, could the administrators live with it? If not, where would they go? What would they do? And, on the other hand, if I left, what negative impact would that have on the Mission? Everyone tried to avoid the subject and to function as if all were normal, but tension between most of the administrators and me became evident.

There was one simplistic solution. It would be so easy, I thought. If only I could convince myself that my growing conviction was wrong. If only I could find something I had missed, a verse that blocked a major artery in my scheme of things, a commentary that would show me the error of my way. I had been exposed to pretribulation thinking most of my life. Nonetheless, I went back and read from my heroes: John F. Walvoord, a good acquaintance and a dean of pretribulationism; Charles C. Ryrie, under whom I had the privilege of taking several courses at Bible college and seminary and for whose theological insight I have the greatest esteem; J. Dwight Pentecost and his standard work *Things to Come*. I also consulted numerous commentaries on Daniel, Matthew, the Gospel of John, 1 Corinthians, 1 and 2 Thessalonians, James, 1 and 2 Peter, 1 John, Revelation; books on the Rapture; books on the Millennium; an unpublished doctoral dissertation on "The Day of the Lord"; articles that were recommended; and back to the earlier mentioned eighty-eight-page refutation. I would read it again; perhaps I had missed something, anything that would allow me *genuine* reasonable doubt for the position toward which I was being increasingly drawn. I prayed for a way out. I wanted it so badly—something, anything that would allow me to walk back into the presence of my board with head down, repentant, apologetic for my error and all the confusion and hurt I had caused. Oh, how I would have welcomed an opportunity to make amends. But I could not find the "reasonable doubt" that I sought, though I searched with my whole heart.

Instead, I found an abundance of arguments which I believe devastate posttribulationism. I read with profit Robert Gundry's well-written posttribulational book, *The Church and the Tribulation,* which identified and then did radical surgery on some areas of pretribulationism, and John Sproule's excellent, if brief and in some areas courageously concessionary, responses to Gundry. I read men like Gleason Archer and Harold Ockenga, who see problems in both pretribulation rapturism and posttribulation rapturism and have championed the mediating position of midtribulationism. They, and others like them, came tantalizingly close, missing the mark, in my view, only because they did not distinguish between the Great Tribulation, which begins at the middle of the seventieth week, and the Day of the Lord, which begins, as will be demonstrated, with the opening of the seventh seal of Revelation. I applaud the honesty of men like Paul Feinberg[1] and Richard Mahue,[2] both minority view pretribulation rapturists, who maintain that the Day of the Lord cannot begin at the beginning of the seventieth week of Daniel, a position pretribulationists largely assume in their writings.[3]

But there was no release for the anguish of my soul. In retrospect, I realize now that I had to travail if there were to be a birth. I should have known that early on. I have always believed that sermons are not so much prepared as they are *given birth to*. Without travail there can be no life. As I studied and prayed, the pains became sharper and came faster. There appeared to be no relief, no anesthesia that could help.

Then one day the phone rang. It was a conference call. On the line were the chairman of the board and the Mission lawyer. They were part of a board-appointed ad hoc committee authorized to act for the board in taking action if quickly needed, assisting me wherever possible, and keeping the board abreast of all developments. Some time had passed since my announcement had shocked the board out of a joyous mood and into a somber, anxious one. They had never heard a presentation of the position I was espousing. They only knew that it was not traditional pretribulation rapturism—that I placed the "catching up" of the church somewhere inside the Tribulation period, not before it. It was time, we agreed, that the board be given that presentation. *After all, the same doctrinal statement stating that the Mission was pretribulational also stated that the Bible was the final authority for doctrine and practice—the ultimate yardstick.*

But there were to be some ground rules. This was not to be an adversarial session. Both the board and I wanted God's will and what would ultimately be best for the cause of Christ and the Mission. First, they clearly understood that I was not fighting for my job and that I was willing to step down, with love for them and absolutely no animosity toward the Mission, the moment they felt it would be in the best interest of the ministry. Second, I was to present my view intellectually and factually but without the force of advocacy—a tightrope walk requiring considerable tactfulness. They were not seeking so much to evaluate the details of the position theologically as to understand the big picture practically. How radical was it? How biblical? How logical? Third, no final decision concerning my status was to be made at that meeting. This latter point was largely due to the efforts of the Mission attorney. He neither rejected nor accepted my view, but he believed in my personal integrity and in my passion for the Word of God. He was convinced that a view I espoused so strongly and with so much at stake could not be without some biblical merit. Perhaps more significantly, he felt that one's view of the timing of the Rapture should not be a divisive issue among believers. During a telephone conversation he said, "Marv, we've got to massage the problem; we can't act hastily; we've got to give it time; we've got to allow the Spirit to work in all of our hearts." He was right, and I realized that the process entered into by God-fearing men was in itself important, whatever the outcome. Within my heart there was a silent chuckle as I reflected on his comment. "We've got to massage the problem"—the words of a lawyer. "We've got to give the Spirit time to work"—the wisdom of a mature believer. I threw away the letter of resignation that he didn't know I was in the midst of writing.

And so I met with the board within those guidelines. There was no hostility; the atmosphere was congenial. For six hours, with the aid of transparencies, as clearly as I could, I enunciated my views. When I concluded, there was a time of silence. From my vantage point, a number of things came into focus. First, most of these men had come to the meeting with an open heart and an open mind. Second, and perhaps most importantly, I am convinced that they realized the position I was espousing was not "off the wall," "simply sensationalizing," or without considerable biblical basis and logic. One board member, who had been doing a great deal of private study, publicly endorsed the position; two others would come to me privately sharing their genuine interest, expressing their appreciation, and promising to pursue the matter further. Others were cautious but warm.

Now the board discussion turned to other matters. Was the position that I presented a legitimate biblical alternative to existing views? The concern was not so much for whether it was right or wrong, but for whether it had merit. And further, could they justify in their own minds opening up the Mission doctrinal statement on the Rapture to accommodate this view? Never was consideration given to changing the doctrinal position to reflect my view. That would have been unfair to the entire Mission family.

The conversation then turned to personal issues. Every board member was associated with a church that was pretribulational; most served on other boards that were pretribulational; their friends were pretribulational; many of the godly pastors who had discipled them and whose remembrances they cherished were pretribulational, as were the Bible colleges and seminaries which some had served and supported much of their lives. Now concern was not simply about the implications for the Mission, but about the personal lives of its personnel as well. I thought to myself, *Could these men, some of whom are up in years, make that kind of decision? And should they have to?* Whatever the outcome, I was pleased to be associated with this fine group of men. They were struggling, some at considerable personal risk, to know and to do God's will.

I had entered that meeting welcoming the opportunity to share, but with the conviction and resolve that little or no potential for the board to broaden the doctrinal statement existed. I would be asked to resign at the conclusion of my study. *There were simply too many hurdles for them to overcome,* I thought. In the transition, I would do all I possibly could to lessen the shock of my departure for staff and constituency. But in the interim, the process remained important and had to be graciously carried forward. I left that meeting buoyed in spirit. It was a long shot, and I knew it. *But perhaps—just perhaps,* I thought—*God would lead that group of men to do what I viewed as being humanly impossible.*

A few days later I walked into the office of one of our administrators. He was not only an esteemed colleague but one of my closest personal friends. With the advent of my change in eschatology (the doctrine of last things), there was no denying that a tension began to exist between us. He shared with me the fact that his emotions, like an elevator, went up and then down. First he would be angry with me, and then he agonized in prayer for me. I purposely had kept him at a distance because I did not want to give the appearance of proselytizing for my view while the board was deliberating, nor did I want to become adversarial with a friend. I apologized for my tactlessness, and we talked for a long time. At the end of our conversation, teary-eyed, he stood up, reached across his desk, and shook my hand. I will never forget his magnanimous statement: "Marv, like you I have been burning the midnight oil. I don't believe that one's view concerning the timing of the Rapture should separate brethren. If the board opens the doctrinal statement to allow for your view without forcing it on others, I'll stay with the Mission for the good of the ministry and the cause of our Lord." I knew full well how much that decision could cost him personally. I also knew that his scholarship was appreciated by our missionaries and field evangelists and that his attitude could have a welcomed ripple effect on them.[4]

I left his office singing to God in psalms, hymns, and spiritual praises. Was the process moving ahead? Were we giving the Holy

Spirit time to work? I thought to myself, in my typical hyperbole, *Is God opening the Red Sea? Could there be a miracle, a way to walk through this dilemma on dry ground?*

I continued to cooperate with the board in the process. They had asked me to meet with the seven administrators to share with them my views in some detail. One of the administrators had, through an extended period of personal study, become convinced of the new position. He was, for me, a source of great encouragement and strength, and some of his insight and suggestions are reflected in this book. At least two others I believed to be sympathetic toward the board's opening up the doctrinal statement to accommodate my view without imposing it upon others.

But there were still four other men. How would they respond? I had already purposed in my heart that I could not allow my view to divide the Mission, not even if the board opened the doctrinal statement to permit my view. A dissenting voice or two—perhaps—but no more than that. We would have all we could handle to keep the Mission going forward with the external flak that was certain to come. We could not absorb that and internal problems too. I was certain that once this book was published and my position known, we could anticipate a substantial loss of support. But I also believed we could tighten our belt—curtail new initiatives—put a freeze on new personnel—cut corners—and *weather the storm*. The shock waves would perhaps last a year to eighteen months. And, in my view, we would be stronger on the other side. We would continue to be a Mission with a message of life in Christ to "the lost sheep of the house of Israel" (Matt. 10:6) and to the rest of the world God so loves, ready, under God, to be a catalyst, calling men to holiness, ready to challenge a lethargic, lukewarm, materialistic church in the tenth decade of the twentieth century to come back to God.

But for the moment at hand, I had to meet with the administrators. I had to present my view with conviction—but without overkill. I perceived then, and continue to believe, that the underlying problem is not the details of the position taken in this book. Rather, it is the pure shock that one's position on a significant area of prophecy is being threatened. The shock is all the greater when it comes internally—from someone *within the camp*. It is my opinion that if men of absolute neutrality, average intelligence, and belief in the authority of the Word of God were given an ideal presentation of the commonly held Rapture views and the one presented in this book, they would choose the latter because of its simplicity, clarity, logic, and, above all, because it would be seen as the fruit of an unstrained, clear, unified, and normative interpretation of the Word of God. But such ideal circumstances do not exist.

I remember sitting in a hotel lobby in Jerusalem with a very close acquaintance who is an Israeli tourist guide. It was after midnight, we were alone, and I was pressing the claims of Christ on his life. We had been talking for some time, as we had done on other occasions, and suddenly he blurted out in anguish, "Marvin, please, please, no more." He was not angry with me. He simply could not cope with the issue at hand. If I were right about Christ, then his father was wrong, his grandfather was wrong, his great-grandfather was wrong, our people had been wrong for nineteen hundred years. I was placing him under tremendous stress.

The issue may have been different, but it was not unlike the pressure I was placing on my colleagues. They had defended pretribulation rapturism for most of their lives, and so had their heroes before them. Now that position was being challenged.

They also had an additional problem. In the structure of the Mission, I was the chief executive, the director, and they were my subordinates. If they accepted or even condoned the position I was espousing, it would appear that they had caved in to my authority. Rightly, none of them wanted to be marked with that kind of weakness and capitulation.

Moreover, I had spent months in personal study before I could even bring myself to an intellectual state where I was able to say that maybe my pretribulation rapturism is wrong. How could I reasonably expect them to reach my conclusions so quickly?

At the initial meeting, the administrators sat for six hours, listened attentively, and afforded me every courtesy. When I concluded, one administrator spoke in support of the position. A second was impressed with its logic and fidelity to God's Word. All, I believed, were convinced in their hearts that I was not grandstanding, sensationalizing, or without biblical argument. None could summarily dismiss my position. They knew that it *could be* right, and I believe that it was intimidating for some of them. A time of discussion followed, not so much about the rightness or wrongness of the position, but about whether it was appropriate to broaden the doctrinal statement to permit my view and about how the fallout would affect the future of the Mission.

Two statements made that day did not escape my notice. The first statement was, "If Marv stays, his position will eventually dominate the Mission." I thought, *Perhaps he is right, and maybe it is inappropriate for me to stay*. But it also occurred to me that the comment was an oblique admission to the strength of my position. These were seminary-trained Bible teachers. If the view I espoused had no biblical basis and strength, the concern that it would one day dominate the Mission would not have surfaced. The second statement was a recommendation that was not adopted. It was a suggestion that each administrator take an important facet of my view and attempt to disprove it. I thought to myself, *There's that reflexive defense again. Why not examine it to see if it's right?* Someone may respond, "But that is against human nature." That is exactly right!

Amazingly, when I finished my presentation to the administrators, the agony of my soul disappeared; the intense labor pain within was gone. In its place was an indescribable peace that had no relationship to the ultimate resolution of the problem. I had attempted with grace, tact, and appropriateness to share my conviction—first with the board and then with the administrators. I had done all I could, as best I could. And now, as they spoke, I sat as if transfixed; not indifferent, but with the peace that passes understanding, ready to move in whatever direction my heavenly Father decreed.

On a number of occasions after that meeting I came very close to resigning. That would have been, for me, very easy and uncomplicated. But would it have been best for the Mission and, more importantly, was it God's will? Each time my mind was brought back to that good advice from the Mission attorney: "We have got to massage the problem. We've got to keep the process moving and give the Spirit time to work."

In May of 1989, the process came to an end. What no one wanted finally came to pass. By the smallest majority, the board could not in good conscience broaden the doctrinal statement to accommodate my view. I, in good conscience, could not sign the existing doctrinal statement. In practical terms that meant I would not be permitted to remain at the Mission. Obviously, it was a traumatic experience for all involved.

Now the book that I did not want to write has become a burning passion of my life. My prayer to God is that I can make clear in print what I am convinced is correct theology. Above all, I do not want to bring dishonor to my Lord or unnecessary confusion to the Body of Christ. But I must proclaim what I perceive, in the deepest recesses of my soul, to be crucial truth for the church I love at this strategic moment of history.

I will write as a lover from within the pretribulational camp, not as an opponent from without, seeking to nudge others to a modification of their view with what I believe to be biblical. I will, therefore, quote pretribulationists in the main, but with absolutely no ill feelings toward my premillennial brethren who hold other Rapture views. For me, the more I have grappled with the issue of the Rapture, the more tolerant I have become of other Rapture positions. There is absolutely no inconsistency in having a strong personal opinion and yet being tolerant of other views.

It is my observation that in recent years the theological trend is away from pretribulationism and toward posttribulationism. Calls that have been made for a new, scholarly book in defense of pretribulationism will not make significant changes in the status quo. The evidence has been sifted, the Scriptures that purportedly support pretribulationism proven scanty, and the arguments made. I believe there are no *hidden veins* in traditional pretribulationism yet to be mined. The position of this book preserves and defends the major premise of pretribulationism that the church is "not appointed . . . unto wrath"—not simply a brief span of wrath, as Robert Gundry suggests, but a substantial period of time encompassing the trumpet and bowl judgments. The issue is, When does the Day of the Lord's wrath begin? This book will not initially be perceived by some as an ally to pretribulationism, but I believe that history will one day substantiate it as such.

I write in great gratitude to those pretribulational scholars from whom I have profited so much and whose names I have found it difficult to bring myself to use when I think they are wrong or inconsistent in their teaching on the Rapture. Consequently, I will sometimes use terms like "pretribulationists say," or "many hold," or "some have suggested," although I have in my files specific names, quotes, and sources. There will be some essential exceptions.

I have written as simply as I can. In the technical sense, I am not a scholar, nor do I write primarily for scholars. But that is not to infer that the book is not scholarly. Much of the writing on prophecy is either highly sensational with little biblical basis or is confusedly technical and beyond the comprehension of the great body of believers who are desperately looking for clear, concise, and helpful teaching. I have never forgotten the words of a beloved professor who, although himself possessing two earned doctorates, said to his students, "Never forget that he who says it simplest says it best."

I write with a great sense of urgency. Conservative, evangelical Christianity, with which I identify, is in grave crisis at the present hour of history. In the church, historic foundations are cracking, values are slipping, humanism is penetrating, and materialism is dominating. I believe that the messages to the seven churches of Asia Minor (Rev. 2–3) are not descriptions of different periods of church history or characteristics of the church during all periods of its history, as pretribulationism is forced to conclude. Rather, the letters to the seven churches are an urgent warning call to *all* Christendom—a call to make one's salvation sure (2 Pet. 1:10)—a call to be *overcomers* (Rev. 2:7, 11, 17, 26; 3:5, 12, 21), not through exemption from the Tribulation by rapture, but by being willing to suffer and die for Christ, if necessary, under the persecution of the Antichrist—always, however, with the blessed hope of rapture before God's wrath is poured out during the Day of the Lord. In absolutely no sense does the potential for suffering before the Rapture negate the "blessed hope" (Titus 2:13). It will be demonstrated that the seals of Revelation 6 represent the climactic actions of unregenerate

Much of the writing on prophecy today is either highly sensational with little biblical basis or is confusedly technical and beyond the comprehension of the great body of believers.

men and that believers will not be exempt from those difficult days. The trumpets and bowls, in contrast, originate with God—they are His final wrath on an unbelieving world. God's children will be delivered from that day. That is the "blessed hope."

The central message of this book—the prewrath Rapture—if heeded by God's servants, could be a catalyst to call them to holiness and genuine revival during this crucial moment of history.

I write with a limited objective in view. I do not want to unduly speculate, nor do I want to confuse. Consequently, much that I view as significant is omitted because it does not deal directly with the issue at hand. Perhaps one day, if God wills it, that material will become a commentary on the book of Revelation. A by-product of the view herein espoused is a clear, logical, and sequential interpretation of the book of Revelation, the implications of which are tremendously significant for this hour of history.

However, the objective of this volume is to demonstrate that the Day of the Lord is the time of divine wrath. It will be recognized as about to begin by the cosmic disturbances associated with the sixth seal (Joel 2:10–11, 30–31; Rev. 6:12–17; cf. Matt. 24:29) and will begin with the opening of the seventh seal (Rev. 8:1). The Rapture of the church will immediately precede the Day of the Lord. The Day of the Lord will begin sometime within the second half of Daniel's seventieth week. I hope to marshal biblical evidence that makes that position clear, logical, and impregnable. I am confident that disagreement in areas like the treatment of "the sons of God" and "daughters of men," the parallel drawn between Abraham and Nimrod, and other matters of that nature will not blur the basic thesis of this book. Some chapters are less controversial, designedly devotional, and of a background nature, but all are very important to the whole.

I write at considerable personal cost—not as an ivory-tower theologian who may theorize but live apart from his theories. To be sincere, however, is not enough. Charles Caldwell Ryrie once quoted Charlie Brown, who, following a baseball game, commented, "How could we lose one hundred and thirty-eight to nothing, and we were so sincere?" Then Ryrie added, "But you did lose, Charlie Brown."

If I am wrong, ten thousand angels arguing my cause would not make it right, and I will have played the fool. If I am right, and one soul for whom Christ died enters the seventieth week of Daniel prepared to be an overcomer, I will be sufficiently rewarded. If that soul refuses the mark of the Antichrist, worships the Son of God only, and remains doctrinally pure like the church of Philadelphia (Rev. 3:7–13), I will rejoice.

# 2

# The Ultimate Absolute of History

Jesus is coming again. That fact is the ultimate absolute of history. In a context in which Jesus was discussing His Second Coming, He proclaimed, "Heaven and earth shall pass away, but my words shall not pass away" (Matt. 24:35). He was underscoring in the strongest possible way the absolute, inviolable certainty of His return. The solemnity of His statement is only heightened by the truth that God has exalted His Word above His name. The psalmist wrote, "Thou hast magnified thy word above all thy name" (Ps. 138:2). If His Word concerning His return is not true, His name is blemished, His character flawed. Unthinkable! "Let God be true, but every man a liar" (Rom. 3:4).

Jesus is coming again. Men can count on it and live in the light of that fact. There is no force in the universe that can successfully thwart the Father's purpose, that His Son will come again.

Almost two thousand years ago the Lord of glory visited and left His incomparable imprint on this planet. All of history and time literally revolve around that fact. When He stepped across the stars to this celestial ball, less than a dot on the face of an infinite landscape, it was "the fullness of the time" (Gal. 4:4). In the vernacular of the late twentieth century, *all systems were go*. It was "the fullness of the time" for the Son of God to make His appearance because of the confluence of divinely appointed events that merged together to make it so.

It was "the fullness of the time" because of Roman roads. It was, in the first century, no empty cliché to say, "All roads lead to Rome," for wherever her armies marched in conquest, her engineers went to build the roads. But those roads would fulfill another purpose. They would literally *pave* the way for the disciples, who would be under sovereign orders to go "into all the world, and preach the gospel to every creature" (Mark 16:15).

It was "the fullness of the time" because of the *Pax Romana*. The worldwide Roman peace was a parenthesis within a long corridor of almost endless wars. It too would afford the disciples great latitude in traveling from country to country. The Roman peace, even if it was compulsory, aided and abetted the early church in its proclamation of the One who alone is the Prince of Peace.

It was "the fullness of the time" because of the Greek language and culture. When the armies of Alexander the Great marched in the third century before Christ in conquest of the bodies of men, his philosophers marched alongside to conquer the minds of men. As a result, when the Son of God appeared on the stage of planet Earth, the Greek language and culture came to dominate much of the world. This commonality of language and philosophy, like the roads that linked nations and the forced peace that subjugated them, would aid the spread of the gospel. Unlike twentieth-century missionaries, who spend years in language study and cultural familiarization, for the first-century missionaries, the Greek language which they spoke was ideal, and cultural shock between nations was minimized. In large measure, those things contributed immensely to the rapid spread of the first-century church.

But the Roman roads, the Roman peace, and the Greek language would have meant little were it not for a fourth reality that characterized that era in history.

It was "the fullness of the time" because there was also a religious expectancy in the hearts of men. Even secular historians suggest that there was a spiritual vacuum, a hungering and thirsting for something more. The "mystery" religions of the Roman world did not work; paganism provided no real satisfaction; and the unbridled licentiousness of much of the idolatrous worship was abhorrent even to some of the more noble pagan souls. In some vague way, unregenerate men began to sense that it was a special moment of history, that deity was going to visit humanity.

For those attuned to scriptural truth, that moment in history was not vague at all. They knew that the sixty-ninth week of Daniel's prophecy (comprising 483 years), which foretold that the Messiah was to be "cut off" (crucified), was near at hand (Dan. 9:25–26).

The all-knowing, omnipotent God is never caught off guard. He does not simply respond to unanticipated human circumstances. In absolute sovereignty, He brought all things into alignment for His purposes. Then, and only then, the infinite, self-existent, eternal God clothed Himself in flesh and an unfallen human nature for the purpose of dying for the sins of the world (Heb. 2:9). Before the divinely appointed time, no force in the universe could have put Christ on the cross. When men tried to take Him prematurely, He escaped out of their midst, for His time had not yet come (Luke 4:28–30; John 8:59; 10:39). When it *was* time, no force could have kept Him off the cross. Jesus said of Himself, "No man taketh it [my life] from me, but I lay it down of myself. I have power to lay it down, and I have power to take it again" (John 10:18). When well-intentioned but impetuous Peter tried to protect his Lord from soldiers, Jesus said to him, "Put up again thy sword into its place . . . Thinkest thou that I cannot now pray to my Father, and he shall presently give me more than twelve legions of angels?" (Matt. 26:52–53).

This same Jesus is coming again. And His coming will be right on schedule—at the right place, in the right way, accomplishing the right things. It will be a second "fulness of the time." Another divinely appointed confluence of events will merge to make it so.

And once again, as men approach the end of the twentieth century, there is, in the hearts and minds of a growing multitude the world over, the conviction that something has to happen—that something must give—that this planet is coming unglued—that foundations are disintegrating—that men in government, philosophy, business, science, education, and the arts not only do not have the answers to pressing, crucial issues of the present hour, but they are not even asking the right questions. Never mind light at the end of the tunnel. Informed, honest voices are asking, "Where *is* the tunnel?" because men have either created their own gods with their darkened minds or have legislated God out of any relevance for life. As a result, men have no foundation upon which to build and no absolutes as a standard of measure.

Within such an atmosphere of humanly unsolvable problems on every side, even many unregenerate men are looking outside of themselves for some kind of help. And an ever-growing number of Christians are looking up for the Son of God to bring harmony out of the discordant, humanly unfixable *mess* that sinful men have orchestrated.

Men in government, philosophy, business, science, education, and the arts not only do not have the answers to pressing, crucial issues of the present hour, but they are not even asking the right questions.

There are numerous reasons for Jesus' return. Jesus is coming again because nature impatiently awaits it. The apostle Paul wrote, "For we know that the whole creation groaneth and travaileth in pain together until now" (Rom. 8:22). With the sin of man came a curse on man's planet (Gen. 3:17–18). As a result, nature itself is waiting, as in travail, for deliverance from the curse of sin at the coming of the Son of Man. Only then will it fulfill its intended, glorious purpose during Messiah's millennial kingdom—when the desert will blossom like a rose, the earth will give its full bounty, and the wolf will lie down with the lamb (Isa. 11:35).

Jesus is coming again because true Christians eagerly anticipate that event. Hear Paul once again: "So Christ was once offered to bear the sins of many; and unto them that look for him shall he appear the second time without sin unto salvation" (Heb. 9:28). The coming of Christ is the blessed hope of every believer. That coming to consummate spiritual union with His own should be as eagerly anticipated by Christians as a bride, ecstatically in love, anticipates union with her beloved bridegroom. The deliverance of His church will be the King's first order of business at His coming.

Jesus is coming again because justice legally demands it. The Lord Himself said, "For wheresoever the carcase is, there will the eagles be gathered together" (Matt. 24:28). This was a familiar Hebraic expression, the meaning of which would be, *moral corrup-*

*tion requires divine judgment* (cf. Job 39:27–30; Rev. 19:17–18). "Wherever the carcass is" conveys the idea of moral corruption, stench, and decay. "There will the eagles be gathered together" implies divine judgment on all corruption (sin and its progeny). If God is holy and just, then He must, of necessity, punish evil. Judgment on unrepentant, wicked men requires His return and will be on the King's agenda at His coming.

Finally, Jesus is coming again because the Bible authoritatively proclaims it. Old and New Testament verses in abundance join their voices to declare that glorious refrain. The apostle Peter noted that the ancient prophets searched regarding "what, or what manner of time the Spirit of Christ who was in them did signify, when he [the Spirit] testified beforehand the sufferings of Christ, and the glory that should follow" (1 Pet. 1:11).

The prophets rightly understood that the Messiah was to suffer and die. Isaiah wrote, "But he was wounded for our transgressions, he was bruised for our iniquities: the chastisement of our peace was upon him; and with his stripes we are healed" (Isa. 53:5). The prophets also understood that He would be exalted and glorified: "Lift up your heads, O ye gates; even lift them up, ye everlasting doors; and the King of glory shall come in" (Ps. 24:9). Their problem, however, related first to the chronology of these events, and then to the fact that the description of suffering and glory for the Messiah appeared incongruous—absurd, incompatible, inappropriate. Yet, the biblical truths were undeniably clear. The Messiah must endure intense suffering and death. In addition, the Messiah must also experience great exaltation and glory. The ancient prophets could not comprehend the relation of these two events to one another. It was as though they looked down the corridor of time and saw two prophetic mountain peaks. The first was the suffering Messiah, the second the glorious Messiah who would follow. For them, the width of the valley between the two peaks was undiscernible. They had no concept of the church age, which spanned the two peaks and has already lasted almost two millennia.

Since ancient Jewish sages were at a loss on how to reconcile the incongruity of suffering and glory and the time sequence of these events, for some of them, at least, there could be but one solution. There must be two Messiahs. One they chose to call Messiah Ben Joseph (Christ, the Son of Joseph). The other they called Messiah

Ben David (Christ, the Son of David). The reasoning that brought them to such a conclusion is clear. In the Old Testament Scriptures, they saw a portrait of a Messiah who would be rejected, suffer, and die. Since Joseph was rejected, sold into slavery, suffered, but eventually delivered his brethren from famine, they said there must be a Messiah Ben (Son of) Joseph—the suffering Messiah. However, they had a second portrait. This one portrayed a glorious Christ who would deliver His people and reign in kingly majesty. He was named after Israel's greatest king. They called him Messiah Ben (Son of) David—the glorious Messiah. The first-century Jewish leaders could not bring themselves to accept the irrefutable fact that their Scriptures spoke not of two Messiahs but of one Messiah who would appear two times—first to redeem and second to judge and reign—with death, resurrection, and an undetermined period of time in between. He came and suffered—that is history. He will come again and be exalted—that is prophecy.

Not only is Jesus coming again, He is coming again in absolute triumph. The first time He came on a donkey (Matt. 21:5–7). The second time He will come on a great white stallion (Rev. 19:11). The first time He came as a lamb in silence: "He was oppressed, and he was afflicted, yet he opened not his mouth; he is brought as a lamb to the slaughter, and as a sheep before her shearers is dumb, so he openeth not his mouth" (Isa. 53:7). He is coming the second time as a lion with roaring: "The LORD also shall roar out of Zion, and utter his voice from Jerusalem, and the heavens and the earth shall shake" (Joel 3:16). The first time He came, He was judged (John 9:39). The second time He will be the Judge (2 Tim. 4:8; Acts 10:42). The first time He came in humility (Phil. 2:5–8). The second time He will come in glory (Matt. 25:31). The first time He came to die (Matt. 20:28). The second time He will come to judge and reign (Rev. 11:15).

If men are willing to identify with Christ in His humiliation and suffering, He will most assuredly identify with them in His exaltation and glory.

Up front and in person, unlike twentieth-century believers, the first-century disciples participated in the Lord's confrontation with and rejection by the Jewish leadership (Matt. 23:13–33). And with that rejection, the die was cast, the chasm formed; reconciliation at that time was impossible. The disciples who had followed him for three exciting and expectant years were crushed. Jesus, their Master and Teacher, was leaving. He had declared that Israel would not see Him again until she was ready to say, "Blessed is he that cometh in the name of the Lord" (Matt. 23:39). In the disciples' minds one question towered above all other questions: "What shall be the sign of thy coming, and of the end of the age?" (Matt. 24:3).

If man's redemption is to be consummated, God's holiness vindicated, the curse lifted, Satan defeated, righteousness established, and the Father's glory manifested—Jesus Christ must return. He will. That singular fact is an ultimate absolute.

# 3

# The Options of "When" Laid Out

As a group of students reached the dormitory lobby, relieved to be out of the chilly night air, they were surprised to see a fellow student rushing down the steps from the upper levels of the building. Her face was pale, and fear was etched across her brow. Almost crashing into her friends, she broke into uncontrollable sobs. It took a few minutes to calm her down, and then this story unfolded.

She had decided to take a nap before spending some time in study. When she awakened, her roommate was not in the room. But there was nothing unusual about that. Students often roamed the large halls and visited other rooms. She dressed and stepped into the hall, but her roommate was still nowhere in sight. No one else was visible either. She walked to another friend's room only to find it vacant. Something was strange. She thought for a moment and then realized what it was. There were no sounds, no voices, no laughter coming from anywhere. She started to go from room to room. In each case the results were the same: Lights were on, books were opened, everything was in place, but there were no girls. She thought, perhaps some of them are in the large community bathroom. In an instant she was there, but no one else was. Concern was now turning to fear. She remembered advice she had once been given: "When you're in a difficult spot, take a deep breath, compose yourself, don't panic." She thought for a moment and then remembered something. One of the girls was having a birthday party. Everyone must be up on the fifth floor celebrating. With a flood of relief coming over her, she quickly climbed the steps, opened the door, and entered the hallway. No one could be seen. But just then she heard voices coming from one of the rooms. At least someone was there. In her relief and excitement, she entered the room without knocking. Expectancy turned to shock. The voices she heard were coming from the radio. Back in the hall she called out, and nobody responded. She screamed, and nobody heard. Fear had now taken over. She was alone, absolutely alone. It was study time, and all students were required to be in the dorm. But about 150 girls had simply vanished. Slowly it came over her, and what her mind had not allowed her heart to believe could no longer be denied. She rushed to the elevator and pushed the button. The elevator did not respond. Of course, she thought, the elevator operator is gone—further confirmation of her worst fears. She rushed to the steps, darted down the five flights of stairs, reached the lobby, and almost collided with her friends.

The college fire alarm had gone off while she napped. It was a drill. But she had not heard the alarm. Her roommate was out of the room, and no one had aroused her. When she awakened, no one was there. The entire college seemed to be abandoned. Everything was as it had been—except there were no people. She was certain that the Lord Jesus Christ had come to rapture the church and that she had been left behind.

After she was calmed, the students had a good laugh. But for me—and I was one of the students in the lobby that evening—from that moment on the Rapture issue would be far more than an academic exercise. It would become a practical and important doctrinal issue.

Closely associated with the timing of the Rapture of the church is the nature of the Millennium. It is important to understand the relationship of the Rapture to the Millennium in any serious consideration of the Rapture's timing.

The word *millennium* is derived from two Latin words, *milus* meaning *thousand* and *annum* meaning *years*. *Millennium* literally means *a thousand years*.

In the book of Revelation the Greek equivalent of the Latin word *millennium* (thousand years) is used six times.

The Bible records that an angel came down from heaven, "And he laid hold on the dragon, that old serpent, who is the Devil and Satan, and bound him a *thousand years*" (Rev. 20:2). And then it is stated that the angel imprisoned Satan "till the *thousand years* should be fulfilled" (v. 3). The apostle John wrote that he saw the souls of martyrs who did not submit to the Antichrist and then gave this commentary: "and they lived and reigned with Christ a *thousand years*" (v. 4). Speaking of the resurrection at the end of the thousand years, he wrote, "But the rest of the dead lived not again until the *thousand years* were finished" (v. 5). John also said that those who participate in the first resurrection "shall reign with him a *thousand years*. And when the *thousand years* are ended, Satan shall be loosed out of his prison" (vv. 6–7).

Six times in six verses the phrase *thousand years* is mentioned in connection with the reign of Christ. While this is the only place where a specific period of time is enunciated, namely a thousand years for the duration of Christ's reign, the concept of Christ's reign and a kingdom age permeates the entire Bible. It is clearly taught that a glorious age will one day be established on the earth.

> And it shall come to pass in the last days, that the mountain of the LORD's house shall be established in the top of the mountains, and shall be exalted above the hills; and all nations shall flow unto it. And many people shall go and say, Come ye, and let us go up to the mountain of the LORD, to the house of the God of Jacob; and he will teach us of his ways, and we will walk in his paths; for out of Zion shall go forth the law, and the word of the LORD from Jerusalem. And he shall judge among the nations, and shall rebuke many peoples; and they shall beat their swords into plowshares, and their spears into pruning hooks; nation shall not lift up sword again nation, neither shall they learn war any more. (Isa. 2:2–4)

It is also taught in Scripture that Christ will rule over that kingdom. Daniel the prophet wrote,

> I saw in the night visions, and, behold, one like the Son of man came with the clouds of heaven, and came to the Ancient of days, and they brought him near before him. And there was given him dominion, and glory, and a kingdom, that all people, nations, and languages should serve him; his dominion is an everlasting dominion, which shall not pass away, and his kingdom that which shall not be destroyed. (Dan. 7:13–14)

The prophet Zechariah succinctly adds his testimony concerning that future kingdom: "And the LORD shall be king over all the earth; in that day shall there be one LORD, and his name one" (Zech. 14:9). The prophet Isaiah confirms that testimony and adds more details:

> For unto us a child is born, unto us a son is given, and the government shall be upon his shoulder; and his name shall be called Wonderful, Counselor, The Mighty God, The Everlasting Father, The Prince of Peace. Of the increase of his government and peace there shall be no end, upon the throne of David, and upon his kingdom, to order it, and to establish it with justice and with righteousness from henceforth even forever. The zeal of the LORD of hosts will perform this. (Isa. 9:6–7)

The New Testament confirms the testimony of that future kingdom. At the Council of Jerusalem, a crucial occasion for the early church, James, the half brother of the Lord, proclaimed:

> Symeon [Peter] hath declared how God first did visit the nations, to take out of them a people for his name. And to this agree the words of the prophets, as it is written: After this I will return, and will build again the tabernacle of David, which is fallen down; and I will build again its ruins, and I will set it up [the Kingdom]; That the residue of men might seek after the Lord, and all the nations, upon whom my name is called, saith the Lord, who doeth all these things. (Acts 15:14–17)

Note the similarity between the phrase "the Lord, who doeth all these things" (Acts 15:17b) and "The zeal of the LORD of hosts will perform this" (Isa. 9:7b). Both are in the context of this future kingdom. A myriad of additional verses speak of this coming kingdom (cf. Isa. 4; 11; 32; 34; 52:1–12; 61:2b–11; 66:10–21; Amos 9:11–12; Zech. 12:8–9; 14:16; Matt. 16:28; 26:29; John 18:36; 2 Pet. 1:11).

For centuries theologians have debated and sometimes fought over the character of that kingdom concerning which the Word of God has so very much to say. Will the return of Christ to rule be premillennial (before the thousand-year kingdom begins), amillennial (a rule in the hearts of men between the first and second comings), or postmillennial (after the spread of the gospel has ushered in the kingdom)?

Premillennialism was clearly the position of the early church for the first four centuries of its existence. Evidence for that fact is considerable and convincing.[1] But while such evidence is weighty, it cannot alone be determinative. Premillennialism, as a system, is based on a literal or normative method of biblical interpretation. In this system, words mean what they normally mean in everyday usage, while at the same time allowing for legitimate figures of speech. The simple thesis of premillennialism is that Jesus will literally return to the earth before (pre) the Millennium (thousand-year kingdom age) begins and that He himself will inaugurate and rule over it. This position is illustrated on the chart below.

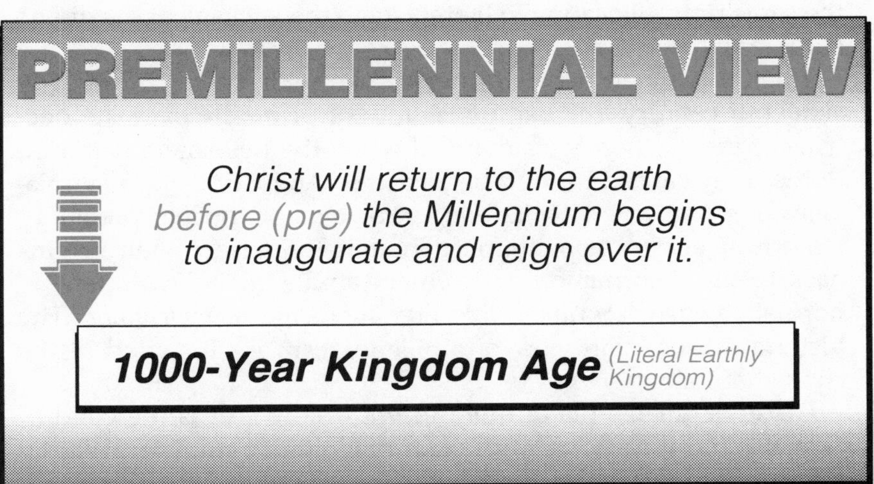


Amillennialism as a system of interpretation was begun in the fourth century. Its architect and primary exponent was the well-known Catholic theologian Augustine. He was convinced that the thousand-year kingdom of which the Bible spoke would be the period of time between the first and second advents of Christ. In time, however, he became disillusioned because the description of the kingdom in the Bible did not fit the reality of the world in which he lived. Therefore, he decided that the kingdom could not be literal. To Augustine, it must (if it were to occur between Christ's first and second comings) be a spiritual kingdom. The kingdom of God, he declared, was "in the hearts" of faithful men, not in an actual literal kingdom on the earth over which Christ would one day rule.

To achieve his ends, Augustine used Origen's allegorizing

methods to interpret much of the Word of God, particularly prophetic sections. The last days were no longer the last days; Israel was no longer Israel; Jerusalem was no longer Jerusalem; the house of David was no longer the house of David; a thousand years did not mean a thousand years—and on and on it went. Under this system of interpretation, the Bible became a subjective patchwork which could be made to say whatever one wanted it to say. It had the added benefit of aiding the emerging Catholic anti-Semitic mood of the time. By allegorizing the Scriptures, it allowed the church to become a new Israel and, as such, acquire for herself all of the blessings promised to the sons of Jacob while, at the same time, allocating to literal Israel (the Jews) all of the divine cursings.

Tragically, when the Reformers broke with Rome in the early sixteenth century, the battle was fought primarily over the doctrine of justification by faith. And when the Reformers departed Rome, they carried in their baggage the Augustinian amillennial view of prophecy with its allegorical method of interpretation. Unfortunately, most mainline denominations trace their origins back to the Reformation and remain amillennial. The letter *"a"* normally negates. So *amillennial* literally means *no millennium*. The historic Augustinian view of amillennialism is illustrated in the chart that follows.

Postmillennialism is of more recent origin. It was the child of Daniel Whitby, a seventeenth-century Unitarian minister. Whitby was convinced that the gospel, like leaven (yeast), would permeate the entire world. As the gospel had its purifying effect on men's hearts, things would get better and better. Eventually men, through the effect of the gospel, would bring in the kingdom. Then, when everything was right, after a thousand years of man's progressive improvement, Christ would return.

Postmillennialists were convinced that the First World War was the war to end all wars. The peace that they believed would follow would be an evidence that the gospel was doing its job of purifying the world. However, the Second World War dashed the hopes of many postmillennialists, and the adherents of this view diminished in number. In recent years, the writings of some credible advocates have given to postmillennialism a modest resurgence. Nonetheless, major theological problems remain intact for postmillennialism, and nineteen hundred years of church history argue directly against this position. There is no evidence that the church, through the spread of the gospel, is purifying the world. Conversely, all one need do is look around to see that the world is polluting the church in perfect fulfillment of 2 Timothy 3:1–5, which describes the decline of the church in the last days. Technology is racing like a roller coaster in a down mode. Today men

**AMILLENNIAL VIEW**

*Between His two comings Christ rules over a spiritual kingdom in the hearts of mankind.*

***Spiritual Kingdom***

***1000-Year Kingdom Age*** *(Non-literal Earthly Kingdom)*

can bypass the heart, transplant the heart and even develop artificial hearts, but they cannot make a bad heart good and prepare it for kingdom living. The spiritual heart remains "deceitful above all things, and desperately wicked" (Jer. 17:9). Scripture makes it clear that the end of the age will not be characterized by world revival. It will be the Antichrist's ultimate *hour of power,* cut short not by the universal spread of the gospel but by the Day of the Lord judgment.

The postmillennial view of the kingdom is illustrated in the chart that follows.

One's view of the Millennium is an important matter—not reserved for the theologian, pastor, or Bible teacher. It is an issue of great significance for every believer.

Its ramifications are substantial, ranging literally across the pages of the Bible from Genesis to Revelation. The very character of God is in view. Does He keep His word? Are His promises literal? Does He have the power to keep them? Will He change His mind? Have things occurred that He did not anticipate? If God's promises to Israel are not literal, it could be argued that His promises to the church are not literal. Maybe the believer does not really have a home prepared in heaven. Perhaps God does not have the power to redeem because He is not omnipotent, or will change His mind about redeeming because He is not immutable. "God forbid [don't even think it]: yea, let God be true, but every man a liar" (Rom. 3:4). God is faithful. He will fulfill all of His promises literally to Israel and to the church. Christ will return to the earth to establish His kingdom. For a classic and still unanswered treatment of this subject, read *The Basis of the Premillennial Faith* by Charles Caldwell Ryrie.

**POSTMILLENNIAL VIEW**

*Man will bring in the Kingdom through the spread of the gospel. Christ will return after (post) its universal acceptance to sit upon His throne.*

***1000-Year Kingdom Age***

A question now arises which is the central issue of this book. All premillennialists are agreed that Jesus will return before the thousand-year kingdom is established. They also generally agree that there is a seven-year period (plus seventy-five days, often ignored but, in actuality, critical [Dan. 12:11–12]) that immediately precedes the kingdom. This seven-year period of time is popularly called the Tribulation period or the seventieth week of Daniel. What premillennial scholars disagree over is the *timing* of Christ's coming in relation to that seven-year period.

The seventieth week plus the seventy-five days referred to by Daniel will have within its borders:

1. The ultimate manifestation of man's rebellion;
2. The revealing of the Antichrist;
3. The apostasy of the nation Israel;

4. The Rapture of the church;
5. The outpouring of God's wrath;
6. The consummation of the "times of the Gentiles";
7. The spiritual rebirth of the nation of Israel;
8. The destruction of the armies of the world at Armageddon; and
9. The defeat of the Antichrist and Satan.

But will Christ's rapture of His church be

Pretribulational—
before the seventieth week of Daniel begins?

Midtribulational—
in the middle of the seventieth week?

Posttribulational—
at or near the end of the seventieth week?

Or, as will be advocated in this book,
Prewrath—at the opening of the seventh seal sometime within the second half of the seventieth week?

The word *rapture,* like the word *millennial,* comes not from the Greek but from Latin. It is the translation of the word *rapere,* meaning *rapid*. It appears in the Latin translation of 1 Thessalonians 4:7. There *rapere,* or *rapid,* is used to translate the Greek expression *caught up*. The words *raptured, snatched,* or *caught up* have come to be used interchangeably. They are used to describe the initial phase of the second coming of Christ, who, by the word of His power, will snatch, catch up, or rapture His true church out of the gravitational pull of this planet to meet Him in the clouds and to remain forever with Him. This event, as noted by many pretribulation rapturists, is a part of the larger truth of a literal second coming of the Lord Jesus Christ.

Pretribulation rapturism represents the belief that Christ will rapture true believers before the Tribulation period or seventieth week of Daniel begins.

This position, widely held by many conservative premillenarians, is relatively new in origin. As an established view, it can be traced back to John Darby and the Plymouth Brethren in the year 1830. Some scholars, seeking to prove error by association, have attempted (perhaps unfairly) to trace its origin back two years earlier to a charismatic, visionary woman named Margaret MacDonald.[2] In any case, neither its recent origin nor its source proves nor disproves its correctness. But if pretribulationism is used as a badge for orthodoxy, one is faced with the perplexing question of what to do with the millions of godly believers who, for almost eighteen hundred years, did not hold to pretribulation rapturism. Among them are men like John Wesley, Charles Wesley, Charles Spurgeon, Matthew Henry, John Knox, John Hus, William Carey, John Calvin, Isaac Newton, George Whitfield, A. B. Simpson, George Mueller, John Newton, Jonathan Edwards, John Wycliffe, John Bunyan, and many others. The argument sometimes advanced that end-time events had not yet been systematized or developed and, therefore, that men were not pretribulational, carries no weight whatever. Men had the Word of God then as men have the Word of God today, and they were responsible to live in the light of its truth. Unsystematized doctrines did not exempt men from responsibility. The fact remains that they were not pretribulational.

Nor can the doctrine of imminency (the belief that Christ could return at any moment without the need for any prophesied event occurring first) in the early church be sustained. Nonetheless, without any historical justification, incorrect statements like the one that follows are sometimes made: "From the days of the apostolic church, the Christians throughout the world have always believed and taught that the church, the Body of Christ, composed of all believers in the Lord Jesus, would be caught away to be with the Lord in the air before the day of earth's greatest travail and sorrow breaks upon the earth." With far greater sensitivity, John F. Walvoord lists eight quotes from church Fathers in an attempt to prove that the early church believed in imminency.[3] Robert Gundry examined Walvoord's list of quotes in historical context and clearly refuted his contention,[4] so much so that pretribulationist John A. Sproule wrote:

> However, another question arises. Is pretribulationism proven by the doctrine of imminency or does the doctrine of imminency derive from an exegetically proven pretribulationism? To find help, the researcher will be disappointed in his search for pretrib. literature on the subject of imminency. Walvoord . . . refers to imminency as the "heart of pretribulationism." Yet he is able to muster

only a few vague quotations from the Early Church Fathers plus a few debatable Scriptures (John 14:1–3; 1 Thess. 1:10, 13–18; 5:6; and 1 Cor. 1:7) to support his statement. However, a contextual examination of these quotations shows them more supportive of posttrib. than pretrib.[5]

Understanding that certain prophesied events had to occur before Christ's return, J. Barton Payne wrote,

> The death of Paul and Peter, the destruction of the Temple at Jerusalem in A.D. 70, and the spread of the gospel [Great Commission] means the early Apostolic Church could not have held an "any moment" view of the Lord's coming.[6]

John Sproule, in summing up his comments on imminence with the refreshing scholarship and integrity that characterized his writing, said,

> Pretribulationism can ill afford to rest upon the shaky foundation of traditionalism and eisegetical [reading into the text what is not there] statements. If its "heart" [i.e., pretribulationism] is a debatable and inductively determined doctrine of imminency then, perhaps, an exegetical "heart transplant" may be in order.[7]

**The *Scofield Reference Bible* . . . more than any other force popularized the pretribulation view of the Rapture.**

If pretribulationism is an evidence of theological integrity, then those saints who lived from the first century to the beginning of the nineteenth century get no ribbon of orthodoxy. Obviously, such a conclusion is totally unwarranted and therefore makes church division over the *timing* of the Rapture (not the fact of it) totally inappropriate.

The pretribulational view made its way to the United States in the 1880s, and with it, unfortunately, came friction and division. Men like Arno Gabelein, Harry Ironside, James Gray, Ruben Torey, and Lewis Sperry Chafer were early champions of pretribulation rapturism. *The Scofield Reference Bible* of 1909 and the revised edition of 1917, which included pretribulation rapturism as a major part of its prophetic teaching, more than any other force popularized the pretribulation view of the Rapture. Untold multitudes became pretribulationists as a result of Scofield's notes which, because attached to his reference Bible, became highly authoritative in the minds of many. Most of the early Bible conferences, Bible colleges, and seminaries, under the influence of those early pretribulationist leaders, adopted the pretribulational position, and the number of adherents continued to grow. Additional champions of pretribulation rapturism include men like Charles Feinberg, John Walvoord, Charles Ryrie, and Dwight Pentecost.

The general view of pretribulation rapturism is charted below.

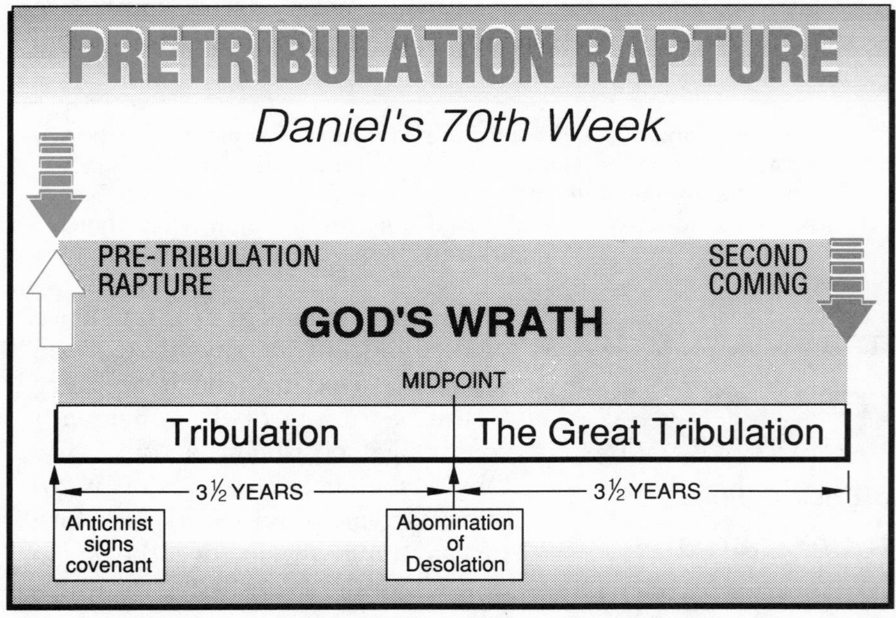


Midtribulation rapturism is even more recent in origin than pretribulation rapturism. A major advocate is Norman B. Harrison who, in 1941, published the book *The End: Rethinking The Revelation*. Other scholars such as J. Oliver Buswell, Harold J. Ockenga, and Gleason Archer also championed this cause. It has been particularly attractive to those who are disenchanted with both pretribulation and posttribulation rapturism. Many of its followers see this as a mediating position. According to midtribulation rapturists, the *catching away* of the church will occur three and one-half years into the Tribulation period, immediately prior to the Great Tribulation. Harrison believed that the wrath of God is to be associated only with the Great Tribulation and that this wrath will be triggered by the opening of the seventh trumpet judgment (Rev. 11). Therefore, midtribulationists would view their position as teaching that the Rapture will exempt the church from God's judgment. Their position is charted below.

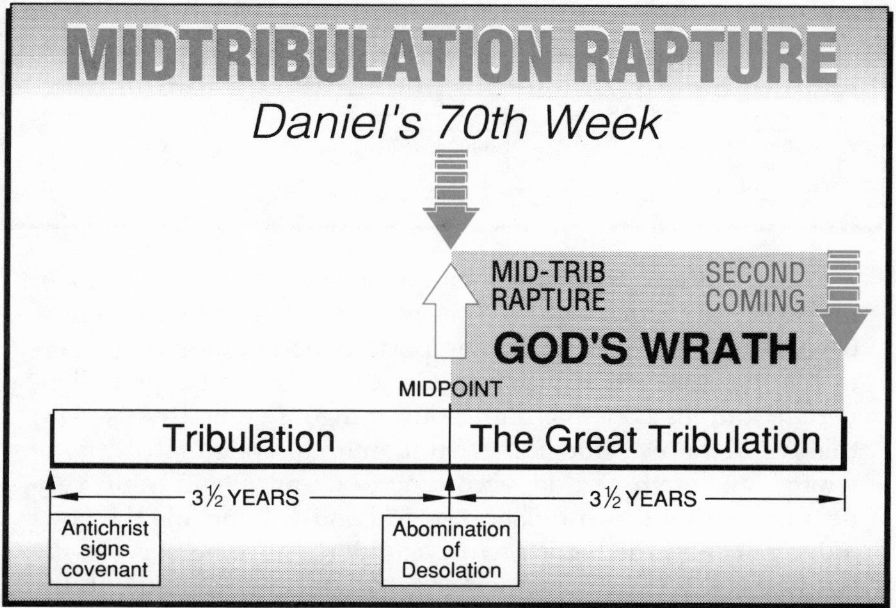


Historic posttribulation rapturism espouses the position that the church will go through the entire seven-year Tribulation period. At the end of that time of wrath, Christ will return to the earth. This view, unlike pretribulationism and midtribulationism, does not exempt the church from the time of God's wrath. Alexander Reese produced what many view as a classic defense of posttribulationism with his book *The Approaching Advent of Christ*. The historic posttribulation rapture position is charted on the following page.

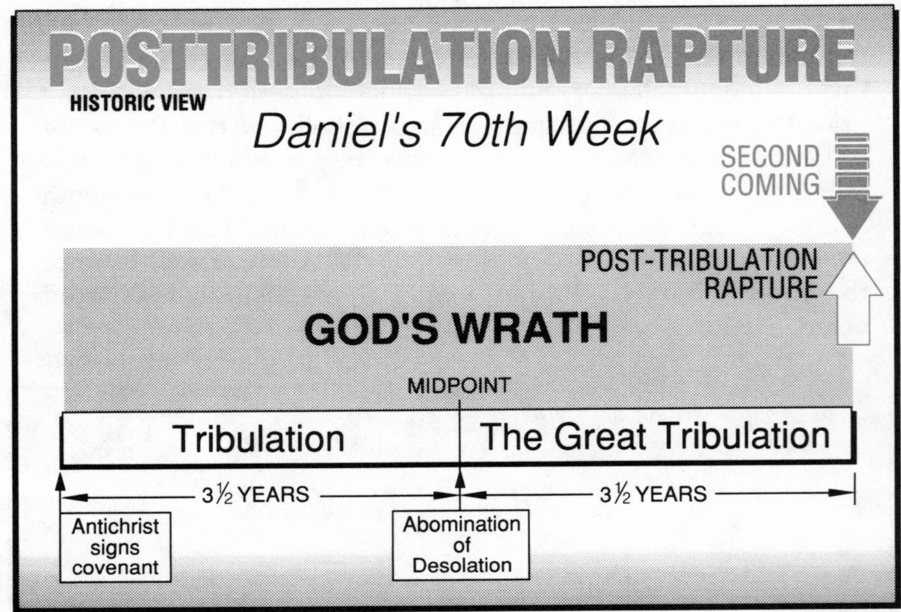


Robert Gundry's posttribulation position, as enunciated in his book *The Church and The Tribulation,* written in 1973 and now beyond its sixth printing, is an important modification of the normative posttribulation position. Gundry is himself a premillennarian, and his book has a gracious and godly tone. In his view, the Tribulation period is not fundamentally a time of divine wrath. The wrath of God, according to Gundry, will begin very near the end of the Tribulation period and will include the bowl judgments and the battle of Armageddon. Since he believes the Rapture will occur before this divine judgment is poured out, the church will be kept from God's wrath—which he understands to cover a very brief period of time.

Walvoord, in a discussion of pretribulation, midtribulation, posttribulation rapturism, and a little-known position called partial rapturism, makes this comment: "It is obvious that only one of these four possible positions is correct."[8] Exception must be taken to Walvoord's statement. It has neither logic to drive it nor evidence to substantiate it. The fact is, it is not "obvious" at all that one of those four views must, of necessity, be correct. Pretribulation rapturism traces its origin to the year 1830; partial rapturism, still with few adherents, to the middle of the nineteenth century; midtribulation rapturism is itself only fifty years old; and posttribulation rapturism has no clearly identifiable origin. The ongoing conflict between the opposing views, the glaring problems, and frequently heard statements like, "I don't know what to believe," or "I'm a posttribulationist because it seems to have fewer problems than pretribulationism," and not infrequently, "I'm a pretribulationist, but I never preach on it," strongly suggest that the prevailing views are, in fact, fatally flawed—and that a fresh new examination not only should be welcomed but warmly encouraged.[9] It certainly cannot cause any more confusion than that which already exists, especially with the proliferation of sensationalizing, and often nonbiblical literature being minted and distributed in greater quantities than ever before.

This book is an attempt to present a fresh examination.

In contrast to the normally held positions of pretribulation, midtribulation, or posttribulation rapturism, the position of this book is called prewrath rapturism. (Interestingly enough, pretribulationism, midtribulationism, and Gundry's posttribulationism would claim they are prewrath too, but their identifying names do not use that designation.) Again, let it be emphasized that every attempt will be made to keep the presentation clear, concise, logical, and biblical. There will be no attempt to climb up the ladder by standing on the shoulders of those with opposing views. Nor will any attempt be made to refute other positions, except where it is impossible for more than one to be on the same rung of the ladder at the same time.

> The Olivet Discourse is Jewish in character, sequential in progression, logical in argument, parallel to the seals of Revelation in nature, covers the seventieth week of Daniel in scope. . . .

The conflict between the varied views revolves around a large number of issues. There are *experts* who say the Greek text surrounding an argument can be translated only one way; yet other *experts* defend another interpretation. (You need only read the linguistic arguments over "keep thee from the hour" [Rev. 3:10] to see how far *expert* testimony can vary regarding a single phrase.) It is not unlike a court scene where prosecutor and defense attorney parade opposing *expert* testimony, and the jury is left totally confused.

The battle rages over issues such as "consistent" dispensationalism; distinction between Israel and the church; differing interpretations of words and concepts such as *coming, age, wrath,* and *tribulation;* the sequence of the book of Revelation; identification of the time of the Day of the Lord; the significance of the seventh trumpet; the context of the Olivet Discourse; the doctrine of imminency; and on, and on, and on it goes. By the time discussions are over, only a theological and linguistic genius could successfully sift through the conflicting arguments and views. So many *trees* have been examined, it is hard to know where the *forest* is. And it is easy to be left thinking you are part of the survivors of Armageddon and thankful that you escaped with only a monumental migraine.

God expects His children to descend and dig deeply for the truth to be found in the inexhaustible treasure chest of His Word. It is the God-ordained method. But occasionally one wonders if rigidity in a position has not caused some interpreters to mine "fool's gold," which shines but has no value.

The basic theses of this book are simple:

1. The Rapture of the church will occur immediately prior to the beginning of the Day of the Lord.
2. The Day of the Lord commences sometime within the second half of the seventieth week.
3. The cosmic disturbances associated with the sixth seal will signal the approach of the Day of the Lord.
4. The Day of the Lord will begin with the opening of the seventh seal (Rev. 8:1).

Everything else will be presented as confirmation of those theses.

The Olivet Discourse (Matt. 24–25) will be a central text. It is the author's contention that the Olivet Discourse is Jewish in character, sequential in progression, logical in argument, parallel to the seals of Revelation 6 in nature, covers the seventieth week of Daniel in scope, answers the dual question concerning the Lord's coming and the end of the age posed by the disciples (which was the catalyst for the Lord's teaching), and encompasses both the

Rapture and the return of Christ within its borders. It will also be demonstrated that the seventieth week of Daniel has three major, distinct, and identifiable periods of time: the "beginning of sorrows," the Great Tribulation, and the Day of the Lord—all found in the Olivet Discourse.

The prewrath rapture is charted below.

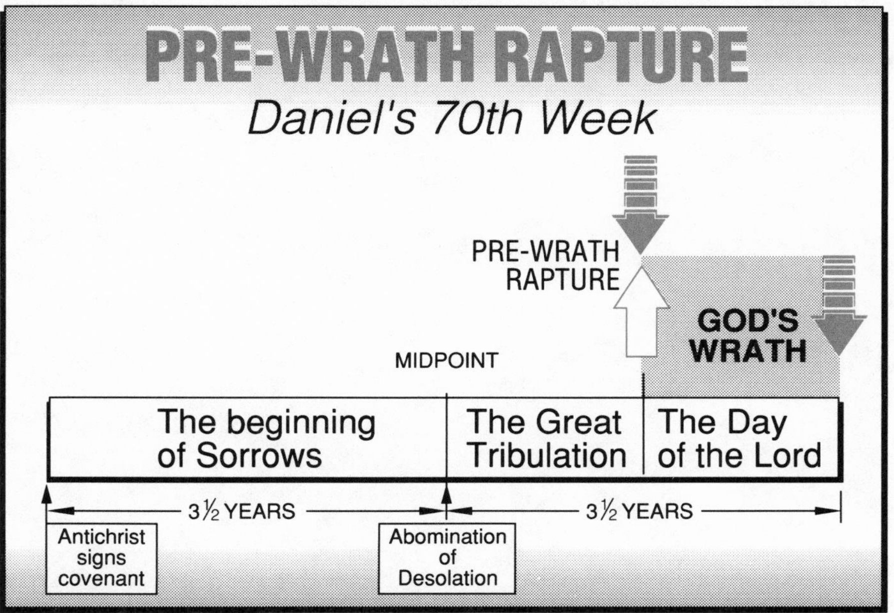

# 4

# The Conflict That Makes It Necessary

The planet earth is on a collision course with its Creator. When that event occurs, it will be the genuine "big bang" (and that, in contrast to the foolish theories of humanistic evolution, such as the relatively recent proposal that suggests the universe began with a "big bang"). The Word of God refers to a future collision between God and man as the Day of the Lord. When it occurs, the impact will be heard around the world.

This inevitable crash was set in motion when man, created in the exalted image of God, heeded the solicitation of Satan to disobey God. In pride, man chose to rebel against his Creator and brought sin and its inviolable consequence, death, into the realm of human experience. As a result, "It is appointed unto men once to die" (Heb. 9:27).

Every broken body, every disturbed mind, every hurting heart—the collective tears of the human race—can trace its ancestry back to the sin of Adam and Eve. The first man was the official representative of all men. What he did in the Garden of Eden, in disobeying God, all men did in him. Future unborn generations were in the loins of Adam and share equally in the consequences of his action (Rom. 5:12).

Before sin entered the arena of human history, there was no death. Adam was not aging; his heart was not growing tired; his hair was not turning gray; his teeth were not decaying. Before sin, Adam did not know the pain of arthritis, the dizziness of high blood pressure, the fear of cancer. Before sin, animals were not carnivorous; weeds did not choke out good plants; rust did not deteriorate metal. Before sin, armies would never have been formed. Natural catastrophes would not have occurred, and men would not lie, cheat, lust, rob, rape, and murder. But Adam chose to sin. And, as the progeny of Adam and Eve, all men are born with a sin nature. Under the controlling influence of that fallen nature, all men commit sinful deeds.

No man, however noble or moral by human standards, can plead exemption. The Word of God is precise on this point. By the divine standard, "all have sinned, and come short of the glory of God" (Rom. 3:23). "There is none righteous, no, not one" (Rom. 3:10). The language is emphatic. Sin separates man from God, and separation from God results in spiritual death. God is light and life (John 1:4); therefore, to exist apart from God is darkness and death. Death is more a qualitative designation than a quantitative one. There is no such thing as total annihilation or cessation of existence—only separation. Man is an eternal being. God breathed into him the breath of life; therefore, he is destined to exist forever. Fundamentally, physical death is separation of the soul from the body. Spiritual death is separation of the soul from God. It is the quality of that existence which is in view. To live in God's presence is life. To live apart from His presence is death. Since man is born with a sin nature, he commits sinful deeds and is spiritually dead. That is the present status of the natural man. If left in that natural condition, he is helpless, hopeless, and forever lost—spiritually dead.

It is at this threshold of human depravity and helplessness that an understanding of what God is really like can begin to dawn on the human soul. Although God is holy and cannot condone man's sin, and although He is just and must punish man's sin, God is also loving and has provided an escape from sin and its consequences. And He has done this in perfect harmony with His own righteousness.

Upon the earth and in the heavens, there is a war raging for the souls of men. This war is spiritual and invisible—the results eternal and irreversible. The battle lines have been drawn. God and Satan are in conflict. The sphere of that conflict is heaven and earth. The created subjects of that conflict are angelic and human. The origin, purpose, and consummation of human history form the tapestry of this universal warfare.

On the earth, the opening skirmish took place in the Garden of Eden. Satan, through the use of a beguiling serpent, with subtlety tempted Adam and Eve. He himself, as "the anointed cherub" (Ezek. 28:14), the highest and most powerful of all created beings, had rebelled against his Creator. Lifted up with pride, he sought to usurp God's throne and sovereignty (Isa. 14:12–17; Ezek. 28:11–19). In his rebellion he declared, "I will ascend into heaven, I will exalt my throne above the stars of God; I will sit also upon the mount of the congregation, in the sides of the north, I will ascend above the heights of the clouds, I will be like the Most High" (Isa. 14:13–14). Satan wore pride like a garment. Five times in this passage he spoke words of sedition against his Creator. He declared "I will ascend," "I will exalt," "I will sit," "I will ascend," and "I will be like the Most High."

Upon the earth and in the heavens, there is a war raging for the souls of men. This war is spiritual and invisible—the results eternal and irreversible.

"I" is the most frequently used of all words. It can also be the most damning, often reflecting the pride of the heart. Was it not Nebuchadnezzar, ruler of one of history's greatest empires, who, while beholding his magnificent hanging gardens and capital city, proclaimed, "Is not this great Babylon, that I have built for the house of the kingdom by the might of my power, and for the honor of my majesty?" (Dan. 4:30)? Nebuchadnezzar's reign inaugurated a period of time referred to in the Bible as "the times of the Gentiles" (Luke 21:24). Because he lifted himself up with pride, he was smitten with insanity for seven years until he acknowledged that the Most High God rules in the kingdoms of men and is the absolute Sovereign of the universe (Dan. 4:33–34).

Pride is always sinful and always punished. The righteous Creator of the universe could not remain passive in the face of such treacherous rebellion as that instituted by Satan. He was cast out of heaven "to sheol, to the sides of the pit" (Isa. 14:15). Much later in time, Jesus would remind Satan, "Thou shalt worship the Lord, thy God, and him only shalt thou serve" (Matt. 4:10).

Satan's unrealized ambition became the very core of his sinful solicitation to Adam and Eve. He wanted to be like God, and so he subtly suggested to the first couple that if they partook of the forbidden tree they would be as God. Here was the supreme appeal to pride.

So subtle, so carefully worded, so eloquently disguised came the enticing, seductive suggestion of the Evil One to Adam and Eve: "For God doth know that in the day ye eat thereof, then your eyes shall be opened, and ye shall be as God, knowing good and evil" (Gen. 3:5). Half-truths are always whole lies. Error is always *served* that way—poison garnished with a little truth. In sinning, Adam and Eve would know "good and evil"—that was true. But they would not become "as God"—that was false. And no computer, however powerful, could calculate the resultant, unending agony and groaning, tears and sorrow of the human race. Satan spoke nothing of those consequences of sin to man's first parents. And with the introduction of sin, the image and likeness of God, in which man had been created, became fatally flawed. The diamond fashioned to reflect the many-faceted brilliance and glory of its Creator was now dark with sin, and Satan was pleased.

Adam had been authorized by God to be king of the earth—to rule and reign, to give names to the animal world, and to subdue all things. For his involvement in sin, Adam and, through him, all men are under divine judgment. Physical death, a curse on the ground, and thorns and thistles are the results (Gen. 3:17–19).

For her involvement, Eve and, through her, all women are being chastened. Physical death, pain in childbearing, and an inclination to usurp the divine design of male leadership within the marriage union were decreed (Gen. 3:16). (This inclination to rule is the probable meaning of the phrase "and thy desire shall be unto thy husband.")

For Satan's involvement, he and all those who followed him have been judged and will one day be consigned to a place of eternal punishment (Gen. 3:14–15; Rev. 20:2–3).

But not only has God decreed judgment upon those who rebelled against Him; He has moved into action with a plan to provide redemption from the curse of sin for all men who will put their faith in Him. To Satan He sovereignly declared, "And I will put enmity between thee and the woman, and between thy seed and her seed; he [Christ] shall bruise thy head, and thou [Satan] shalt bruise his heel" (Gen. 3:15). The serpent strikes the heel—that is why men wear boots in places where snakes are present. In the case of Christ, the wound would be painful but neither final nor determinative—Christ would rise from the dead.

The divine decree that the *seed of the woman* would one day bruise his head was taken seriously by Satan. He moved swiftly to counter the divine thrust against him. Since the seed that would inflict him with a fatal wound would come from humanity, he rushed to corrupt the human race. The beginning of that tragic saga is the substance of Genesis 6.

The "sons of God" who procreated with the "daughters of men" were fallen angelic beings (Gen. 6:2). Despite the protest of those who reject such identification, the evidence is strong and compelling, the reason clear and logical. By corrupting the human race through the unnatural offspring of human women and fallen angelic beings, the seed destined to crush Satan's head could never be born. To suggest, as some have, that this incident describes intermarriage between the righteous line of Seth and the unrighteous line of Cain is unconvincing and appears to ignore the larger context. The fallen angels who participated in this perverted act are most probably "the angels who kept not their first estate, but left their own habitation" (Jude 6a). It is these angels who, according to Jude, are "reserved in everlasting chains under darkness unto the judgment of the great day" (Jude 6b). The actions of these fallen angels are compared to Sodom and Gomorrah and the sin of "going after strange flesh" (Jude 7). In the case of Sodom and Gomorrah, homosexuality is in view; in the case of the fallen angels, taking on physical form and cohabiting with women is in view.

The apostle Peter makes the same association as does Jude. He speaks of "the angels that sinned" and are "delivered . . . into chains of darkness, to be reserved unto judgment" (2 Pet. 2:4). He relates these "angels that sinned" with the destruction of the world by flood (2 Pet. 2:5) and, like Jude, associates this judgment with that of Sodom and Gomorrah (2 Pet. 2:6).

It cannot be demonstrated from Scripture that angels are sexless beings, as some suggest. It is true that God intended angels to neither marry nor be given in marriage (Matt. 22:30). And that is precisely the point. The sin perpetrated by the union of the "sons of God" and the "daughters of men" was the creation of a mongrel race through the perverted union of fallen angels and mortal women. It was unnatural and contrary to the divine intent. This action was a satanic attempt, through his demon emissaries, to corrupt the human race so that the divinely promised *seed of the woman* of Genesis 3 could not be born. If successful, man could not be redeemed; Satan could not be defeated; God could not be sovereign; and righteousness and justice would lie mortally wounded.

Grotesque stories about beings that are half man and half demon do not trace their origin to Greek mythology but to antediluvian (preflood) history. Books on this theme often occupy far more space on most bookstore shelves than do books on the Bible and theology. The present fascination of millions with demonism, witchcraft, astrology, the occult, and the New Age movement is a significant barometer of growing satanic influence as the end of the age closes in.

Satan's diabolical scheme to thwart God's purpose and keep sinful, unforgiven man forever under his evil dominion appeared to be succeeding. Clearly, man was standing at the brink of inescapable disaster. "And GOD saw that the wickedness of man was great in the earth, and that every imagination of the thoughts of his heart was only evil continually. And it repented the LORD that he had made man on the earth, and it grieved him at his heart" (Gen. 6:5–6).

Was this to be the ignominious end of man created in the image of God? Was Satan, after all, to be the victor? At that darkest moment, a glimmer of light shone through, couched in these most encouraging of all words: "But Noah found grace in the eyes of the LORD" and "Noah was . . . just . . . perfect in his generations, and . . . walked with God" (Gen. 6:8–9). He and his immediate family had not been contaminated by the progeny of the "sons of God" and "daughters of men."

God commanded this man to build an ark, and build it he did—on dry ground, although it evidently had not yet rained on the earth. The fountains of the great deep had not yet been broken up (Gen. 7:11). For 120 years, Noah and his sons built while men laughed and ridiculed. A boat on dry ground—how absolutely ludicrous, men thought. And then one day, without warning, something new occurred on earth. Water began to fall from heaven. It began to rain and rain and rain. And then God Himself shut the door to the ark (Gen. 7:16). Men were inside before the rain started, or they did not get inside. Still it rained, hour after hour, day after day. The water rose, the flood spread to the highest mountains, and all but a remnant of mankind perished. Wicked and perverted men were drowned, but mankind was saved. Noah, his wife, three sons, and three daughters-in-law—eight souls from among all of humanity—disembarked from the ark. Then Noah built an altar and called on the name of the Lord (Gen. 8:20). God was pleased, and He "blessed Noah and his sons, and said unto them, Be fruitful, and multiply, and fill the earth" (Gen. 9:1). The *seed of the woman,* which was to crush Satan's head and redeem men (Gen. 3:15), remained intact in the loins of Noah and his family. The heavenly angels must have sighed a sigh of relief. The obituary of mankind was not to be written.

But Satan would not remain passive in the wake of this major setback. He empowered a man by the name of Nimrod. Nimrod was ruler of ancient Babylon. "He was a mighty hunter before the LORD" (Gen. 10:9). This hunting capability does not refer to prowess in the field as, for instance, in the case of Esau, who was "a skillful hunter, a man of the field" (Gen. 25:27). Nimrod was a hunter of the *souls* of men. God commanded that men be spread abroad across the earth (Gen. 9:19). Nimrod, in defiance of God, was the prime mover in building the tower of Babel, a presumptuous attempt to "reach unto heaven" (Gen. 11:4). The zodiac and astrology trace their origin to Nimrod and the tower of Babel. It was with Nimrod that the pervasive "mother and son" worship had its origin. History records the fact that Nimrod's wife, Semiramis, came to be called the "Supreme One," the priestess. Early in their religion the legend developed that she was impregnated by a sunbeam and gave birth to a son named Tammuz—clearly an attempt at a counterfeit virgin birth. One day, while out hunting, Tammuz was killed by a wild boar. Semiramis was so bereft that she wept and cried and would not eat for forty days, and at the end of those forty days, Tammuz rose from the dead—an attempt at a false resurrection. It was from this forty-day period, when Semiramis mourned for her son Tammuz, that the observance of Lent, with its mourning and self-denial, had its origin—not from the Bible. This was the beginning of the systematic "mystery" religion of Babylon. In time, the worship of Semiramis, who came to be called "the Queen of Heaven" (see Jer. 7:18; 44:15–30), spread across the civilized world. In Assyria, her name was Ishtar, and her son was Bacchus; in Egypt, she was known as Isis, and her son as Osiris; in India, she was Isi, and her son was Iswara; in Asia, Cybele and her son Deoius; in Greece, Aphrodite and her son Eros; and in Rome, Venus and her son Cupid.

The belief in Mary as the perpetual virgin and her co-mediatorship with Christ, her Son, as enunciated by the Roman Catholic Church, is the ultimate perpetuation of the false religious system begun by Nimrod, the great hunter of the souls of men. It is for this express reason that the apostle John identified Rome as "THE MOTHER OF HARLOTS" (Rev. 17:5). She seduces men to commit spiritual adultery with her rather than to experience true spiritual union with the Son of God (the *seed of the woman* promised in Gen. 3:15). Not without reason, then, John identified Rome, seated as she is on seven mountains (cf. Rev. 17:9), as "MYSTERY, BABYLON" (Rev. 17:5). She perpetuated the false religious system begun by Nimrod, founder of Babylon. At the end time, out of a revived Roman Empire or Western European confederation of nations, will come her most diabolical progeny, the Antichrist. Empowered by Satan, whose offspring he will be, the Antichrist will be the ultimate hunter of the souls of men. During the Great Tribulation men will be commanded to bow to the image of the Antichrist. Those who comply will receive his mark and give him their allegiance. Those who do not comply will be hunted down and slain (Matt. 24:15–22; Rev. 13:11–18).

But the Lord of all things, the Lover of men, whom He created in His own image, was not indifferent to the satanic devices or to man's plight.

Not far removed from Babylon was another city. It was inhabited by a people given over to idolatry. Situated along the Euphrates River, it was known as Ur of the Chaldeans. There was one man (Abram; later named Abraham by God; Gen. 17:5) in that city, however, who was not idolatrous. How he came to be different from his contemporaries, we are not told. But there is an ancient Jewish tradition that suggests that Abraham's father Terah was an idolator and that he had a shop in the city of Ur in which he sold idols. One day, suggests the tradition, Terah told his son Abraham to watch the business until he returned from some errands. Once again, as he had done on so many past occasions, Abraham looked around at the idols in his father's shop. They came in all sizes, shapes, and materials, but one idol in a corner was much taller than all the others and it had a large ax in its hands. Abraham's glance focused on that largest of all the idols. Then, his decision made, he went into action. Carefully slipping the ax out of the idol's hands, Abraham moved about and systematically used that ax to destroy all of the idols except the one from which the ax was taken. His work done, Abraham carefully slid the ax back into the hands of this largest and only remaining idol. Soon his father returned to discover that his inventory of idols had been smashed beyond recognition or repair. "Abraham," Terah inquired of his son in a loud voice, "What happened to the shop? To my idols? To my business?" Somewhat sheepishly, Abraham pointed to the one remaining idol with the ax firmly in its hands and said, "That idol went about destroying all of the other idols," to which his father responded, "Idols cannot see; idols cannot hear; idols cannot move. It is impossible that that idol is responsible for this." At that moment Abraham interrupted his father and inquired, "Father, have your ears heard what your mouth has spoken?"

In biblical history, Abraham became known as the father of the faithful (Rom. 4:11). God called this man to leave Ur and travel to a land that He would show him (Gen. 12:1). And there in the Negev Desert, in the land of Canaan, God would teach this man to trust Him.

To Abraham God gave a series of unconditional promises in what has become known as the Abrahamic covenant (Gen. 12; 15; 17; 22). Chief among them was the promise that "in thee shall all families of the earth be blessed" (Gen. 12:3). Looking backward in time, this promise to Abraham identified him as the channel through which the *seed of the woman* was to come (Gen. 3:15). Looking forward in time, this promise pointed to a lowly people (the Jew), in an insignificant land (Israel), within an obscure village (Bethlehem). There, in a stable for animals, a righteous Jewish maiden, a virgin named Miriam (her proper biblical name) gave birth to the Lamb of God. Nine months earlier, the Holy Spirit had come upon her, and the power of the Highest had overshadowed her (Luke 1:35).

The entire Old Testament is a history of the nation Israel and her vicissitudes. From Abraham to the incarnation, her glory and her ignominy, her victories and her defeats alike are chronicled. The mention of other nations and peoples of the world are only referred to in passing when, in one way or another, for good or bad, they impacted the descendants of Abraham, Isaac, and Jacob and the land of Israel.

The entire Old Testament is a history of the nation Israel and her vicissitudes. From Abraham to the incarnation, her glory and her ignominy, her victories and her defeats alike are chronicled.

This entire period of time, from Abraham to the birth of Christ, is described in the Bible this way: "And she [Israel], being with child, cried, travailing in birth, and pained to be delivered" (Rev. 12:2).

With Nimrod originated the false religious system of "mother and son" worship and its adherents including Romanism, out of which the Antichrist, the false seed, will one day come (Dan. 9:26; Rev. 13:1; 17:3–6).

With Abraham, through whom God promised universal blessing, originated a true spiritual system of worship of God and a people (the Jew) out of which the true Christ would come (Rom. 9:3–5; Gal. 3:8–9).

Two men, Nimrod and Abraham; two systems, the self-work of Romanism and the faith principle of biblical Judaism and out of which came true Christianity; two seeds, Satan's son (the Antichrist) and God's son (the true Christ); two peoples, the followers of Antichrist represented by the revived Roman Empire during the seventieth week and the followers of the true Christ who during that same period are willing to suffer and die if necessary for their sovereign Lord. These peoples and systems have been in conflict since the beginning of human history. Not without reason, therefore, Rome has been the greatest and most consistent persecutor of the sons of Abraham throughout history. It was Roman legions that destroyed Jerusalem and the temple in A.D. 70. It was Rome that scattered the Jews throughout the world in A.D. 135, forbidding their return to Jerusalem under punishment of death. It was Roman (allegorical) theology in the fourth century that fostered fifteen hundred years of anti-Semitism. It was Queen Isabella and King Ferdinand who, in 1492, launched the Spanish Inquisition, compelling Jews to convert to Roman Catholicism or be killed, imprisoned, or driven from the land. Centuries later, the Roman papacy, bribed by the gifts of churches and holy sites in Israel by Mussolini, remained silent during the Nazi Holocaust, thus contributing to the death of perhaps hundreds of thousands of Jews. The persecution of the Jewish people by Rome, in whatever lands their power permitted it during the past nineteen hundred years, is both extensive and well documented—right up to the present hour of history. Harsh words, these, but true—not against a people but a system, a false religious system under the control of Satan.

When, in the fullness of time, Christ was born in Bethlehem, Rome was the unchallenged world power. Herod the Great, who ruled over Israel, was himself an Edomite. His grandfather was a proselyte to Judaism. Herod, a Gentile, educated in Rome, and, like his grandfather, a convert to Judaism, was not a descendant of Abraham through Jacob; he was not of the tribe of Judah; he was not in the lineage of David. Herod had no credentials that would allow him to rule over Israel. He was placed in power and kept in power by imperial Rome, whose servant he was. When Herod, as a Roman puppet, killed all the male children in Bethlehem two years of age and under (Matt. 2:16), this was a satanic attempt to kill the *seed of the woman* promised in Genesis 3:15, the seed that would come through the family of Abraham. The Bible describes Satan's attack through his servant Herod this way: "and the dragon stood before the woman [Israel] who was ready to be delivered, to devour her child [Christ] as soon as it was born" (Rev. 12:4). But forewarned by God, Joseph, Mary, and the child had fled to Egypt.

Revelation 12 through 14 form a trilogy of thought. First, chapter 12 speaks of a woman (Israel) who gives birth to a child (Christ) and of Satan who, when his false religious system (Romanism) is unable to kill Christ, assails the Jewish people through whom Christ came into the world. If he cannot get them to bow to him, he will attempt to kill them so that they cannot bow to the true Christ. The ultimate manifestation of this scheme will occur during the Great Tribulation, "the time of Jacob's trouble" (Jer. 30:7; Dan. 12:1; Matt. 24:21).

Second, in Revelation 13 the emergence, at the end of the age, of the Antichrist (vv. 1–10) and his false prophet (vv. 11–18) is foretold. *Anti* means both *against* and *in place of*. The purpose of the Antichrist will be to oppose the true Christ and to have worship directed toward himself and Satan, who empowers him (2 Thess. 2:3–4; Rev. 13:4). Here, then, is the manifestation of the wicked one's ultimate goal—"to be like the Most High" and receive the worship of men which belongs alone to God and His Christ.

Third, in Revelation 14 the apostle John wrote, "And I looked and, lo, a Lamb stood on Mount Zion, and with him an hundred forty and four thousand, having his Father's name written in their foreheads" (v. 1). Here is presented the manifestation of the true Christ on Mount Zion with 144,000 souls who have not bowed to the Antichrist and received his mark. They are called "virgins" (Rev. 14:4). Normally this has been understood to mean that they did not marry or were eunuchs. Perhaps, however, the answer is to be found in the spiritual realm and their refusal to prostitute themselves and bow to the Antichrist (Isa. 57:3, 4, 8). They did not receive his mark—they did not commit spiritual adultery with Rome, "THE MOTHER OF HARLOTS" (Rev. 17:5). This 144,000 represent 12,000 men from each of the 12 tribes of Israel who will remain chaste for Christ in a still-future day. "These were redeemed from among men, the first fruits unto God and to the Lamb" (Rev. 14:4) and are clearly precursors (since they are "the first fruits") of others from among Israel who will be redeemed. This is the prelude to four of history's most momentous events: (1) the judgment of the nations (Rev. 14:17–20); (2) the defeat of the Antichrist, which immediately follows the destruction of Babylon with its false religious system (Rev. 17:5, 14); (3) the establishment of the millennial kingdom, which is consummated with the defeat of Satan, and the Great White Throne Judgment (Rev. 20:1–6, 10–14); and (4) the ushering in of the eternal state (Rev. 21:22).

# 5

# But First the Counterfeit

Allow it to be said without apology and with biblical justification that man without God is hopelessly lost. He is like a blind man in a dark room looking for a black cat that is not there. Man does not know from whence he came or whither he is headed. Man is totally bankrupt. He possesses in himself absolutely nothing of incorruptible and enduring value. His best scientific, philosophical, and educational achievements have not even identified, let alone explained or resolved, the real issues of life. With all of his astounding technological advance, he has not nudged his fellows one inch heavenward. In the words of Scripture, unsaved men are "Ever learning, and never able to come to the knowledge of the truth" (2 Tim. 3:7).

However, there is divine design, purpose, continuity, and consummation in human history. The sin that started in the Garden of Eden will have its last hurrah at the temple on Mount Moriah at Jerusalem. It will be the final attempt to enthrone man in the place of God.

The trip-hammer, the flash fire, the catalyst for this ultimate sin is referred to in the Bible as "the abomination of desolation."

Few texts of Scripture have greater prophetic significance than do these words of the Lord: "When ye, therefore, shall see the abomination of desolation, spoken of by Daniel the prophet, stand in the holy place (whosoever readeth, let him understand)" (Matt. 24:15). The parenthetical phrase, "(whosoever readeth, let him understand)," was given to mark out and underscore the crucial nature of what the Lord had just spoken. There will be a terrible abomination; it will make the temple a desolation. This abomination will be standing in the holy place, and it was predicted by Daniel the prophet. Daniel wrote, "And he [the Antichrist] shall confirm the covenant with many [some of the Jewish people] for one week [seven years]; and in the midst of the week he shall cause the sacrifice and the oblation to cease, and for the overspreading of abominations he shall make it [the temple] desolate" (Dan. 9:27).

To better comprehend this still-future abomination by the Antichrist, who will come out of the revived Roman Empire, it should be noted that the prophet also predicted an earlier abomination which has already occurred at the temple through a man who came out of the Grecian Empire. Daniel wrote of that event this way: "Yea, he magnified himself even to the prince of the host, and by him the daily sacrifice was taken away, and the place of his sanctuary was cast down" (Dan. 8:11). In other words, Daniel gave an historical precedent of an abomination which occurred at the temple in chapter 8 to help men comprehend the still-future abomination recorded in chapter 9 and to which the Lord referred in Matthew 24.

In the year 323 B.C., Alexander the Great died. Not only had he captured, in his brief lifetime, a substantial part of the known world, but, with great fervor he spread Greek culture, religion, and language into that world. This Grecian philosophy of life became known as Hellenism.

With the death of Alexander, his kingdom was divided among four of his generals. One of those four generals controlled a large area to the north of Israel known as Syria and established the Seleucid Dynasty. A second general ruled over the Egyptian Empire to the south of Israel and established the Ptolemaic Dynasty.

For about the first one hundred years, the little province of Israel was under the rule of Egypt. Eventually, because of power struggles and political intrigue, Israel came under the sway of Syria. A state of war now existed between Syria and Egypt that would last for decades. Trapped in the middle, as if between the anvil and the hammer, the little Jewish nation existed in a state of uncertainty. At times she literally did not know to which empire she belonged, Syria to the north or Egypt to the south, and, therefore, to whom she was to render allegiance and pay taxes.

As a result of these geographical/political realities, two Jewish parties arose. One party, more religiously conservative, favored Egyptian rule. Egypt, as a unified nation with an ancient indigenous culture, was less Hellenistic and, therefore, was in a position to give the Jews a greater measure of religious freedom. The other Jewish party, more religiously liberal, favored Syrian rule with its Hellenistic culture which the Syrians forced on conquered peoples to help unify their expanding empire. This latter group of Jews was little concerned about the negative Hellenistic impact on their religious life and the worship of Jehovah. Many of those nonreligious Jews, mostly among the aristocracy, changed their Hebrew names to Greek names, instituted Greek athletic games, and began to dress according to Greek fashion.

In this electrified atmosphere there arose a Syrian leader named Antiochus Epiphanes. He would rule Syria from 175 to 164 B.C.

Antiochus had launched a successful military campaign against Egypt and then returned home. However, in the year 168 B.C., he went down to Egypt a second time. The purpose of this expedition was to consolidate his earlier victory and bring Egypt under Syrian domination. History records that on this occasion he was met by a courier empowered by the senate in Rome who, at that time as an expanding military power, opposed Syria's conquest of Egypt.

The choice he was offered was clear: He must break off his attack against Egypt or face war with Rome. Frustrated in his attempt to expand his kingdom at the very moment of apparent success, he started home. On the way, Antiochus marched his armies into Israel and stopped in Jerusalem. There he had his soldiers kill a pig on the altar of the temple where sacrifices were normally offered by the priests in the worship of Jehovah. To the Jewish people, this sacrifice of a ceremonially unclean animal to a heathen deity was an abomination of great magnitude. But, with even greater desecration, Antiochus Epiphanes had an image of his chief god, Zeus Olympus (significantly, as will be seen, this heathen deity was fashioned as a man and with the face of Antiochus himself), carried into the temple—even into the Holy of Holies itself. He then demanded that the people bow down to worship his god. Many Jews would not bow to the statue of a heathen deity, and history records that as many as eighty thousand people were slain, while others fled.

Antiochus was not a fool, simply up to mischief, and an understanding of why he did what he did is crucial for a clear understanding of related prophetic truth.

There were three major steps in ancient conquests. They were simple, basic, and brilliant. The first step was to engage the enemy on the battlefield and defeat him. The second step was to humiliate the enemy once he was defeated. Lastly, the defeated enemy was assimilated into the triumphant nation's culture and government.

When ancient armies marched into war, they marched under the ensign and supposed protection of their pagan gods. For them, there was little concept of one true, universal, omnipotent God. Rather, they viewed gods as localized, finite deities. Each nation had its own plurality of gods which they worshiped. The army that was victorious in conflict was, therefore, thought to be the army with superior deities. To humiliate a vanquished foe, the second step was to enter the temples of their gods and carry the icons away and then later, in great pomp, place them in the temples of the triumphant army at the feet of their own gods. This was the height of humiliation for the defeated nation. The final step was to assimilate the defeated foe by getting them to worship the triumphant nation's gods. The logic went like this: *Our gods are greater than your gods because our army defeated your army. Where are your gods? They're at the feet of our gods. Isn't it reasonable and beneficial to worship our gods?*

Once a defeated nation began to worship the gods of their conquerors, they were easily assimilated. That normally meant they would not rebel, would serve the conqueror's army, and would pay tribute. Religion was used as an instrument for political assimilation. This concept is clearly illustrated in the Bible. After Nebuchadnezzar defeated Israel, he went into the temple at Jerusalem and took the vessels (there were no idols or statues of Jehovah) used in the worship of the Lord back to his temples. Later, his grandson Belshazzar used those sacred vessels in a licentious party (Dan. 5:1–2). As a result, God told the king his kingdom would be taken from him that very night (Dan. 5:23–29).

When Antiochus Epiphanes had his soldiers carry the image of his chief deity into the Jewish temple, he was seeking to assimilate the Jewish nation into his kingdom. He could not have Egypt, but at least he thought he would have Israel assimilated into the very fabric of his nation through Greek culture and religion. They would pay taxes to Syria, serve in her army, and be a geographical buffer zone between Syria and Egypt should the latter one day plan a counterattack.

Antiochus did not have to accomplish the normal first step through conquest. At that moment of history, Israel was a weak and defenseless people. They had no army to be defeated. But they had to be humiliated. To that end, Antiochus had a pig killed on the altar in sacrifice to his god and then had the statue of Zeus Olympus carried into the Temple of Jehovah.[1]

Antiochus knew that he already had considerable support from the Hellenistic (nonreligious) Jews. He anticipated that the rest of the nation would fall in behind. However, he seriously miscalculated. Under the godly priest Mattathias and his five sons, the third known in history as Judas Maccabaeus (Judah the Hammer), a guerrilla-style resistance began. Within three years, Antiochus and his Syrian army were driven from Israel.

After his departure, the immediate priority of faithful Jews was the cleansing and rededicating of the temple on Mount Moriah at Jerusalem. There had been an abomination (the parading of a heathen deity in the likeness of a man into the temple built for God) which had made the temple a desecrated desolation for three years. This cleansing of the temple resulted in a new, joyous holiday for the Jewish people.

As a matter of fact, every time someone wanted to destroy the Jewish nation, the Jews added another holiday. Pharaoh tried it, and God gave them Passover. Haman tried it in the book of Esther, and they celebrated Purim. Antiochus tried it, and it resulted in Hanukkah, or "the feast of the dedication" (John 10:22). In our own day, Hitler tried it, and his failure eventuated in the rebirth of the Jewish nation and its independence day.

In broad outline, the conflict between Syria and Egypt and its implications for Israel with the desecration of the temple is described by the prophet Daniel in an extended passage of Scripture (Dan. 11:21–32). It is also alluded to by the prophet Zechariah (Zech. 9:11–17).

This historic portrait of the "abomination of desolation" (the introduction of the image of a man into the temple built as an habitation for God) under Antiochus Epiphanes, who arose out of the Grecian Empire, gives a frame of reference for understanding the still-future prophetic "abomination of desolation" under the Antichrist, who will arise out of the revived Roman Empire (sometimes referred to as a ten-nation confederation in Europe).

Biblically, the term *antichrist* is sometimes broadly used to describe the attitude and philosophy (spirit) of this unregenerate world system toward God (1 John 4:3). That attitude and philosophy will ultimately be personified in one being who will himself be called the Antichrist (1 John 2:18, 22). Antiochus was a precursor of this coming man. The prefix *anti* comes from a Greek preposition meaning both *against* and *in place of*. For that reason, the Antichrist is described in these words, "Who opposeth [against] and exalteth himself above [in place of] all that is called God" (2 Thess. 2:4). When Satan rebelled against his Creator, he sought to be both *against* and *in place of* God (Isa. 14:13–14). Whenever an antichrist is referred to, the dominant idea is *opposition to* and *substitution of* God (see e.g., Dan. 11:36; Rev. 13:11–17). That antichrist attitude characterized the ongoing opposition of this unregenerate world toward its Creator.

Does it strain credibility to suggest that man—intelligent, informed, sophisticated, modern man—would ever bow to the image of a man? That at the end of history, men will seek to deify a man? It should not, because that is precisely where human history is unerringly heading. When the Antichrist appears on the stage of history, he will be the most attractive and persuasive of all men.

Clarence Larkin, in his helpful commentary on Revelation, wrote concerning the Antichrist: "He will be a 'composite' man. One who embraces in his character the abilities and powers of Nebuchadnezzar [of Babylon], Xerxes [of Persia], Alexander the Great [of Greece], and Caesar Augustus [of Rome]. He will have the marvelous gift of attracting unregenerate men, and the irresistible fascination of his personality, his versatile attainments, superhuman wisdom, great administrative and executive ability, along with his powers as a consummate flatterer, a brilliant diplomatist, a superb strategist, will make him the most conspicuous and prominent of men. All these gifts will be conferred on him by

Satan, whose tool he will be."[2] Let it be added that Larkin's superlatives are not an overstatement. For negative purposes Antichrist will be the consummate superman.

Empowered by Satan and aided by his false prophet, an image of the Antichrist (a man) will be enthroned at the temple (built for God alone) in Jerusalem. His purpose will be assimilation of the Jewish people through the religion of humanism. Concerning man's response to that coming event, the apostle Paul wrote, "And for this cause God shall send them [unregenerate Jews] strong delusion, that they should believe a lie" (2 Thess. 2:11). Literally, the text says they should believe "the" lie—a specific, definitive, and identifiable lie. It was the lie of Satan in the Garden. He said, "In the day ye eat thereof . . . ye shall be as gods" (Gen. 3:5). What began as rebellion and self-exaltation in the Garden of Eden will find its final, short-lived glory and certain demise in the rebuilt temple on the mountains of Jerusalem. Deification of man is the "theology" of humanism. And its deadly venom has spanned history from Adam to the present day.

Humanistic philosophy rests on four major pillars. The first is *atheism,* the belief that there is no God, no Sovereign, no Creator, no Being to whom man must one day give account. Those who hold such a view can easily be described. The Bible says, "The fool hath said in his heart, There is no God" (Ps. 14:1; 53:1).

The second pillar of humanism is *evolution*. If the first pillar is accepted, the second follows quite naturally. If there is no Creator, the only explanation for man's existence is that he evolved from some lower form of life. To believe that man evolved is unrealistic, nonscientific insanity. The evolutionists' ridicule of those who believe that God exists is prompted by the fact that the very belief in God condemns their unbelief.

The third pillar of humanism, *moral relativity,* comes logically out of the first two. If there is no God and man has evolved, there can be *no absolutes* for living. There is nothing solid or eternal upon which to build one's life. Righteousness is rightness, and rightness, by definition, is conformity to a standard. The standard of rightness is God Himself. But if there is no God, there is no standard. If man evolved, he is *still* evolving, and all is in flux and change. There is no foundation; all is quicksand.

The fourth pillar is pragmatic and relates to values and lifestyle. If atheism and evolution are true and no absolutes exist, then *amo-*

*rality,* which means *no morality,* reigns. According to this fourth pillar, there is no right or wrong—only likes and dislikes, your way and my way, efficiency and inefficiency, expediency and inexpediency. "I did it my way," "Do your own thing," "If it feels good, do it," "It's your thing; I can't tell you what to do"—these are all slogans that express the logical and amoral outworking of humanism.

Mark it well—the dignity, nobility, and worth of mankind are inseparably wed to the truth that God created man in His own image. He breathed into him the breath of life so that man became a living soul—an everlasting being. But if there is no God and man has evolved, there is no basis for dignity, nobility, or worth for mankind. He is simply a higher order of animal being—but an animal.

Out of such thinking, knowingly or unknowingly, comes the proabortion mentality. After all, if man is only an animal, then *what is so wrong about terminating an unwanted pregnancy?* And in time, such contemporary thinking will ask, *What's wrong with terminating the elderly who have outlived their usefulness?* Pets and other animals by the tens of thousands are put to sleep every day.

If there are no absolutes, no God-given eternal standards of right and wrong, then what is wrong with homosexuality, adultery, drugs, alcoholism, and wickedness and perversions of every other kind which have invaded and virtually dominate the present hour of history?

That is precisely where planet Earth is at the present moment. Humanistic thinking has captured and now controls the minds of most men. How exceedingly relevant are the words of the apostle Paul, "Be not conformed to this world" (Rom. 12:2). That is, be not fashioned, molded, shaped, put in a box, wrapped, and tied with the ribbon of this world's philosophy. It is the philosophy of Satan, the supreme enemy of men's souls. Every time we turn on the television, read a newspaper, go to work, send our children to secular school, we are bombarded by a humanistic philosophy based upon the supposition that there is no God, that man evolved, that there are no absolutes. So why not do your own thing? Yes, it is that bad!

Paul said, "Be not conformed to this world." But tragically, this world's humanistic philosophy is squeezing many of God's children so tightly that they would be nigh unto spiritual death if that were possible.

What must be done to get out of this suffocating grasp? Paul continued, "but be ye transformed by the renewing of your mind" (Rom. 12:2). As believers we must not allow the external, godless philosophy of this unregenerate world system to come upon us to shape and mold our thinking. Rather, we must be "transformed," spiritually *metamorphosized,* like a caterpillar which becomes a butterfly. We must permit the indwelling Spirit within us to take full control of our lives. How is that done? "By the renewing of our minds"—by saturating our intellects with the truths of the living and powerful Word of God.

Humanistic thinking has captured and now controls the minds of most men. How exceedingly relevant are the words of the apostle Paul, "Be not conformed to this world."

In the end, Satan will not triumph. The Antichrist will not prevail. Man will not be deified. The combined forces of darkness, although powerfully arrayed against the divine purpose, will not succeed. The omnipotent Father has spoken: "Yet have I set my king upon my holy hill of Zion" (Ps. 2:6).

The enemies of our God and His Christ will be destroyed (2 Thess. 2:8; Heb. 2:14; Rev. 20:10–15). And then, "every knee should bow . . . and . . . every tongue should confess that Jesus Christ is Lord, to the glory of God, the Father" (Phil. 2:10–11). As Isaac Watts beautifully declared:

> Jesus shall reign where'er the sun
> Does His successive journeys run,
> His kingdom spread from shore to shore
> Till moons shall wax and wane no more.

But before that indescribably glorious time arrives, there are rivers to forge, mountains to climb, and dangers to flee. So please read on.

# 6

# The Background That Must Be Understood

The time was about A.D. 30; the month, April; the city, Jerusalem; the occasion, the approaching Passover; the location, the Mount of Olives. Three of the seven holidays which God gave to Israel—Passover, Pentecost, and Tabernacles—required attendance at the temple on Mount Moriah at Jerusalem (Ex. 23:14–17; 34:23; Deut. 16:16). Historians suggest that in A.D. 30 hundreds of thousands of Jews converged on the temple at the Passover. From the Mount of Olives, overlooking the Kidron Valley and the Temple Mount, Jesus and His disciples could hear the sounds, smell the smells, see the sights, and sense the excitement of the priests as they prepared for the great multitudes who would soon descend upon them for the purpose of worshiping Jehovah. Jesus had been ministering for three years; His time had come; He was ready. Jews from all over the Mediterranean world were back in Israel. This was the time He would choose to press His messianic claim upon the people.

His command to get a donkey and a colt must have jolted the Lord's disciples into action. They were familiar with the prophetic message of the prophet Zechariah, "Rejoice greatly, O daughter of Zion; shout, O daughter of Jerusalem; behold, thy King cometh unto thee; he is just, and having salvation; lowly, and riding upon an ass, and upon a colt, the foal of an ass" (Zech. 9:9). At last, they must have thought, He is going to claim the throne of David and throw off the yoke of Roman oppression. Amid growing anticipation, Jesus was placed upon the donkey and started down the Mount of Olives. The people, in typical Eastern custom when a king approached, spread their garments in the way, and others "cut down branches from the trees, and spread them in the way. And the multitudes that went before, and that followed, cried, saying, Hosanna to the Son of David! Blessed is he that cometh in the name of the Lord! Hosanna in the highest!" (Matt. 21:8–9). The crowds were quoting directly from Psalm 118. This song was traditionally sung by Jewish people at the Feast of Tabernacles amid the waving of palm branches and emphasized ultimate and perfect deliverance. *Hosanna* literally means *save now* or *deliver now*. They were not speaking of the *new birth* or of *being born again*. They understood none of those things.

The crowds referred to Jesus as the "Son of David," their rightful King. The credentials of Jesus were impeccable: He was a Son of Abraham, of the tribe of Judah, of the family of David. He had a legal right to rule over Israel. Multitudes were calling on Him to lead a rebellion against Rome, as later false messiahs would unsuccessfully attempt to do. In the midst of the clamor and commotion, Jesus continued down the Mount of Olives, across the Kidron Valley, up Mount Moriah, through the Eastern Gate, and straight ahead to the temple. The one requisite for Jesus to establish His kingdom and rule over the nation of Israel was repentance of sin on the part of the people (the reason for the necessity of repentance will be discussed in due course).

"And Jesus went into the temple of God, and cast out all them that sold and bought in the temple, and overthrew the tables of the moneychangers, and the seats of them that sold doves, And said unto them, It is written, My house shall be called the house of prayer, but ye have made it a den of thieves" (Matt. 21:12–13). Why this violent, righteous indignation on the part of the Lord? What was so terrible about changing money or selling animals for sacrifice? Many Jewish families had made long, difficult, dangerous journeys back to Jerusalem from all over the world. When they returned to the holy city, they carried with them the coins of the nations from which they came. But those coins were struck with the imprints of human kings; and that, to the religious leaders of the temple, was idolatrous. Such coins could not be given at the temple as part of the mandatory tithes and offerings required under the Mosaic Law. They had to be exchanged for Jewish coins which Rome permitted to be minted—and which had no imprint of a man upon them. And so, the religious leadership established, as it were, *The First National Bank of Jerusalem*. Right in the temple area, they exchanged money and charged an inordinate rate. Also, an animal was required for Passover sacrifice. Lambs and doves were needed in abundance, and they had to be without spot and blemish—to meet priestly approval. A concession for selling animals was, therefore, established, and once again prices were inflated. The leadership had established *big business* at the temple, and it evidenced an internal heart attitude that was neither pure nor holy toward God. Is it any wonder, therefore, that Jesus turned over the tables of those who changed money and sold animals and proclaimed, "My house shall be called the house of prayer, but ye have made it a den of thieves" (Matt. 21:13)? The fact that they were condemned as "thieves" suggests the problem was not in the exchanging of money or selling of sacrificial animals but in the excessive charges and priestly corruption associated with these practices.

The people of Israel had been called upon to repent of their sin. That repentance was not forthcoming. Concerning their lack of repentance, Jesus would say, "If thou hadst known, even thou, at least in this thy day, the things which belong unto thy peace! But now they are hidden from thine eyes" (Luke 19:42).

He had offered them so much, and they had refused. His heart was broken. He left the temple and mourned over the city of Jerusalem; and had you been there, you would not have described that event as men describe it today. Somehow, men have chosen to call it the *triumphal entry*. There was nothing triumphal about it. He had called on His beloved people to repent, but the leaders and many of the people would have none of that.

The next day, the Pharisees took counsel as to how they might entangle Him in His speech. Jesus had condemned the leadership because of their sin and unrighteousness. Multitudes were now following this Prophet from Nazareth. He had to be silenced, so the Pharisees devised a question whereby they thought they could trap Him in His speech (Matt. 22:15). They were not looking for answers. That would have been commendable. Rather, they simply wanted to discredit Christ. And so, they sent their disciples, along with the Herodians, to pose their question. The Pharisees and the Herodians hated each other, but they banded together against Jesus. Their hatred of Him was obviously greater. The Herodians were more a political entity than a religious one. They supported the Herodian dynasty started by Herod the Great. These rulers were appointed and empowered by Rome; therefore, the Herodians were supporters of Roman rule and were detested by the overwhelming majority of Jews.

The question the leaders put to Jesus was simple: "Is it lawful to give tribute unto Caesar, or not?" (Matt. 22:17). That sounds very simple and straightforward: Do we pay taxes to Rome, or not? They thought that their question had put Jesus on the horns of an unsolvable dilemma. If He said no, that would be treasonous; and with Roman loyalists (the Herodians) present, that could mean imprisonment or death. If He said yes, with Pharisees present to spread the word, the multitudes who detested paying taxes to Rome would have turned from Him.

Jesus gave neither answer. Perceiving their wickedness, He inquired, "Why test me, ye hypocrites? [He knew they weren't really looking for answers.] Show me the tribute money. And they brought unto him a denarius. And he saith unto them, Whose is this image and superscription? They say unto him, Caesar's. Then saith he unto them, Render, therefore, unto Caesar the things which are Caesar's; and unto God, the things that are God's" (Matt. 22:18–21). Dumbfounded, defeated, amazed, but unrepentant, they left.

That same day the Sadducees came to Him. In large measure, they were the ultra-conservatives of that day. They were the aristocracy, and they controlled the priesthood and the temple. The stellar hero of the Sadducees was Moses, and since Moses wrote the first five books of the Old Testament, they venerated those five books above the rest of the Jewish Scriptures. And, unlike the Pharisees with whom they were always feuding, they denied the doctrine of resurrection. Therefore, their question revolved around resurrection. They wanted to demonstrate how ludicrous it was to believe in resurrection. They based their question on the ancient law of the kinsman-redeemer (Deut. 25:5–6). The Law of Moses stated that if a man died without a child, the surviving brother was to marry the deceased brother's wife and raise up a seed. This law was given for two purposes: first, that the name of the deceased not perish in Israel (Deut. 25:6); and second, that the family inheritance not be lost (Lev. 25:25–34). This gracious, God-given law of the kinsman-redeemer is the central theme of the book of Ruth. Naomi's husband had died; her two sons had died; the family name was about to perish and the inheritance (family allocation of land) would be forever lost. But godly Boaz, kinsman to the deceased, married Ruth, redeemed the family inheritance, and raised up a seed for his deceased brother. From the union of Boaz and Ruth would come King David, and eventually through that lineage the Lord Jesus Himself would come according to the flesh (Rom. 1:3). As a result, mankind will not perish from the earth, and His birthright (inheritance) to rule as King of this planet will not be lost.

But the Sadducees took this God-given law to an extreme, unjustified position. First, they reminded the Lord that Moses had given the law (Matt. 22:24). Then they presented a hypothetical case: A man married a woman and died without an heir. In obedience to the law, the next brother married the deceased brother's wife, and he died without an heir; then the third brother, fourth brother, fifth brother, sixth brother, and seventh brother. Each in turn married her, and each died without an heir. And last of all, the woman died. The story finished, the Sadducees were ready to pose their question to spring their trap. They inquired with sickening piety, "In the resurrection whose wife shall she be of the seven? For they all had her" (Matt. 22:28). Quite a question, from men who did not even believe in resurrection.

But the Lord answered, and in doing so, He made two observations. First, He said, "Ye do err, not knowing the scriptures" (Matt. 22:29). You, who pride yourselves in being followers of Moses, do not really know what Moses taught. What a condemnation! Second, He said, You do not know "the power of God" (Matt. 22:29). Their faith was lifeless. They had never experienced the power of God in their own lives; therefore, they could not comprehend that power which could raise the dead. Jesus informed them that their question was irrelevant, because in heaven there is neither marriage nor giving in marriage (Matt. 22:30). None of the seven brothers would be married to her in the resurrection. Further, since the Sadducees not only rejected resurrection but also denied the existence of angels, He discomfited them a little more by comparing man's state in the resurrection with the angels of God who neither marry nor procreate.

But the Lord was not done. Now He went on the offensive.

"But as touching the resurrection of the dead [since they had raised the question], have ye not read that which was spoken unto you by God, saying [He took them back to the account of God's appearing to Moses at the burning bush, Ex. 3:14–15], I am the God of Abraham, and the God of Isaac, and the God of Jacob?" (Matt. 22:31–32). Then the Lord destroyed their inaccurate theology with one irrefutable, cutting observation: "God is not the God of the dead, but of the living" (Matt. 22:32b). The patriarchs Abraham, Isaac, and Jacob had been dead for centuries, but God appeared to Moses and said, "I am the God of Abraham, and the God of Isaac, and the God of Jacob." The whole argument revolved around the tense of the verb. God did not say, "I *was,*" but "I *am* the God of Abraham, and the God of Isaac, and the God of Jacob." They were still alive, although they had died centuries before, and God was still their God. Resurrection life was real. The Sadducees were wrong, and this was demonstrated by Moses, the very one they exalted and presumed to follow.

How wonderful it would have been if the Sadducees had cried out in repentance, "We see it! We see it! Resurrection is real! Eternal hope is ours!" But such was not the case. "They were astonished at His doctrine" (Matt. 22:33) but unrepentant. They had tried to entrap Him but, because of their hardened hearts, they only trapped themselves.

One group of opponents yet remained. The Pharisees were the Lord's major antagonists. They were religious—so very religious and so very lost (not unlike multitudes of religiously dead people today). One of their members, "a lawyer, asked him a question, testing him, and saying, Master [what hypocrisy], which is the great commandment in the law?" (Matt. 22:35–36). A New Testament "lawyer" was one steeped in the Mosaic Law (not a lawyer in the contemporary sense). The question seemed, on the surface, to be simple and straightforward, easy enough to answer—except for the fact that the rabbis had determined that there were 613 laws, not simply the Ten Commandments. And there was heated debate among the Jews as to which was the greatest of all the laws. There were even two schools of thought: followers of Rabbi Shammai and followers of Rabbi Hillel. Once again, the Lord appeared to be placed on the horns of a dilemma. No matter how He responded, they thought, He would alienate a great segment of the Jewish people, and the goal of *entangling Him in His speech* would be achieved. But such would not be the case. "Jesus said unto them, Thou shalt love the Lord, thy God, with all thy heart, and with all thy soul, and with all thy mind. This is the first and great commandment [law]. And the second is like it, Thou shalt love thy neighbor as thyself. On these two commandments hang all the law and the prophets" (Matt. 22:37–40). His answer seemed simple, but what Jesus did was to cite both of the combating schools of thought. From one school, He said, *Love God*—that is *vertical,* between man and God. From the other school, He said, *Love man*—that is *horizontal,* between man and man. Their ambush did not work. The religious leaders were silenced but unmoved.

Three major groups within Israel—the Herodians, the Sadducees, and the Pharisees—each in turn tried to entrap the Lord in His speech. They attempted to trip Him up, to discredit Him before the multitudes, because at the temple He had discredited them before the people when He had brought their corrupt practices to light.

Now the Lord, in some of the strongest language found anywhere in the Bible, condemned the hypocrisy of the nation's religious leaders. They had been confronted by the One who is "the way, the truth, and the life" (John 14:6) and yet rejected Him. Seven times the Lord said, "Woe unto you, scribes and Pharisees, hypocrites!" (Matt. 23:13, 14, 15, 23, 25, 27, 29) and then demonstrated their hypocrisy, ending the pronouncements by calling the scribes and Pharisees, "Ye serpents, ye generation of vipers, how can ye escape the damnation of hell?" (Matt. 23:33).

Then, left with a heart that was breaking, with tension and pathos, Jesus cried out in agony of soul for His own brethren: "O Jerusalem, Jerusalem, thou that killest the prophets, and stonest them who are sent unto thee, how often would I have gathered thy children together, even as a hen gathereth her chickens under her wings, and ye would not!" (Matt. 23:37).

They had killed the prophets; they had rejected the messengers who had been sent through the centuries—that was nondebatable biblical fact. And now, the Son of God was present—never mind the prophets and the messengers—and they were rejecting Him also. He wanted to gather them as a hen gathers her chickens under her wings—lovingly, tenderly, protectively, providingly, intimately.

But they would not have Him to rule over them. They had not repented. As a result, the Lord declared, "Behold, your house is left unto you desolate" (Matt. 23:38). Hardly could a statement be more devastating. When the Lord said, "Your house is left unto you desolate," He was not talking about New England Cape Cods or Southern colonials or posh condominiums or sprawling ranchers. He was talking about their temple on Mount Moriah. He had already said, concerning the temple, "My house shall be called the house of prayer, but ye have made it a den of thieves" (Matt. 21:13). To understand what was in view, it is imperative that the origin of the temple be considered.

The first temple had been built more than nine hundred years before Christ. King David had expanded the borders of Israel, defeated her enemies, brought a measure of prosperity, and made Israel a world power. Evidently, as he looked at the heathen nations round about him, he saw the magnificent temples built to house their gods. But they were gods conceived in men's minds and fashioned out of wood, stone, and metal by men's hands. In contrast, King David worshiped and served Jehovah, the true and living God, the Holy One of Israel, the only uncaused cause, the self-existent God; and King David wanted to build a house for his God.

The Lord was pleased with David's heart attitude, but King David was a soldier, a man of war, and he would not be permitted to build the house for "The Prince of Peace" (Isa. 9:6). He would, however, be permitted to gather the materials for the house (1 Chron. 22:1–5). His son Solomon would build the house (1 Chron. 17:1–12). In time, the magnificent Solomonic temple was completed, and although God is omnipresent and "the heaven of heavens cannot contain [Him]" (2 Chron. 6:18), He chose, in a localized sense, to dwell among His people within His temple and to manifest His glory there. The children of Israel would be permitted in a unique sense to see the holiness, justice, truth, goodness, grace, long-suffering, faithfulness, and mercy of God—what He was truly like. This divine presence among His people was an incomparable privilege which no other nation had ever known. Israel alone, in a specialized sense, possessed the divine presence, power, provision, and protection.

But about four centuries later, the prophet Ezekiel described the departure of the glory of God from the temple. His description is one of the most heartrending stories in all the Word of God. The Sovereign of the universe, the One who cast the stars into space, who spoke the world into existence, who fashioned man from the dust of the ground, who breathed into man the breath of life, the One of whom it is said, "Heaven is my throne, and the earth is my footstool" (Isa. 66:1), and who chose Israel as His "peculiar treasure" (Ps. 135:4), was driven out of the temple by His people's grievous sin (Ezek. 8:6).

Not without reason, the gospel of Matthew stands first in the New Testament. It is the logical bridge between the Old Testament and the New Testament.

First, the glory of God departed from over the ark of the covenant between the cherubim in the Holy of Holies to the threshold of the temple (Ezek. 10:4). It was almost as if the glory of God had paused there at the threshold to say, "Don't drive Me away. I want to be your God. I want you to be My people. But I am a holy God, and you are a sinful, unrepentant people. Repent of your sin, and I will stay." Then the glory of God moved from the threshold of the temple to the east gate of the Lord's house (Ezek. 10:19). And once again, it was as if the glory of God paused, hesitated, hoping for a repentance that would allow Him to remain but which never materialized. Finally the glory moved from the Eastern Gate, across the Kidron Valley, and over the Mount of Olives on the east side of the city (Ezek. 11:23). The nation had forced the withdrawal of the presence of God from their midst by their grievous, continuous sin. With that event, over Israel was written the word *Ichabod,* meaning *the glory is departed* (1 Sam. 4:21).

Then almost six hundred years later, history would repeat itself. Jesus was God in flesh. In Him dwelt all the fullness of the Godhead in bodily form (Col. 2:9). In Christ the glory of God could return to the temple once again. The central message of the Gospel of Matthew is "Repent, for the kingdom of heaven is at hand" (Matt. 4:17; cf. Matt. 10:7).

Not without reason, the Gospel of Matthew stands first in the New Testament. It is the logical bridge between the Old Testament and the New Testament. No defense for a message that called for repentance had to be made by Matthew. The Jews of the first century knew that the worst thing which had ever befallen the nation was the withdrawal of the divine presence from the temple because of national sin. If that glory were to return in the person of Christ, the nation must repent of its sin. On Palm Sunday, Jesus went to the temple to see if that repentance had occurred. The temple was the heart, soul, and pulse of Israel. If there were genuine repentance, it would have been evidenced at the temple. What the Lord found were changers of money, sellers of animals, a corrupt system, and hypocritical leaders—but no repentance.

And so Jesus, with a broken heart, said, in effect, *I (for My part) would have gathered you; you (for your part) would not have Me. Your house is left unto you desolate. The glory is not returning now. And you will not see Me until you are ready to say* [they were not ready then], *Blessed is he who comes in the name of the Lord* (see Matt. 23:37–39).

Now the hopes of the disciples were dashed on rocky shoals they had not anticipated. They had followed Jesus for three long years. They were sure He was going to ascend the throne of David, and, as His disciples, they would have positions of honor, power, and prestige. But something seemed to have gone terribly wrong. Jesus had alienated the Jewish leadership; a wide chasm had opened between them. Their Master had said that He was leaving, and men would not see Him for an indefinite period of time. One question arose in the minds of the disciples. It towered above all else. "Tell us, when shall these things be? And what shall be the sign of thy coming, and of the end of the age?" (Matt. 24:3).

# 7

# The Question That Had to Be Answered

The die was cast—the decision was final—Jesus was leaving. Israel's tragic plight was now sealed. They had brought it on themselves. During three years of public ministry, Jesus had pleaded with His nation to repent of their sin and acknowledge His messianic claim to rule over them. His credentials were impeccable. The lineage from which He sprang, the village in which He was born, the city in which He was raised, the compassion He demonstrated, the courage He displayed, the wisdom He evidenced, the miracles He performed, the message He proclaimed, the authority He exhibited ("Never man spoke like this man," John 7:46)—all collaborated to attest to His messiahship. It was with justifiable reason, therefore, that the disciples thought He was going to become King of Israel—that finally the yoke of ruthless, relentless Roman persecution would be broken. At last, they believed, under Messiah's rule Israel would once again know the greatness and glory which had been theirs almost a thousand years earlier under mighty King David and his wise son, King Solomon.

But their hopes and dreams notwithstanding, it would not be—not for that hour of history. Through the centuries, the Jewish leadership had corrupted the inspired writings of Moses and the prophets of Israel with their oral law and vain traditions. Only a vestigial skeleton of pure, God-given Judaism remained.

Many of the Pharisees were corrupt hypocrites. In the words of the Lord, they were whitewashed sepulchers (Matt. 23:27)—well-manicured on the outside but decaying and smelling on the inside. They had become "blind leaders of the blind" (Matt. 15:14). The holiness of Jesus condemned their sin, and the truth of Jesus rebuked their error. And tragically, through lies, distortion, manipulation, and false witnesses, they misled the Jewish people. This, in spite of the fact that His flawless life and selfless ministry met all the criteria set forth in the sacred writings of their ancient sages, the very Scriptures to which the Jewish leadership outwardly claimed allegiance.

Soon now, at the appointed time, in the omniscient plan of God the Father, the steps of God the Son would unerringly wind their way to a hill outside the northern wall of the city of Jerusalem. There He would, as the true Passover Lamb, "taste death for every man" (Heb. 2:9).

Jesus knew in intimate detail what was to befall Him in less than a week at Calvary. He knew the humiliation, pain, and death He was facing. With a saddened heart—amazingly, not for Himself but for His beloved nation—He informed His followers that He was leaving. He tempered the shock of His departure, however, with the certain promise of His return. Concerning His beloved nation He said, "Ye shall not see me henceforth, till ye shall say, Blessed is he that cometh in the name of the Lord" (Matt. 23:39).

Now one question towered above all else in the disciples' thinking. It consumed them in importance and cried out to be answered. All of Israel's national hopes were linked inseparably to the promised Messiah. Jesus, the disciples realized, was that Messiah. But the national leadership rejected His messianic claims, and He was leaving to return another day. Therefore, the disciples asked, "What shall be the sign of thy coming, and of the end of the age?" (Matt. 24:3).

Understanding the significance of the word *sign* and what the disciples were requesting of the Lord in asking for a sign is a key that opens the door to comprehending a great deal of end-time events.

The word *sign* occurs 119 times in the Bible. The first usage is in Genesis in the context of God's creative acts and the beginning of human history. The sun, moon, and stars were, in the divine scheme of things, intended to be "for signs, and for seasons" (Gen. 1:14). The final usage is in Revelation, the last book of the

Bible, in the context of God's final judgment on the earth. "And I saw another sign in heaven, *great* and *marvelous,* seven angels having the seven last plagues, for in them is filled up the wrath of God" (Rev. 15:1). Signs were placed in heaven at creation and will be manifest in heaven at God's final judgment.

It may appear obvious, but signs are for seeing. That is, men are called upon to see, look at, behold signs. Signs are intended to be conspicuous, not hidden. The Bible speaks of signs appearing (Mark 24:30), being shown (Matt. 13:22), being accomplished before people (John 20:30), in the midst of people (Acts 2:22), and among people (2 Cor. 12:12). By their very nature signs are to be public.

Signs are also miraculous. The concept of biblical signs and miracles is so closely intertwined that sometimes the Hebrew or Greek words usuallly rendered as *sign* are literally translated *miracle* (see Ex. 7:9; Num. 14:22; Deut. 11:3; John 2:11, 23; 12:37). Often the words *signs, miracles,* and *wonders* occur in tandem (see Ex. 7:3; Deut. 4:34; 6:22; 34:11; Acts 2:22; 8:13). Signs were placed by God, as it were, at crucial forks in the road of redemptive history to say to men and women of faith, *This is the way, walk ye in it*. Signs were to confirm, identify, or mark out someone or something as genuine, authentic, the "real McCoy." Signs were posted to reveal truth and were authenticated by a miracle or wonder.

> If God chose to authenticate truth with signs, it should not be surprising that Satan attempts to authenticate his lies with counterfeit signs or miracles (Matt. 24:24).

If God chose to authenticate truth with signs, it should not be surprising that Satan attempts to authenticate his lies with counterfeit signs or miracles (Matt. 24:24).

Signs relate primarily to the Jewish people. The apostle Paul, writing to the church at Corinth, said, "The Jews require a sign, and the Greeks seek after wisdom" (1 Cor. 1:22). It was the Jewish people who kept requesting signs to validate truth (Matt. 12:38; 16:4; Mark 8:11; Luke 11:29).

Signs are more directional in nature than chronological. They tell men *which way* rather than *what time*. When the disciples inquired of the Lord, "What shall be the sign of thy coming, and of the end of the age?" (Matt. 24:3), they were not so much asking *when* will the end occur, but *how* will men recognize it when it does?

When God sent Moses back to Egypt to deliver the children of Israel, He equipped His servant with a rod. God said to Moses, "And thou shalt take this rod in thine hand, wherewith thou shalt do signs" (Exod. 4:17). In the court of the Pharaoh of Egypt, Moses used that rod to perform signs which were miraculous and supernatural. They were given to authenticate and confirm that it was the self-existent God of the Hebrews who had sent Moses into the courts of Pharaoh to redeem the children of Israel. Try as they would, however, the wise men and sorcerers of Egypt, although empowered by Satan, could only partially duplicate the signs given by God through His servant Moses (Exod. 7:8–13).

Centuries later the apostle John, in giving the reason for penning the Gospel that bears his name, wrote, "And many other signs truly did Jesus in the presence of his disciples, which are not written in this book; But these [signs] are written, that ye might believe that Jesus is the Christ, the Son of God; and that believing ye might have life through his name" (John 20:30–31). John chose a series of miracles from among the many that Jesus performed. These miracles were chosen because they authenticated and substantiated that Jesus was the promised Messiah and the Son of God.

Jesus Christ is the preincarnate (that is, He existed before He took on human flesh), self-existent (that is, He has always been and owes His origin to no one and nothing) Son of God. He is coequal and coeternal with God the Father and God the Holy Spirit. But at a precise moment in history, Jesus would be born of a human mother on the planet Earth. The preincarnate (before flesh) Son of God would become the incarnate (in flesh) Son of man. He would be both undiminished deity and perfect humanity—the God-Man, who alone could meet every need of the human heart.

But how would men recognize Him when He appeared? How would they know with absolute certainty? How could He be picked out from among the myriads of men who would live and die on the earth?

Here was a crucial fork in the road of human history, so God would place a sign—not a small placard which could be inadvertently passed by, but a giant billboard, as it were, which all could see. It would be unusual, miraculous, supernatural—something which satanic power could not successfully duplicate. The sign would be given to confirm and authenticate—to leave no doubt concerning the identity of the Son of God. He would make His appearance in the "fullness of time" (Gal. 4:4), and men of faith would be able to recognize Him.

The sign was promised by God more than seven hundred years before it appeared. An unrighteous king was then ruling over the kingdom of Judah. His name was Ahaz. To this king God gave a promise that the military attack being planned against him by the ten northern tribes of Israel would not succeed (Isa. 7:3–9). Although Ahaz was a godless king, this coalition to the north could not be permitted to kill off the Davidic lineage through which the true Messiah was to come. To confirm His promise, God invited King Ahaz to request a sign—nothing easy or commonplace, but something miraculous and supernatural. To this faithless king God said, "Ask a sign of the LORD, thy God; ask it either in the depth, or in the height above [this was an invitation to test the LORD, to have Him bare His right arm of power, to move the muscle of omnipotence]. But Ahaz said, I will not ask, neither will I test the LORD" (Isa. 7:11–12).

God turned, therefore, from the unbelieving king to the whole house of Israel. He would give them a sign—not a sign concerning the impending invasion but a sign to identify the righteous King who would bring certain, eternal deliverance.

To Israel God said, "Therefore the Lord himself shall give you a sign; Behold [signs were made for beholding], the virgin shall conceive, and bear a son, and shall call his name Immanuel" (Isa. 7:14). The birth of a child through a virgin obviously was unique, unprecedented, and miraculous—it would require supernatural power. It would be a bona fide, unimpeachable sign to identify the Messiah and Savior of the world when He appeared.

Parenthetically, those who debate over the translation of the Hebrew word *almah* and whether it means *virgin* or *young maiden* are sifting out the fly and swallowing the camel. The birth of the child was to be a sign. Divine signs, by definition, are miraculous and supernatural. *Virgin* is the only legitimate translation of *almah* in the context of Isaiah 7:14 and in light of the divine statement that the birth would be a sign.

And so the long centuries moved agonizingly on, one century after another, one generation after another, and the sign which God had promised did not appear. Doubtless, with the passing of time, some ridiculed the promise of a sign, others ignored it, and many forgot it. Only a few, like the righteous priest Zacharias, his wife Elizabeth (Luke 1:5–6), and godly Simeon, continued to wait for "the consolation of Israel" (Luke 2:25).

It must have been a clear Judean night; the latter rains were now past; the stars were shining brightly; the hills surrounding Bethlehem were never more beautiful. A solemn hush fell over all things; the shepherds were watching their sheep. And then it happened, as if a dream; but it was real. Earth was visited by heaven! An angel appeared and said to the shepherds, "Fear not; for, behold, I bring you good tidings of great joy, which shall be to all people. For unto you is born this day in the city of David a Savior, who is Christ the Lord. And this shall be a sign unto you: Ye shall find the babe wrapped in swaddling clothes, lying in a manger" (Luke 2:10–12). The sign of which the angelic messenger spoke was not, "Ye shall find the babe wrapped in swaddling clothes, lying in a manger," although that is the almost universal interpretation. There was nothing unusual about a child being wrapped in swaddling clothes. That the child was wrapped in swaddling clothes and lying in a manger suggests poverty, but certainly there was nothing miraculous or supernatural about it. Those details were simply given so that the shepherds could locate the child in Bethlehem.

The sign which God gave was the virgin birth—it was the fulfillment of the words of the prophet Isaiah, "The virgin shall conceive, and bear a son" (Isa. 7:14). The shepherds raced to Bethlehem to find the child. And they found Him wrapped in swaddling clothes, lying in a manger. When they entered, they bowed; they worshiped; they arose; and they left. They had no need to inquire, "Where is the proud father?" They knew that He was virgin-born.

Before them lay the Son of God because the eternal God was His Father, and the Son of man because the Jewish maiden Miriam (or Mary), who never knew a man, was His mother (Luke 1:34–35).

Seven centuries earlier, the Sovereign of the universe had promised a sign (the virgin birth), a miracle to substantiate that God was dwelling among men. In the little village of Bethlehem, which lies along the patriarchal highway, running north and south through Palestine, the sign was posted for all men to see.

In time, the Son of God grew to manhood. At the age of thirty, the Lord Jesus Christ embarked on His public ministry. Thirty was the traditional age at which Jewish rabbis could officially begin their teaching. Jesus functioned as a rabbi, but His ministry was short-lived. At age thirty-three, after only three and one-half years of preaching and teaching, His life ebbed away as he torturously suffocated on a Roman cross.

By any standard, the span of His ministry was brief, but it cannot be measured like the shooting meteor that lights up the dark sky for a brief instant only to be remembered no more. Rather, it was like the dawning of a new day as the sun moved from below the horizon to directly overhead. Men could see its rays and feel its heat—and they still can.

For most men, the rays of the truth He taught are too bright, and the heat exemplified in His holy living is too hot.

Once the Lord began His ministry, the scribes and Pharisees came to Jesus to ask for a sign (Matt. 12:38–40; 16:1–4; Mark 8:11–12). Jews require a sign! They were asking for something miraculous, something supernatural, something that would authenticate and substantiate what they viewed as His revolutionary teaching. They wanted to know, *By what right, by whose authority, under whose ensign do You do these things? Give us a sign,* they challenged. He responded by saying, "There shall no sign be given" (Matt. 12:39). But they were persistent; they would not be put off. Again they asked for a sign (Matt. 16:1).

Jesus declared, "A wicked and adulterous generation seeketh after a sign" (Matt. 16:4). His point was clear and forceful: Had His brethren been faithful to Moses and the prophets of Israel (that is, to their own Old Testament Scriptures) they would have known by what right, by whose authority, and under whose ensign He taught and did the things which the Pharisees now questioned. They had become an adulterous generation. They had committed spiritual adultery. They substituted the traditions of men for the truth of God, all the while proudly proclaiming their orthodoxy.

Finally, in response to their persistent request for a sign, Jesus said that only one sign would be given. "For as Jonah was three days and three nights in the belly of the great fish, so shall the Son of man be three days and three nights in the heart of the earth" (Matt. 12:40).

The sign Jesus gave to substantiate and authenticate all that He said and did in His life and death was His resurrection. He gave the same response to a request for a sign on another occasion. He said, "Destroy this temple [His body], and in three days I will raise it up" (John 2:19), and He did (Matt. 28:1–6).

Outside the northern wall of Jerusalem, where multitudes still pass by, the place where the sign was posted can still be seen. In the midst of an ancient but still beautiful garden is an empty tomb. The angel's stirring message cannot be silenced. Like a rippling pond, it echoes the glorious truth: "He is not here; for he is risen . . . Come, see the place where the Lord lay" (Matt. 28:6).

There was a sign to authenticate and substantiate *when* the Messiah appeared on earth—the virgin birth. There was a sign to authenticate and substantiate *all* that He did in life and death—His resurrection. Now the disciples inquired, "What shall be the sign of thy coming, and of the end of the age?" (Matt. 24:3). It was the one question, above all others, that cried out to be answered.

# 8

# And What of the Tribulation Period?

One of the most frequently used terms in any discussion concerning future events and the Rapture of the church is the term *tribulation*. This, in turn, leads to a discussion of the Great Tribulation, its significance, and its duration.

In this chapter, the terms *tribulation* and *great tribulation* will be discussed.

The designation *the tribulation period* should properly be omitted from any honest consideration of the time of the Rapture of the church. The term *tribulation period* is normally used by pretribulation rapturists as a synonym for the seventieth week of the book of Daniel (Dan. 9:27); that is, to describe the seven years that immediately precede Christ's physical return to the earth to establish His millenial kingdom. Although popular and used by many competent preachers, teachers, and theologians, such a designation has no biblical justification.

The Greek word *thlipsis,* translated *tribulation* or *affliction* in many English Bibles, occurs twenty times in the New Testament. Tribulation conveys the idea of pressure, affliction, anguish, persecution, and trouble. It is most frequently used in nonprophetic settings, as for instance, "In the world ye shall have *tribulation:* but be of good cheer; I have overcome the world" (John 16:33). Or again, "knowing that *tribulation* worketh patience; and patience, experience; and experience, hope" (Rom. 5:3–4). And Paul wrote to the church at Corinth, "Who comforteth us in all our *tribulation,* that we may be able to comfort them who are in any trouble, by the comfort with which we ourselves are comforted of God" (2 Cor. 1:4).

Only six verses of Scripture can be clearly identified as using the word *tribulation* in a prophetic context. Two others (Rom. 2:2–9, and 2 Thess. 1:6) may have prophetic significance but have no bearing on the chronology of the Tribulation. Of the six, one of these uses is found in the Old Testament. Moses said to Israel, "When thou art in *tribulation,* and all these things are come upon thee, even in the latter days" (Deut. 4:30). Since no clearly definitive time period can be identified by the phrase "in the latter days," the word *tribulation* in this context must be interpreted in the light of its clear usage in the New Testament.

Of the five clear prophetic uses of the word *tribulation* or *affliction* in the New Testament, four appear in the Gospels in the teaching of the Lord, and the fifth occurs in the book of Revelation.

In His Olivet Discourse teaching, the Lord said, "For then shall be *great tribulation,* such as was not since the beginning of the world to this time, no, nor ever shall be" (Matt. 24:21). Two points are germane to that statement. First, the time of the tribulation of which the Lord speaks is directly related to the desecration of the temple (the abomination that maketh desolate) and the warning to flee Jerusalem (Matt. 24:15–20). The desecration of the the temple, it is widely agreed, occurs in the middle of Daniel's seventieth week (Dan. 9:27; Rev. 12:6,14), specifically, three and one-half years into it. Second, the word *tribulation* in this text (Matt. 24:21) has the adjective "great" before it. Thus, the Lord is speaking of the Great Tribulation. Eight verses later He once again uses the word *tribulation*. He taught, "Immediately after the *tribulation* of those days shall the sun be darkened, and the moon shall not give its light, and the stars shall fall from heaven, and the powers of the heavens shall be shaken" (Matt. 24:29). There can be no doubt that the tribulation which the Lord has in view in Matthew 24:29 is the Great Tribulation to which He had just referred in Matthew 24:21.

The second gospel writer recorded the Lord's Olivet teaching on the Tribulation this way: "For in those days shall be *affliction* [this is the Greek word *thlipsis* normally translated *tribulation*], such as was not from the beginning of the creation which God created unto this time, neither shall be" (Mark 13:19). This usage of the word *tribulation* is once again intimately and uninterruptedly linked to the desecration of the temple and the warning to flee in the middle of the seventieth week (Mark 13:14–18). Again, a brief five verses later, these words are recorded: "But in those days, after that *tribulation,* the sun shall be darkened, and the moon shall not give its light" (Mark 13:24). The association of this verse with that which precedes it and with the Matthew account which exactly parallels it leaves no room for doubt. Of the four times the Lord spoke of *tribulation* in a prophetic context, He was speaking of the Great Tribulation which begins in the middle of Daniel's seventieth week—precisely three and one-half years into it.

In each instance where the *Great Tribulation* is used in a prophetic setting, it always refers to the persecution of God's elect by wicked men, never to the wrath of God being directed toward mankind. Prophetically, therefore, the Great Tribulation speaks of man's wrath against man, not God's wrath against man.

The word *tribulation* is found one more time in a clear prophetic context. The apostle John wrote, "And one of the elders answered, saying unto me, Who are these who are arrayed in white robes? And from where did they come? And I said unto him, Sir, thou knowest. And he said to me, These are they who came out of the *great tribulation* [lit. *the tribulation the great*]" (Rev. 7:13–14). Here, once again, the adjective "great" is found, and the reference is to the Great Tribulation, which begins not at the inauguration but in the middle of the seventieth week of Daniel.

A clear fact emerges from an examination of the word *tribulation* as used in the Bible. In a prophetic context, it is used to describe only the period of time that begins in the *middle* of Daniel's seventieth week—never of the first half of it. *Based on that indisputable fact, to call the entire seven-year time frame the tribulation period is to coin a technical phrase and superimpose it upon the Scriptures, reading into the biblical text that which it does not itself declare.*

Someone may object, "But isn't the seventieth week of Daniel a time of great difficulty? Isn't it a time when the scroll, found in the right hand of God the Father, is being opened by the Son of Man [Rev. 5:5–7] and when the seals, trumpets, and bowls are bringing history to consummation?" That is true. But in no sense does that justify giving that period the technical designation *the tribulation period*. There have been many periods of history of intense pressure, affliction, persecution, and trouble. But they are not called the Tribulation period. During the Roman siege of Jerusalem between A.D. 68 and 70, tens of thousands of Jews were killed or enslaved, and multitudes more fled for their lives. It was a time of intense trouble and persecution, but that is not called the Tribulation period. In the fourteenth century, an estimated twenty-five million people died from the black plague in Europe; it was a time of extreme distress and pressure, but that is not called the Tribulation period. During the Civil War, fifty thousand men died in three days at Gettysburg. It was a time of great national distress—Americans were killing Americans and brothers were killing brothers—but that is not called the Tribulation period. From 1938 until 1945, during the Second World War an estimated forty million people died throughout the world, including six million Jews. It was a time of great distress and persecution, but that is not called the Tribulation period. There is no basis for calling a particular period of time characterized by pressure, affliction, or anguish the Tribulation period. And more importantly, as will later be argued, most of that difficult seven-year period cannot be directly attributed to action by God or be properly defined as the time of God's wrath.

Someone else may object, "But isn't it simply a matter of semantics—a choice of words—it really doesn't mean anything? What's the difference if it is called the seventieth week of the book of Daniel or the Tribulation period?" The answer to that question is, it means a great deal. If the seventieth week of Daniel is inappropriately given the technical designation the Tribulation period, and believers are reminded that they are "not appointed . . . to wrath" (1 Thess. 5:9), that they are "saved from wrath through him" (Rom. 5:9), and that they "are not in darkness, that that day should overtake [them] as a thief" (1 Thess. 5:4), an *a priori* case is built for pretribulation rapturism on a false foundation. If the seventieth week is the Tribulation period, or "the time of wrath," and God's people are exempt from "wrath," the matter is settled. But such an argument is both unbiblical and illogical and cannot be allowed to stand.

If, in fact, the first three and one-half years are not part of the

Tribulation period and God's wrath does not start, as pretribulationists assume, at the beginning of the seventieth week of Daniel but considerably further into it, they have built their argument on a foundation that will crumble.

It would be terribly inaccurate and unjust to suggest, as has been done, that many Christians are pretribulational simply because they want to escape the Tribulation period. It would be equally inaccurate to suggest that pretribulation rapturism does not offer comfort that is appealing. No normal person welcomes tribulation, and all the more so if that tribulation is initiated by God. The use of the phrase *tribulation period* (coined by men but not justified in the Bible) creates, at the very least, a built-in bias for pretribulationism. Therefore, the term *the seventieth week of Daniel,* a term with biblical justification, is preferred. It will frequently be used to describe the seven-year period that precedes Christ's physical return to the earth. When the terms pre-, mid-, or posttribulationism are used in this book, they will be used to communicate in terms that are familiar but with the clear understanding that such terms have no biblical basis.

A second and related term has been touched upon. Now it must be examined further. It is the term *Great Tribulation*. The Great Tribulation is specifically referred to five times, as has already been noted (Matt. 24:21, 29; Mark 13:19, 24; Rev. 7:14). The starting point of the Great Tribulation can be clearly established. It coincides with the desecration of the temple by the Antichrist in the middle of the seventieth week (Dan. 9:27; Matt. 24:15). Pretribulation rapturists are generally agreed on that point. They also concur that the Great Tribulation is three and one-half years in duration and coincides with the last half of the seventieth week of Daniel.

Some expositors, such as the gifted Greek scholar Kenneth Wuest, call the entire seventieth week of Daniel the Great Tribulation. Wuest wrote, "The next prophetic event will be the Day of Christ or the Rapture of the Church. Following that will come the great tribulation, a period of seven years, the seventieth week of Daniel (9:24–27)."[1] This view totally ignores the biblical data that insists that the Great Tribulation begins at the midpoint when the image of the Antichrist is set up in the tribulation temple. Louis Sperry Chafer, whose memory is rightly revered by multitudes of students, made the same erroneous assessment. He wrote, "Concerning the great tribulation period, it has been observed that it is the seventieth week of seven years which was predicted by Daniel."[2]

It is fair to say, however, that the large majority of pretribulation rapturists would view the entire seven years of Daniel's seventieth week as the Tribulation period and the last three and one-half years as the Great Tribulation. Charles Ryrie's comment on Daniel 12:7 is typical: "The events of the Tribulation will be consummated when the three and one-half times (the last three and one-half years of that seven-year period) come to a close. These last three and one-half years constitute the great tribulation" (cf. Matt. 24:21).[3] This view is illustrated in the chart below.

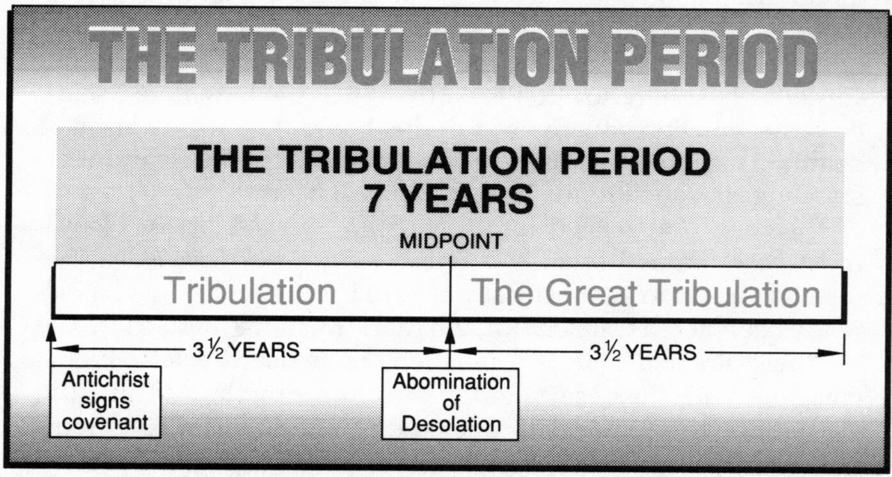


But now another crucial issue arises: Does the Word of God teach that the Great Tribulation is three and one-half years in duration, as pretribulation rapturism insists? Or is that an unfounded assumption with no biblical justification? The Lord, in His Olivet Discourse, spoke of the coming Great Tribulation which would begin in the middle of Daniel's seventieth week (Matt. 24:21). In the next verse He declared, "And except those days should be shortened, there should no flesh be saved: but for the elect's sake those days shall be shortened" (Matt. 24:22). A normative understanding of the Lord's teaching is quite clear. The only possible antecedent to "except those days be shortened" is the Great Tribulation. The Lord is teaching that the Great Tribulation will be cut short. The exact same truth is taught in the gospel of Mark: "For in those days shall be affliction [tribulation], such as was not from the beginning of the creation which God created unto this time, neither shall be" (Mark 13:19). Again this truth is presented, *"And except that the Lord had shortened those days, no flesh should be saved; but for the elect's sake, whom he hath chosen, he hath shortened the days"* (Mark 13:20). Once more, it is the Great Tribulation that is shortened.

It is beyond refutation that the seventieth week of Daniel is not shortened. Daniel was told, "Seventy weeks [of years] are determined upon thy people" (Dan. 9:24). The seventieth week is the last seven-year period of Daniel's prophecy. It is clear that the last three and one-half years are not shortened. This period of time is designated in days: "And the woman fled into the wilderness, where she hath a place prepared by God, that they should feed her there a thousand two hundred and threescore [1,260] days" (Rev. 12:6). "A thousand two hundred and threescore days" is forty-two months (the Jewish biblical month based on the moon is thirty days), and forty-two months is three and one-half years.

The time period is also directly designated in months: "And there was given unto him [the Antichrist] a mouth speaking great things and blasphemies, and power was given unto him to continue forty and two months" (Rev. 13:5); that is, three and one-half years. The same period is also referred to in years: "And to the woman [Israel] were given two wings of a great eagle, that she might fly into the wilderness, into her place, where she is nourished for a time [one year], and times [two years], and half a time [one-half year], from the face of the serpent" (Rev.12:14; cf. Rev. 12:6). Once again, the period is three and one-half years.

This, then, is clear. The entire seventieth week is not shortened. The last three and one-half years of that seventieth week are not shortened. What the Lord Himself teaches is shortened is the Great Tribulation. It is less than three and one-half years in duration. It begins in the middle of the seventieth week, but it does not run until the end of the seventieth week.

The Great Tribulation will be cut short for "the elect's sake" (Matt. 24:22). In light of this truth, the Lord's teaching regarding His return takes on added significance. "Immediately after the tribulation [Great Tribulation] of those days shall the sun be darkened, and the moon shall not give its light, and the stars shall fall from heaven, and the powers of the heavens shall be shaken. And then shall appear the sign of the Son of man in heaven; and then shall all the tribes of the earth mourn, and they shall see the Son of man coming in the clouds of heaven with power and great glory" (Matt. 24:29–30). The Lord is speaking of an event (cosmic disturbance) which occurs after the Great Tribulation but *before* the end of the seventieth week.

The entire seventieth week is not shortened. The last three and one-half years of that seventieth week are not shortened. What the Lord Himself teaches is shortened is the Great Tribulation.

The following facts cannot be set aside: (1) The Great Tribulation begins in the middle of the seventieth week, but it does not run to the end of that week. It is cut short. (2) *Immediately* after the Great Tribulation, there will be cosmic disturbances; these phenomena will signal the coming of the Son of Man from heaven. (3) This coming commences *before* the end of the seventieth week, and is consummated after the end of the seventieth week (Rev. 19:11). For pretribulationism to be sustained there must be *another* coming at the beginning of the seventieth week. Evidence for such an event is simply nonexistent. It will later be demonstrated that following the cosmic disturbances (the sixth seal, Rev. 6:12–14), the Lord's coming from heaven will be for the purpose of rapturing the church before the Day of the Lord's wrath begins with the opening of the seventh seal.

There simply can be no question on this point. The cosmic disturbances concerning which the Lord taught (Matt. 24:29) and which parallel the sixth seal (Rev. 6:12–13) signal the coming of the Son of man in heaven. This sign will occur *after* the Great Tribulation but *before* the end of the seventieth week. The cosmic disturbance (the sun will be darkened, the moon shall not give her light, and the stars shall fall from heaven) will result in a darkened universe. It will be the manifestation of the glory of God which will dispel that darkness. The natural light of the heavenly bodies will be shut off (darkened) and then the supernatural light (the glory of God) will be revealed. The manifestation of God's glory was called by the Jewish people *shekinah* (dwelling) and indicated God's presence. Here then is the answer to the question posed by the disciples, "What shall be the sign of Thy coming, and of the end of the world?" (Matt. 24:3). God's presence will be known through the universal manifestation of His glory. He will rapture the church before He begins to pour out His wrath (the trumpet and bowl judgments) on an unrepentant world. Cosmic disturbance will precede Christ's coming to rapture the church and judge the wicked. The following chart illustrates that truth.

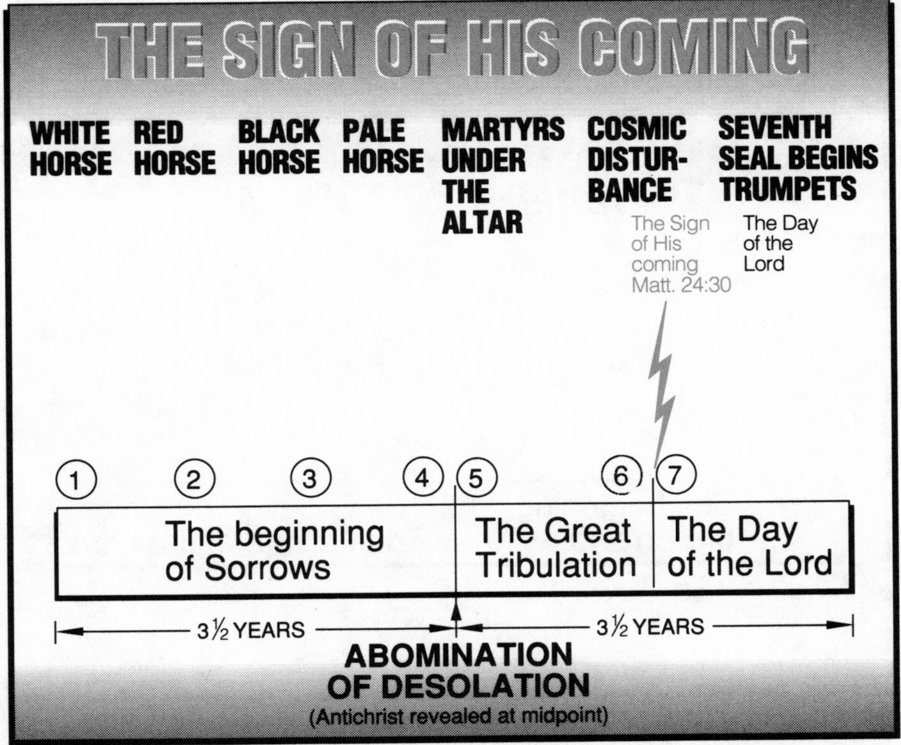


The shortening of the Great Tribulation to less than three and one-half years is one of the most important truths to be grasped if the chronology of end-time events is to be understood. It literally is the key that reveals the sequence to Matthew 24–25 and the chronology of the book of Revelation with the opening of the seals, trumpets, and bowls. Because pretribulation rapturists do not recognize the cutting short of the Great Tribulation (i.e., making it less than three and one-half years), they are logically forced to place the sixth seal at the end of the seventieth week in their interpretation of Matthew 24:22, if they are consistent, and are then faced with the unsolvable dilemma of what to do with the trumpet and bowl judgments of the book of Revelation which arise out of the opening of the seventh seal. It is, above all else, for that reason that a logical, unforced, chronological unfolding of Revelation has evaded pretribulational, premillennial commentators and, in large measure, is the explanation for the fact that the last book of the Bible has largely remained an unsolvable riddle for students of the Word to this very hour.

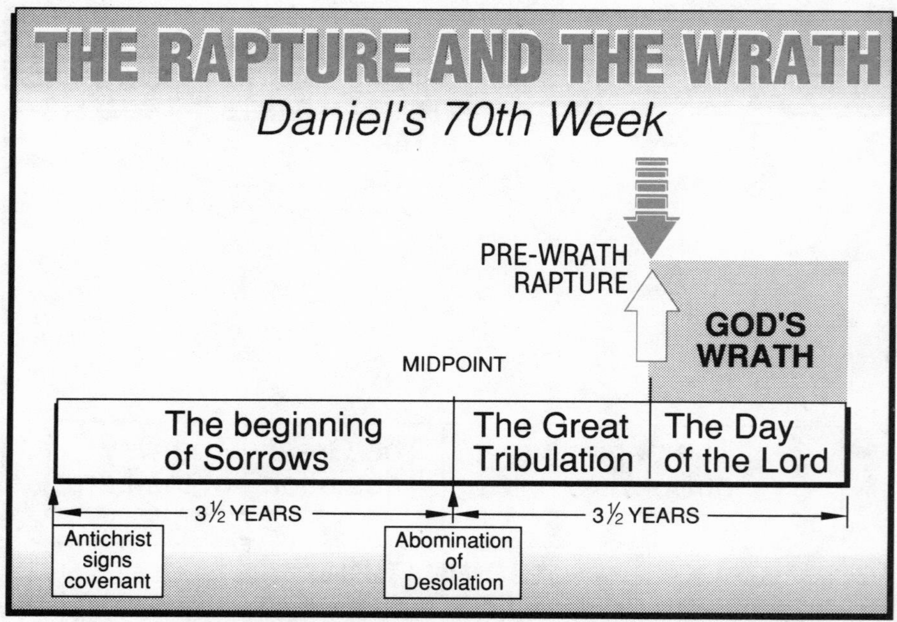


To sum up, then, God will cut the Great Tribulation short; that is, bring it to a conclusion before the seventieth week is concluded. The Great Tribulation will be followed by cosmic disturbance, which will indicate that the Day of the Lord is about to commence. At that time God's glory will be manifested. Speaking broadly, "that day" will have two objectives. First, the Rapture of the church will occur; that will then be followed by the Lord's judgment of the wicked as He begins His physical return to the earth.

# 9

# And Then the Day of the Lord

Jesus is coming again. That fact is an inviolable absolute, an immutable certainty. Among the major purposes for that coming will be the vindication of God's holiness through the judgment of the wicked. The very character of God demands that He one day judge this sinful planet and bring man's rebellion to an end. The Bible refers to that still-future day of judgment as *the Day of the Lord* (Joel 1:15). The certain reality of the awesome judgment of that day should be a catalyst for holy living. It will be the supreme fulfillment of the truth, "Be not deceived, God is not mocked, for whatever a man soweth, that shall he also reap" (Gal. 6:7). The Day of the Lord is one of the most important truths to comprehend if the full-orbed scheme of end-time events is to be understood.

Although a substantial portion of God's Word is given to the subject of the Day of the Lord, it has often been ignored or downplayed in the Rapture debate. Writers frequently simply assume that the Day of the Lord begins with the Tribulation period. For instance, David Cooper, who describes the entire seventieth week as the Great Tribulation, has written, "The 'Day of the Lord' is the great tribulation, which is thus designated in various passages of the Old Testament."[1] In point of fact, nowhere in the Old Testament is the Day of the Lord ever designated as the Great Tribulation or made synonymous with the whole of the seventieth week of Daniel. On another occasion, after quoting Isaiah 13:9–10, which speaks of the Lord's wrath and cosmic disturbances, he writes, "A glance at the context from which this passage was taken shows the prophet was talking of the Day of the Lord, the Tribulation period."[2] The context shows it was the Day of the Lord. It does not, however, show it was the Tribulation period. John Walvoord, commenting on the phrase *the Day of the Lord* in 1 Thessalonians 5:2, says that it is the period of time immediately following the Rapture of the church; that is, the Tribulation period.[3] But that is only an assumption and cannot be biblically demonstrated. Zane Hodges, addressing the same subject, has written, "But since Jesus delivers us from the wrath to come, that affirmation becomes an assertion that the Thessalonians are to be delivered from the calamities of the Day of the Lord." For Hodges, "the wrath to come" occurs during the Day of the Lord, which he equates with the Tribulation period. Like Walvoord and Cooper, he simply assumes that the Day of the Lord includes the entire seventieth week of Daniel or the Tribulation period.[4] But no biblical evidence to support that position is given.

When interpreting 1 Thessalonians 5:1–11, a most important text on the Rapture, many other sincere commentators, without intent, have likewise simply assumed that the Day of the Lord encompasses the entire Tribulation period.

In verse 2 of that classic text, Paul declares, "For yourselves know perfectly that the day of the Lord so cometh as a thief in the night." In verse 4 he gives additional insight: "But ye, brethren, are not in darkness, that that day [the Day of the Lord] should overtake you as a thief." And then in verse 9 Paul gives a word of great encouragement: "For God hath not appointed us to wrath but to obtain salvation [deliverance] by our Lord Jesus Christ." From these statements, an erroneous conclusion is sometimes drawn. The reasoning that leads men to that conclusion follows this path:

1. The Day of the Lord will come "as a thief in the night" (v. 2)—that is a correct biblical statement.
2. You (believers) "are not in darkness, that that day [the Day of the Lord] should overtake you" (v. 4)—correct again.
3. "For God hath not appointed us to wrath but to obtain salvation [deliverance]" (v. 9)—once again, correct.

4. Therefore, the reasoning continues, since the Day of the Lord begins with the Tribulation period, and the believer is not appointed unto wrath, the believer is raptured before the Tribulation period begins. That *conclusion,* however, is *incorrect.*

The error of such logic is that it *assumes* that the Day of the Lord commences when the seventieth week of Daniel begins. But a careful examination of the biblical data will clearly indicate that *it does not!* The false assumption just mentioned is perhaps the single greatest error in the debate concerning the timing of the Rapture. If expositors get the starting point of the Day of the Lord right, the timing of the Rapture becomes clear. It is true that the Rapture *will occur* before the Day of the Lord, as pretribulationists contend. That is precisely what Paul is teaching in 1 Thessalonians 5 and 2 Thessalonians 2. Further, not only does the Rapture occur *in connection with* the Day of the Lord—but the Rapture occurs *on the very day* the Day of the Lord begins (Luke 17:22–36). But the Day of the Lord does *not* begin when the Tribulation period begins—it begins with the opening of the seventh seal of Revelation 8:1. That fact will be clearly established in the next chapter and is illustrated in the following chart.

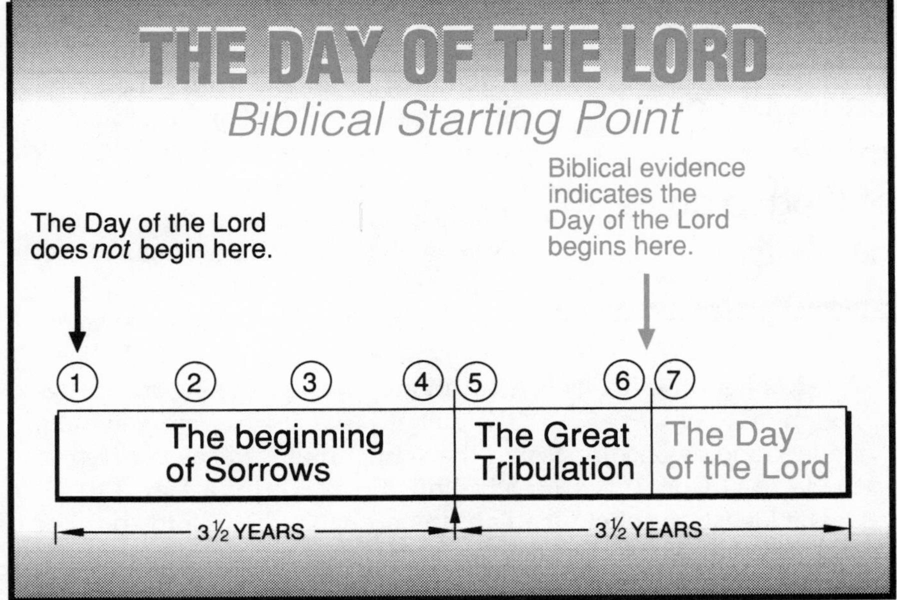

Noted Bible scholar F. F. Bruce called the Day of the Lord "the day when Yahweh (the Lord) was expected to vindicate Himself."[5] Colin Brown defined the Day of the Lord this way: "It designates God's decisive intervention in history for judgment."[6]

The Day of the Lord should be viewed in contrast to Man's Day. Wuest correctly defined Man's Day as "that time starting with Adam's fall until the second advent when unsaved man has liberty under the permissive will of God to do as he pleases."[7] It is only after the cup of man's iniquity is full, his rebellion complete, his attempt at self-deification through the Antichrist manifest, that the Day of the Lord will commence. When it does, it will be the most devastating time of judgment the world has ever known. Men will quake in fear from the wrath of a holy God in that day. Here will be manifested the ultimate reality of Jonathan Edwards's famous sermon, "Sinners in the Hands of an Angry God."

Wuest correctly defined Man's Day as "that time starting with Adam's fall until the second advent when unsaved man has liberty under the permissive will of God to do as he pleases."

*The Day of the Lord* is a term referred to repeatedly in the Old and New Testaments. It is one of the most important terms to understand in a discussion of prophetic truth. Therefore, its usage in the Word of God must be carefully examined. Eight prophets use the specific term *the Day of the Lord* a total of nineteen times. Three New Testament writers—Luke, Paul, and Peter—use the term *the Day of the Lord* in four uncontested passages (Acts 2:19–20; 1 Thess. 5:2–4; 2 Thess. 2:1–2; 2 Pet. 3:9–10). Seven additional passages using the designation "day of Christ" or "the day of Jesus Christ" are generally understood as encompassing the same time frame as the Day of the Lord (1 Cor. 1:8; 3:13; 5:5; Phil. 1:6, 10; 2:16; 2 Tim. 4:8).

The Jewish prophet Obadiah was probably the first to speak of that day. He wrote: For *the day of the Lord* is near upon all the nations. As thou hast done, it shall be done unto thee; thy reward shall return upon thine own head (Obad. 15).

Here is a prophetic utterance that declares that the Day of the Lord will be a time of judgment upon the nations. In the context of the book of Obadiah, that judgment will be in response to the nations' treatment of Israel. As they have done to Israel, God will do to them.

The dominant theme of the prophet Joel is the Day of the Lord. For example:

> Alas for *the day!* For *the day of the LORD* is at hand, and as a destruction from the Almighty shall it come . . . Blow the trumpet in Zion, and sound an alarm in my holy mountain. Let all the inhabitants of the land tremble; for *the day of the LORD* cometh, for it is near at hand; *A day* of darkness and of gloominess, *a day* of clouds and of thick darkness, like the morning spread upon the mountains; a great people and a strong; there hath not been ever the like, neither shall be any more after it, even to the years of many generations . . . The earth shall quake before them; the heavens shall tremble; the sun and the moon shall be dark, and the stars shall withdraw their shining: And the LORD shall utter his voice before his army; for his camp is very great; for he is strong who executeth his word; for *the day of the LORD* is great and very terrible, and who can abide it? . . . And I will show wonders in the heavens and in the earth: blood, and fire, and pillars of smoke. The sun shall be turned into darkness, and the moon into blood, before the great and the terrible *day of the LORD* come. (Joel 1:15; 2:1–2, 10–11, 30–31)

Joel described that day in very somber terms as a time of indescribable destruction from the Almighty. When God blows "the trumpet in Zion," it will be in anticipation of the final judgment of Israel for her sins. But Joel has more to say about that future day:

> Multitudes, multitudes in the valley of decision; for *the day of the LORD* is near in the valley of decision. The sun and the moon shall be darkened, and the stars shall withdraw their shining. The LORD also shall roar out of Zion, and utter his voice from Jerusalem, and the heavens and the earth shall shake; but the LORD will be the hope of his people, and the strength of the children of Israel. (Joel 3:14–16)

Here the prophet hinted at the hope for Israel that other biblical writers also clearly proclaim. At the end of the Day of the Lord, a surviving remnant will be gloriously saved (Zech. 12:10; Acts 15:14–17; Rom. 11:25).

Amos, who was called by God from being a pincher of figs to become a proclaimer of God's prophetic Word, spoke to Judah, the southern kingdom, concerning that coming day. The Jewish people mistakenly thought the Day of the Lord would be a time of judgment on the nations but one of deliverance for Israel—that they would experience salvation without purification. But Amos warned:

> Woe unto you that desire *the day of the* LORD! To what end is it for you? *The day of the* LORD is darkness, and not light, as if a man did flee from a lion, and a bear met him; or went into the house, and leaned his hand on the wall, and a serpent bit him. Shall not *the day of the* LORD be darkness, and not light? Even very dark, and no brightness in it? (Amos 5:18–20)

Isaiah, the greatest of the Old Testament evangelists and a prophet who prophesied from within the royal palace, wrote:

> For *the day of the* LORD of hosts shall be upon every one who is proud and lofty, and upon every one who is lifted up, and he shall be brought low; and upon all the cedars of Lebanon, that are high and lifted up, and upon all the oaks of Bashan, and upon all the high mountains, and upon all the hills that are lifted up, and upon every high tower, and upon every fortified wall, and upon all the ships of Tarshish, and upon all pleasant pictures. And the loftiness of man shall be bowed down, and the haughtiness of men shall be made low; and the LORD alone shall be exalted in *that day*. And the idols he shall utterly abolish. And they shall go into the caves of the rocks, and into the holes of the earth, for fear of the LORD, and for the glory of his majesty, when he ariseth to shake terribly the earth. In *that day* a man shall cast his idols of silver, and his idols of gold, which they made each one for himself to worship, to the moles and to the bats; To go into the clefts of the rocks, and into the tops of the ragged rocks, for fear of the LORD, and for the glory of his majesty, when he ariseth to shake terribly the earth. (Isa. 2:12–21)

When God "ariseth to shake terribly the earth," men will seek to flee to the caves and holes of the earth for protection. Their wealth will be worthless in that day. It will be the catastrophic economic crash, not of Wall Street, but of the world. But Isaiah continued:

> Wail; for *the day of the LORD* is at hand; it shall come as a destruction from the Almighty. Therefore shall all hands be faint, and every man's heart shall melt; and they shall be afraid. Pangs and sorrows shall take hold of them; they shall be in pain like a woman that travaileth. They shall be amazed one at another, their faces shall be as flames. Behold, *the day of the LORD* cometh, cruel both with wrath and fierce anger, to lay the land desolate; and he shall destroy the sinners out of it. For the stars of heaven and the constellations thereof shall not give their light; the sun shall be darkened in its going forth, and the moon shall not cause its light to shine. And I will punish the world for its evil, and the wicked for their iniquity; and I will cause the arrogancy of the proud to cease, and will lay low the haughtiness of the terrible. I will make a man more rare than fine gold, even a man than the golden wedge of Ophir. Therefore, I will shake the heavens, and the earth shall remove out of its place, in the wrath of the LORD of hosts, and in *the day* of his fierce anger. (Isa. 13:6–13)

The prophet Ezekiel, who ministered during the Babylonian captivity, warned against the false prophets. Men who profess to be messengers of God will proclaim a false message in the days immediately prior to the Day of the Lord.

> Thus said the Lord GOD: Woe unto the foolish prophets, that follow their own spirit, and have seen nothing! O Israel, thy prophets are like the foxes in the deserts. Ye have not gone up into the gaps, neither made up the hedge for the house of Israel to stand in the battle in *the day of the LORD*. They have seen vanity and lying divination, saying, The LORD saith. And the LORD hath not sent them; and they have made others to hope that they would confirm the word. Have ye not seen a vain vision, and have ye not spoken a lying divination, whereas ye say, The LORD saith it; albeit I have not spoken? Therefore, thus saith the Lord GOD; Because ye have spoken vanity, and seen lies, therefore, behold, I am against you, saith the Lord GOD. (Ezek. 13:3–8)

But Ezekiel's message was not finished. He was commanded to speak further concerning the Day of the Lord, to forewarn the nations that a day of reckoning and accountability would arrive also for them one day. "Son of man, prophesy and say, Thus saith the Lord GOD: Wail ye. Alas for *the day!* For *the day* is near, even *the day of the LORD* is near, a cloudy *day;* it shall be the time of the nations" (Ezek. 30:2–3).

The prophet Zephaniah, who called Judah to repentance and warned of impending judgment (the Babylonian captivity), also foretold the climactic Day of the Lord judgment:

> The great *day of the LORD* is near, it is near, and hasteneth greatly, even the voice of *the day of the LORD;* the mighty man shall cry there bitterly. *That day* is *a day* of wrath, *a day* of trouble and distress, *a day* of waste and desolation, *a day* of darkness and gloominess, *a day* of clouds and thick darkness, *a day* of the trumpet and alarm against the fortified cities, and against the high towers. And I will bring distress upon men, that they shall walk like blind men, because they have sinned against the LORD; and their blood shall be poured out like dust, and their flesh like the dung. Neither their silver nor their gold shall be able to deliver them in *the day of the LORD's wrath,* but the whole land shall be devoured by the fire of his jealousy; for he shall make even a speedy riddance of all those who dwell in the land. Gather yourselves together, yea, gather together, O nation not desired, before the decree bring forth, before *the day* pass like the chaff, before the fierce anger of the LORD come upon you, before *the day of the LORD's anger* come upon you. Seek the LORD, all ye meek of the earth, who have kept his ordinances; seek righteousness, seek meekness; it may be ye shall be hidden in *the day of the LORD's anger*. (Zeph. 1:14–2:3)

That description of destruction is almost incomprehensible. It is like a battle plan of God's wrath.

That description of destruction is almost incomprehensible. It is like a battle plan of God's wrath. It will be a day of wrath, a day of trouble, a day of distress, a day of waste and desolation, a day of darkness and gloominess, a day of clouds and thick darkness, a day of the trumpet and alarm against the fortified cities. This will not be the time of "Gentle Jesus meek and mild." This will be the wrath of holiness. Men will not mock or scorn God on that occasion. Justice will triumph in that day.

The prophet Zechariah, who foretold the cataclysmic events that are to befall the city of Jerusalem, added this crucial testimony concerning the Day of the Lord:

> Behold, *the day of the LORD* cometh, and thy spoil shall be divided in the midst of thee. For I will gather all nations against Jerusalem to battle; and the city shall be taken, and the houses rifled, and the women ravished; and half of the city shall go forth into captivity, and the residue of the people shall not be cut off from the city. Then shall the LORD go forth, and fight against those nations, as when he fought in the day of battle. And his feet shall stand in *that day* upon the Mount of Olives, which is before Jerusalem on the east, and the Mount of Olives shall cleave in its midst toward the east and toward the west, and there shall be a very great valley; and half of the mountain shall remove toward the north, and half of it toward the south. (Zech. 14:1–4)

Zechariah spoke of that day being a time of divine judgment on Jerusalem, but he also viewed it as a time of judgment against the nations because of their treatment of Israel.

There remains a word from the last of the Old Testament prophets concerning that future day. It is a message that holds out some hope. Before the Day of the Lord begins, God will send a messenger to call the nation of Israel to repentance. Malachi, God's spokesman about four hundred years before Christ, recorded: "Behold, I will send you Elijah, the prophet, before the coming of the great and terrible *day of the LORD;* And he shall turn the heart of the fathers to the children, and the heart of the children to their fathers, lest I come and smite the earth with a curse" (Mal. 4:5–6).

It is not left to the Old Testament prophets alone to speak of the Day of the Lord. Luke wrote: "And I will show wonders in heaven above, and signs in the earth beneath: blood, and fire, and vapor of smoke. The sun shall be turned into darkness, and the moon into blood, before that great and notable *day of the Lord* come" (Acts 2:19–20).

The apostle Paul in both of his Thessalonian epistles spoke of the Day of the Lord. His teaching assumes an understanding of the Old Testament significance of the Day of the Lord.

> For yourselves know perfectly that *the day of the Lord* so cometh as a thief in the night. For when they shall say, Peace and safety, then sudden destruction cometh upon them, as travail upon a woman with child, and they shall not escape. But ye, brethren, are not in darkness, that that day should overtake you as a thief. (1 Thess. 5:2–4)

> Now we beseech you, brethren, by the coming of our Lord Jesus Christ, and by our gathering together unto him, that ye be not soon shaken in mind, or be troubled, neither by spirit, nor by word, nor by letter as from us, as that *the day of the Lord* is present. (2 Thess. 2:1–2)

Peter also wrote of the Day of the Lord:

> The Lord is not slack concerning his promise, as some men count slackness, but is long-suffering toward us, not willing that any should perish, but that all should come to repentance. But *the day of the Lord* will come as a thief in the night, in which the heavens shall pass away with a great noise, and the elements shall melt with fervent heat; the earth also, and the works that are in it, shall be burned up. (2 Pet. 3:9–10)

A compendium from the prophets' description of the Day of the Lord reveals the following. The Day of the Lord will be:

- A time when God "ariseth to shake terribly the earth" (Isa. 2:19, 22).
- A time of destruction from the Almighty (Isa. 13:7; Joel 1:15).
- A time of divine wrath and fierce anger (Isa. 13:13; Zeph. 1:15; 2:2).
- A time when God will punish the world for its evil and the wicked for their iniquity (Isa. 13:11).
- A time when God's indignation and fury will be directed against the nations (Isa. 34:1–2; Zeph. 1:14–2:3; Zech. 14:3; Obad. 15).
- A time when God's vengeance will be revealed (Isa. 34:8).
- A time of darkness in the heavens (Isa. 34:4; Joel 2:31; 3:14; Isa. 13:9–10).
- A time of fire from the Lord (Joel 2:3, 5, 30; Zeph. 1:18; 3:8).

It will be a day of clouds, thick darkness, gloominess, wrath, trouble, distress, and terror (Zeph. 1:15; Ezek. 30:3).

When considering the prophetic description of the Day of the Lord, a number of important factors must be kept in view.

First, the prophets were God's spokesmen. They proclaimed their messages by divine revelation and authority. God knows the beginning from the end. It should not be surprising, therefore, that God's prophetic spokesmen spoke of end-time events. That is but one way God demonstrates His omniscience. After all, the Day of the Lord is the fulfillment of the end which God planned before the beginning (Isa. 46:10).

Second, the prophets sometimes used a near specific period of divine judgment as a basis for prophesying concerning the eschatological (last) great judgment, or Day of the Lord. In this instance, the two (the near and the far) almost appear to merge together (Isa. 13:6; Joel 1:15; 2:1, 11). And sometimes the prophets spoke directly of the future eschatological Day of the Lord, the cataclysmic climax to man's sinful epochs of existence (Isa. 2:12). Those passages which spoke of a near judgment always anticipated the eschatological or final Day of the Lord. The prophets, in their prophetic visions and messages, often saw as a comprehensive whole that which history unfolds as separate, chronological events.

> After all, the Day of the Lord is the fulfillment of the end which God planned before the beginning.

Third, all divine judgment does not come under the heading the Day of the Lord. For instance, the worldwide Noahic flood, although a severe divine judgment, is never called the Day of the Lord (Gen. 6:5–7). Nor is the destruction of Sodom and Gomorrah, another divine judgment, called the Day of the Lord (Gen. 18:20–32; 19:13, 27–29).

Fourth, the Day of the Lord will be a time of judgment upon Israel when she will be brought into account for her sins (Isa. 40:2; cf. Isa. 17:4–8; 33:10–14; Zech. 13:8–9; Mal. 3:2–5; 4:1), and upon the Gentile nations for their rebellion, unrepentance, and persecution of Israel (Rom. 2:3, 5–6, 8–9; Obad. 15). R. V. G. Tasker has made this important observation: "The expression 'the Day of the Lord' at the time of the rise of the great prophets of Israel denoted an event to which the Israelites were looking forward as the day of Jehovah's final vindication of the righteousness of His people against their enemies. One of the tasks of the prophets was to insist that in fact the Day of the Lord would be a day on which God would vindicate His own righteousness not only against the enemies of Israel (the nations), but also against Israel herself."[8]

The Day of the Lord is a time of almost indescribable and incomprehensible judgment. It is a time of "darkness, and not light . . . . Even very dark, and no brightness in it" (Amos 5:20).

There is no blessing associated with the Day of the Lord. It is the most awesome period of divine judgment the world will ever know. Nonetheless, and amazingly, some Bible teachers insist that the Day of the Lord is a time of darkness and light, judgment and blessing, night and day. They do so by starting the Day of the Lord at the beginning of Daniel's seventieth week and then extending it through the millennial kingdom. The former (Daniel's seventieth week) is viewed as the time of judgment; the latter (the Millennium) as the time of blessing (a second period of judgment is said to occur near the end of the Millennium, based on 2 Peter 3:10). In discussing the Day of the Lord, Dwight Pentecost, in his classic and often very helpful volume on prophecy, suggests that "the Day of the Lord is that period of time beginning with Israel after the Rapture at the beginning of the Tribulation period and extending through the second advent and the Millennial age."[9] Similarly, The *Scofield Reference Bible* teaches that the Day of the Lord will *begin* with the translation (Rapture) of the church and will terminate with the cleansing of the heavens and the earth before bringing into existence the new heavens and the new earth.[10] Finally, another noted scholar, D. Edmond Hiebert, suggests that as a prophetic period, the Day of the Lord is inaugurated with the Rapture of the church as described in 1 Thessalonians 4:13–18, covers the time of the Great Tribulation, and involves Christ's return to earth and the establishment of His messianic reign.[11] These men represent the majority view of pretribulation rapturism: that the Day of the Lord will begin with the Rapture and continue through the Millennium. The traditional pretribulation rapture position for the Day of the Lord is charted below.

Strong exception must be taken on biblical grounds, with both the traditional starting point of the Day of the Lord and its completion. The time of the completion of the Day of the Lord is not crucial to the prewrath rapture position being presented in this book. Its starting point, as already indicated, is crucial. Both Paul and Peter warn the church to be looking for the Day of the Lord. Paul wrote to the church at Thessalonica,

> But ye, brethren, are not in darkness, that that day should overtake you as a thief. (1 Thess. 5:4)

And Peter admonished believers,

> Seeing, then, that all these things shall be dissolved, what manner of persons ought ye to be in all holy living and godliness, looking for and hasting unto the coming of the day of God, in which the heavens, being on fire, shall be dissolved, and the elements shall melt with fervent heat? (2 Pet. 3:11–12)

But for completion of thought, the termination point of the Day of the Lord will now be considered. The next chapter will discuss the starting point.

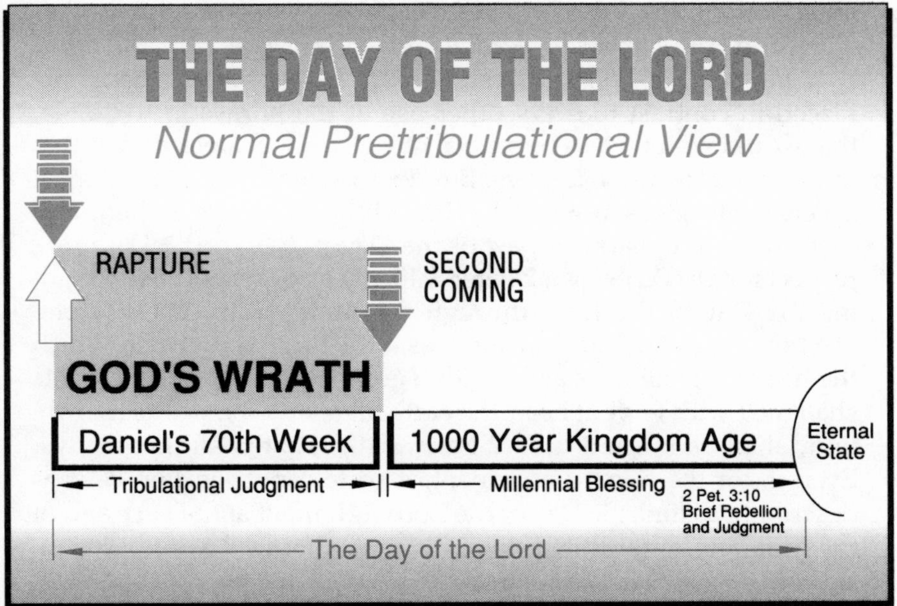


Concerning the termination point of the Day of the Lord, four arguments are advanced to show that the Day of the Lord cannot include the Millennium, as pretribulationism normally teaches.

First, *the description of the Day of the Lord in the Old Testament is exclusively a time of devastating judgment*. No blessing is associated with it. When blessing is mentioned, it is only incidental and given as a chronological marker (for example, after the Day of the Lord there will be blessing, Isa. 11; 35; 60). In contrast, the major description of the Millennium is a time of unprecedented blessing. William Barclay has written, "Many of the most terrible pictures in the Old Testament are of the Day of the Lord (Isa. 22:5; 13:9; Zeph. 1:14–16; Amos 5:18; Jer. 30:7; Mal. 4:1; Joel 2:31). Its main characteristics were as follows: (1) It would come suddenly and unexpectedly. (2) It would involve a cosmic upheaval in which the universe was shaken to its very foundations. (3) It would be a time of judgment."[12]

There is no blessing associated with the Day of the Lord in the texts that describe it. Pretribulationist Richard Mahue said: "The prominent theme of the Day of the Lord prophecies is God's judgment for sin. It is present in every Day of the Lord passage. The blessings of Christ's Millennial reign are *subsequent to* and *as a result of* the Day of the Lord, but *they are not part of it*."[13]

Second, *the supposed exegetical basis for extending the Day of the Lord through the Millennium rests solely on one verse of Scripture.* Placed in contrast to every other use of the phrase in the Bible, that would nonetheless be sufficient if it could be determined that that is what the verse teaches. But does it? Pentecost suggests that 2 Peter 3:10 gives warrant for including the entire Millennium (one thousand years) as part of the Day of the Lord.[14] With due respect for Dr. Pentecost, 2 Peter 3:10 gives no support for extending the Day of the Lord through the Millennium. Peter wrote, "But *the day of the Lord* will come as a thief in the night, in which the heavens shall pass away with a great noise, and the elements shall melt with fervent heat; the earth also, and the works that are in it, shall be burned up" (2 Peter 3:10). That is all that it says. Even if, for the sake of argument, it were conceded that Peter is describing a climactic Day of the Lord judgment at the very end of the Millennium (and it certainly is not), that fact would give no authority whatever for making the kingdom age part of the Day of the Lord. If 2 Peter 3:10 is placed at the end of the Millennium, it would teach that there will be a second prophetic Day of the Lord judgment near the end of the Millennium.

Perhaps, sensing the deficiency of evidence for making the Millennium part of the Day of the Lord, some commentators have compounded the error by attempting to make millennial texts referred to as "in that day" synonymous with the Day of the Lord. Charles Ryrie, whose scholarship is outstanding and study Bible superb, attempts to substantiate the continuation of the Day of the Lord through the Millennium position by citing a number of verses as evidence.[15] One such verse is "*In that day* shall the branch of the LORD be beautiful and glorious, and the fruit of the earth shall be excellent and splendid for those who are escaped of

Israel" (Isa. 4:2). Ryrie equates the phrase "in that day" in a millennial context with the Day of the Lord. However, the phrase "in that day" is not a technical term restricted to one period of time. The context must determine the meaning of "in that day." In the above cited verse, the phrase "those who are escaped of Israel" is unquestionably millennial and refers to those from among Israel who will survive the Day of the Lord to enter the Millennium. Ryrie offers a second text to support the Day of the Lord continuing through the Millennium: "And *in that day* thou shalt say, O LORD, I will praise thee; though thou wast angry with me, thine anger is turned away, and thou comfortedst me" (Isa. 12:1; see also Isa. 19:23–25; Jer. 30:7–9). The same truth is in view; namely, that Jews who survive the wrath of the Day of the Lord will enjoy the blessing of the Millennium. Once again, the phrase "in that day" in a millenial setting cannot arbitrarily and without biblical justification become the Day of the Lord. There simply is no biblical basis for making millennial texts that speak of "in that day" part of an extended Day of the Lord.

Third, *if Peter is speaking of a Day of the Lord at the end of the Millennium, there must be two distinct prophetic occasions called the Day of the Lord*. As has been demonstrated, the Millennium cannot properly be included in the Day of the Lord. Therefore, the Millennium cannot be used as some kind of cement to hold together a Day of the Lord judgment during Christ's Second Coming and another Day of the Lord one thousand years later. If 2 Peter 3:10 is speaking of a Day of the Lord near the end of the Millennium, there must be two distinct prophetic events called the Day of the Lord. The prophets, however, knew nothing of that. They spoke of the Day of the Lord with the definite article—they knew of only one such event.

Fourth, *2 Peter 3:10 is not describing a judgment at the end of the Millennium*. What it is describing is the one climactic, eschatological (final) Day of the Lord that occurs in connection with the Lord's second coming during the latter part of the seventieth week of Daniel. Justification for that statement is based upon the following evidence.

1. The immediate context of 2 Peter 3:10 argues strongly that Peter is speaking of a Day of the Lord that will occur in connection with Christ's second coming. Peter's comment in verse 10, "But the day of the Lord will come as a thief in the night, in which the

heavens shall pass away with a great noise, and the elements shall melt with fervent heat; the earth also, and the works that are in it, shall be burned up," cannot be segregated from the immediate context.

In verse 4 there arises the question, "Where is the promise of his coming?" The word translated *coming* is *parousia*. It is used a total of twenty-four times in the New Testament. Sixteen times it is used of Christ's coming, and in each instance it is used of His second coming before the Millennium begins. Here, and here alone, it must refer to the end of the Millennium if 2 Peter 3:10 is speaking of a Day of the Lord at the end of the Millennium. A further issue is this: Pretribulation rapturists are almost universally premillennial, and premillennialism teaches that Christ will literally and physically return to rule over the earth during the millennial kingdom. The question "Where is the promise of His coming?" (2 Pet. 3:4) applied to the end of the Millennium makes no sense, since Christ will already be present and ruling during His millennial kingdom.

In verse 6 Peter reminds his readers that in the days of Noah "the world that then was, being overflowed with water, perished." Although the word *perished* was used to describe the flood judgment, it was neither the end of the earth nor of all life. After the flood, Noah, his family, and the animals disembarked from the ark and replenished the earth. In the same manner, when Peter speaks of "the heavens and the earth which are now, by the same word are kept in store, reserved unto fire against the day of judgment and perdition of ungodly men" (v. 7) and "the elements shall melt with fervent heat; the earth also, and the works that are in it, shall be burned up" (v. 10), he is not talking of total annihilation of the earth any more than the earth *perishing* in the days of Noah was total annihilation. He is talking of nonannihilative judgment during the Day of the Lord as the prophets foretold, but in connection with Christ's return before the Millennium begins.

In verse 9 Peter declares, "The Lord is not slack concerning his promise, as some men count slackness, but is long-suffering toward us, not willing that any should perish, but that all should come to repentance." The subject in view is salvation. The apostle is teaching that the Lord will not come sooner because He is long-suffering and not desiring that any should perish. Once He comes, judgment must fall, and so He is giving men a chance to repent. The Millennium is a fixed, one thousand-year period of blessing. There is no long-suffering or delay of His coming, waiting for men to repent, associated with it. He will already be present.

2. When Paul speaks in 1 Thessalonians 5:2 of the Day of the Lord, which all agree is associated with Christ's second coming, he says that it will come as a "thief in the night." Peter uses the exact same language in describing the Day of the Lord: "But the day of the Lord will come as a thief in the night" (2 Pet. 3:10). It is possible to have the same expression used for two totally different events separated by a thousand years—but not likely. Further, no theological reason for the Day of the Lord coming "as a thief in the night" at the end of the Millennium is even hinted at in the Word of God. Once again it must be asked, how can the Day of the Lord come "as a thief in the night" when Christ, according to pretribulation rapturism, is already present? The Millennium is *His* earthly rule. And how can it be unexpected when the Millennium is exactly one thousand years in duration?

3. The chronology of Isaiah 65 and 66 clearly teaches that the heavens and the earth will be renovated *before* the Millennium begins, not at its end; and there is no justification for changing the chronology of those two chapters. Isaiah wrote, "For, behold, I create new heavens and a new earth, and the former shall not be remembered, nor come into mind" (Isa. 65:17). Compare 2 Peter 3:13 where the same expression, "new heavens and a new earth," is used. Following the creation of the new heavens and earth, a partial listing of millennial blessings is given. Jerusalem will be restored and blessed (vv. 18–19); life expectancy will be expanded (v. 20); men will build houses and inhabit them, they will plant vineyards and eat the fruit of them (vv. 21–22); "The wolf and the lamb shall feed together, and the lion shall eat straw like the bullock" (v. 25). The new heavens and the new earth of which Isaiah speaks are renovative and precede the Millennium.

It is the Day of the Lord judgment during the latter part of the seventieth week of Daniel which impacts both the heavens and the earth and which will result in the need for a renovation of the heavens and the earth before the Millennium begins. Peter, like all of the other writers, is speaking of the Day of the Lord destruction, which will occur before the Millennium begins.

4. The apostle Paul gives the timing for the Rapture of the

church. Writing to the Corinthians he said, "Behold, I show you a mystery: We shall not all sleep, but we shall all be changed, in a moment, in the twinkling of an eye, at the last trump" (1 Cor. 15:51–52). In context, Paul is not simply speaking about resurrection but of the believer's future glorified body and the fact that one generation will escape physical death by rapture. That Rapture will occur at the last trump. The last trump is the final outpouring of God's wrath.

A cursory examination of the book of Revelation will indicate that all seven trumpets are contained in the seventh seal, and the seven bowls are contained in the seventh trumpet. Therefore, the trumpets and bowls are contained in the seventh seal. They are a comprehensive whole, the final wrath of God—the last trump.

If Peter's Day of the Lord is at the end of the Millennium, then so too is the Rapture—for it must immediately precede the last trump, the final outpouring of divine wrath. Such a placement for the Rapture is impossible; and once again, Peter's Day of the Lord cannot occur near the end of the Millennium.

5. A comparison of Scripture with Scripture argues conclusively that Peter's Day of the Lord is not to be viewed as a separate event occurring near the end of the Millennium. It is to be identified with the one Day of the Lord to which the ancient prophets referred. Isaiah, in a clear Second Coming Day of the Lord passage, wrote:

> All *the host of heaven shall be dissolved,* and the heavens shall be rolled together like a scroll; and all their host [heavenly bodies] shall fall down as the leaf falleth off from the vine, and like a falling fig from the fig tree . . . For it is the day of the Lord's vengeance, and the year of recompenses for the controversy of Zion. (Isa. 34:4, 8)

Isaiah said the heavens would be dissolved, and the heavenly bodies would fall to the earth before Christ's second coming.

The apostle John, in describing the opening of the sixth seal, again before the second coming of Christ, used the same language as Isaiah:

> And, lo, there was a great earthquake, and the sun became black as sackcloth of hair, and the moon became like blood; and the stars of heaven fell unto the earth, even as a fig tree casteth her

> untimely figs, when she is shaken of a mighty wind. *And the heaven departed as a scroll* when it is rolled together; and every mountain and island were moved out of their places. (Rev. 6:12–14)

Like Isaiah, John spoke of cosmic disturbances, heavenly bodies falling to the earth, and the mountains and islands moved out of their places before the Lord's return.

And both agree with Peter, who wrote, "But the Day of the Lord will come as a thief in the night, in which *the heavens shall pass away with a great noise,* and the elements shall melt with fervent heat; the earth also, and the works that are in it, shall be burned up" (2 Pet. 3:10).

Isaiah said, "All the host of heaven shall be dissolved" (Isa. 34:4). That is precisely the word which Peter used to summarize the heavens passing away, the elements melting with a fervent heat, and the earth being burned up (2 Pet. 3:10–11).

John observed, "And the heaven departed as a scroll" (Rev. 6:14).

Peter noted, "The heavens shall pass away with a great noise" (2 Pet. 3:10; see also Micah 1:3–4; Isa. 64:1–2; Zeph. 1:8, 3:8).

All three passages speak of destruction, first in the heavens and then encompassing the earth. Isaiah and John are universally understood to be speaking of the Day of the Lord in connection with Christ's second coming. There is no justification for placing Peter's Day of the Lord at any other time.

6. Peter's clear intent in writing 2 Peter 3 makes placing his Day of the Lord at the end of the Millennium impossible. The following salient facts bear that out. Peter noted:

- In the last days there would be scoffers walking after their own lusts (v. 3).
- They would ridicule the biblical promise of Christ's return to judge men (v. 4a).
- Their reasoning was based on their presumption of an uninterrupted flow of history. Things would continue as they always had (v. 4b).
- Contrary to the philosophy of the scoffers, God *did* intervene in the course of human events through the universal Noahic flood (v. 6).

- It is clear that the present heavens and earth are reserved for judgment, not by water (flood) but by fire (v. 7).
- Judgment has been withheld by a long-suffering God, giving man the opportunity to repent (vv. 8–9).
- The Day of the Lord will come as a thief in the night, and the heavens and the earth will be judged by fire (v. 10).
- In the light of that certain fact, men are to live holy lives looking for the coming of Christ (vv. 11–12). Here is a major reason why pretribulationists want to put 2 Peter 3:10 at the end of the Millennium. How can men look for something, as Peter exhorts them to do, that is imminent and signless?

Peter's whole argument revolves around the fact that God invaded the flow of human history with the Noahic flood. And He will do so once again during the Day of the Lord. To prove that Peter's Day of the Lord occurs at the end of the Millennium is impossible. It requires that Peter bypass Christ's second coming to become King of kings and Lord of lords as an evidence of divine intervention in history. Such a conclusion—a necessary requisite if Peter's Day of the Lord is placed at the end of the Millennium—is simply indefensible.

Premillenniallist Robert Culver summed up the timing of Peter's Day of the Lord succinctly:

> As to time, the new heavens and new earth anticipated by Peter and other prophets are to appear at the beginning of the Millennium, and that in nature and extent the conflagration which introduces the new heavens and new earth shall consist of a strictly limited renovation rather than annihilation of the existing natural order.[16]

In the light of such clear exegetical evidence for placing Peter's Day of the Lord before Christ's second coming, it is perplexing that some try to extend it through the Millennium.

Of far greater significance, however, in terms of the timing of the Rapture, is the *starting point* of the Day of the Lord. That becomes the dominant theme of the next chapter.

# PART II

# THE DAY OF THE LORD

# 10

# Cosmic Disturbance

The issue developed in this chapter is crucial. It deals with a main artery leading directly to the heart of the rapture issue. It will be demonstrated that if the Day of the Lord does not start at the beginning of the seventieth week of Daniel, pretribulation rapturism is fatally flawed. It is not a matter of a hole in the dike that can be plugged—it is a veritable flood that cannot be averted. If, on the other hand, as the thesis of this book contends, the Day of the Lord starts with the opening of the seventh seal, then it will be seen that the church must enter the seventieth week of Daniel, there to experience testing and then deliverance by rapture before the Day of the Lord begins.

Soldiers are not tested during rest and relaxation in the comfort and safety of the rear echelon. They are tested in the thick of the conflict. The soldiers of Alexander the Great were anxious to experience battle and prove their loyalty and courage to their great leader in combat. Only then could the soldier cut an "A" for *Alexander* into his body. It was a mark *(stigmata)* he was proud to bear. The apostle Paul had this concept in mind when he wrote, "for I bear in my body the marks *(stigmata)* of the Lord Jesus" (Gal. 6:17). When the Antichrist is personally present—empowered by Satan (Rev. 13:4) and demanding that the world bow down and worship—the true church will be given its greatest opportunity to demonstrate unfailing love and devotion to her sovereign Lord, by refraining from bestowing upon a false lover the glory due only to her true Bridegroom.

To preach rapture before the consummate battle of the ages is to suggest, in military terms, being *absent without leave* (AWOL). And somehow, however well-intended, men have developed a theology to justify that absence. The faithful soldier volunteers for the front lines, even when he could be permitted to stay behind. The analogy of a soldier is not inappropriate for the believer. Paul wrote to Timothy, "Thou, therefore, endure hardness, as a good soldier of Jesus Christ. No man that warreth entangleth himself with the affairs of this life, that he may please him who hath chosen him to be a soldier. . . . If we suffer, we shall also reign with him" (2 Tim. 2:3–4, 12). A good soldier knows he is never to underestimate the enemy. Ask any Marine drill sergeant. It is a cardinal rule of warfare. To do so is to invite death or injury. To tell the church that it will not be present during a significant part of the seventieth week of Daniel is to court disaster. Such an attitude will result in a church totally unprepared for the conflict, laboring under the misconception that they will not be present. But sermonizing is not enough. Let the Word of God alone be the final arbiter.

The vast majority of pretribulational writers believe that the Day of the Lord will begin with the Rapture of the church—that it will encompass the entire seventieth week and beyond. The position of *The New Scofield Reference Bible* is typical. It states that the Day of the Lord "will begin with the translation of the Church and will terminate with the cleansing of the heavens and the earth."[1]

Of more than passing interest, however, is the fact that this was not Scofield's original view. At first he began the Day of the Lord, not at the beginning, but at the end of Daniel's seventieth week. In the first edition of his study Bible (1909) he wrote, "The day of Jehovah (called, also, 'that day' and 'the great day') is that lengthened period of time beginning with the return of the Lord in glory."[2] Louis Sperry Chafer, in his *Systematic Theology,* also started the Day of the Lord at Christ's second coming to the earth. He described the Day of the Lord in this manner: "This lengthened period of a thousand years begins, generally speaking, with the second advent of Christ and the judgments connected therewith, and ends with the passing of the present heaven and the present earth."[3]

Here are two stellar personalities, among the most influential pretribulation rapturists who ever lived—one the editor of *The Scofield Reference Bible,* the other the founder and distinguished first president of Dallas Theological Seminary. Both originally started the Day of the Lord, not at the beginning of the seventieth week but at its end at the second coming of Christ. Scofield changed his position in later editions of his study Bible. This became important when, in the 1917 edition, he made pretribulation rapturism a major facet of his work. And distinguished students of Chafer (like John F. Walvoord, Charles Feinberg, Charles Ryrie, and Dwight Pentecost, to mention only a few) have substantially modified their mentor's position to reflect a starting time for the Day of the Lord at the beginning of the seventieth week. These are great men of God.

The church, particularly dispensational premillennialism, owes them a debt it can never repay. But they are men; and as such, they are fallible. Without inappropriate humility, it is admitted that their scholarship and piety far exceeds that of the author of this volume. Nevertheless, it is boldly affirmed that they erred in starting the Day of the Lord at the beginning of the seventieth week. They rightly realize, as has the vast body of pretribulational teachers, that the Rapture must precede the Day of the Lord. Therefore, if the Rapture is pretribulational, the Day of the Lord must commence with the beginning of the seventieth week. A few, like Paul Feinberg[4] and Richard Mahue,[5] while acknowledging that the Day of the Lord starts at or beyond the middle of the seventieth week, attempted (in this author's mind, unsuccessfully) to sustain pretribulation rapturism. To do so, they have placed at least three and one-half years between the Rapture and the starting point of the Day of the Lord.

The Scriptures do not allow that kind of extended gap between the Rapture and the Day of the Lord judgment. The Word of God teaches that the Day of the Lord wrath will commence immediately after the church is raptured. In a classic Second Coming text, the Lord taught, "For as the lightning, that lighteneth out of the one part under heaven, shineth unto the other part under heaven, so shall also the Son of man be in his day" (Luke 17:24). The phrase "in his day" is a clear reference to the Day of the Lord. In this connection the Lord said, "And as it was in the days of Noah, so shall it be also in the days of the Son of man. They did eat, they drank, they married wives, they were given in marriage, until *the day* that Noah entered into the ark, and the flood came, and destroyed them all" (Luke 17:26–27). The point of the Lord's teaching is clear. Noah entered the ark, then the judgment began—on the same day. For emphasis, the Lord gave another illustration of the same truth: "But the *same day* that Lot went out of Sodom, it rained fire and brimstone from heaven, and destroyed them all" (Luke 17:29). On the same day that Lot fled Sodom, the Lord judged Sodom. That this deliverance of the righteous and immediate judgment of the wicked are used to illustrate the Second Coming there can be no doubt. The Lord's next words were, "Even thus shall it be in *the day* when the Son of man is revealed" (Luke 17:30).

*Deliverance of the righteous immediately precedes judgment of the wicked. To postulate a period of time between rapture (deliverance) and wrath (judgment) is to contradict the Scriptures.*

If the Day of the Lord begins with the opening of the seventh seal, the Rapture cannot be pretribulational. The chart that follows illustrates that truth.

*Ryrie has rightly stated that "the Day of the Lord is a watershed between pre- and posttribulationism."*[6] *It is also a watershed between pretribulation rapturism and prewrath rapturism, as presented in this book.*

But what are some of the major arguments that pretribulation rapturists use to defend the premise that the Day of the Lord starts at the beginning of the seventieth week of Daniel?

First, pretribulationism suggests that the Day of the Lord is the time of God's wrath, and that the Tribulation period is, by its very designation, also a time of wrath. Therefore, the Day of the Lord begins at the start of the Tribulation period.

That assessment is made or assumed repeatedly in pretribulation literature. The fallacy of that logic is that nowhere in the Word of God is the seventieth week ever referred to as the Tribulation period (see Chapter 8). Nor can it be demonstrated that the opening of the seals reflects an outpouring of God's wrath. Not until the opening of the sixth seal, which initiates cosmic disturbance, does God begin to actively intervene in the affairs of men. With the opening of the seventh seal His wrath is about to commence.

Second, some pretribulationists argue that the second, third, and fourth seals of Revelation 6 indicate war, famine, and pestilence. War, it is suggested, is a method of God's judgment (Lev. 26:21–28; Ezek. 14:21); famine is a method of God's judgment (Deut. 11:17; Ezek. 4:16–17); and pestilence is a method of God's judgment (Num. 11:33; 16:46). And these seals are opened in the first part of the seventieth week of Daniel. Since the Scriptures indicate that these instruments of death are expressions of God's wrath (and the Day of the Lord is a time of God's wrath), the Day of the Lord must, therefore, start at the beginning of the seventieth week.

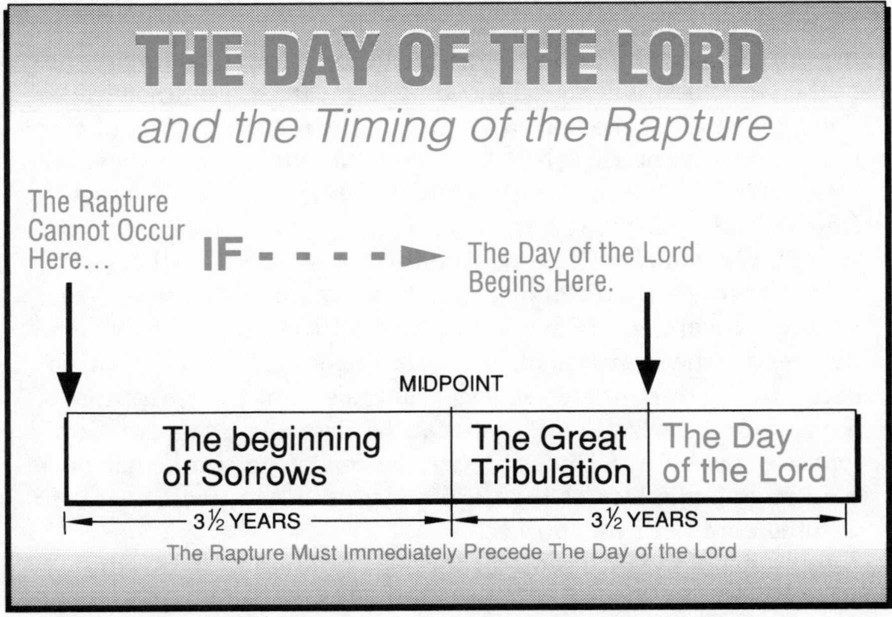


This is a classic illustration of erecting a straw man and then knocking it down. There is no question that God has sometimes used war, famine, and pestilence as means of judgment. That is a given—but it begs the question. The issue is not whether God has used war, famine, and pestilence as a means of judgment, but whether the war, famine, and pestilence of the seals (Rev. 6) originate with God or man. Men also start wars; men also cause famine; and men also generate pestilence. What is conspicuous by its absence on the part of those who advance the view that the seals are God's judgment, is any convincing explanation of the first and fifth seals. The first seal depicts a white horse and rider (Rev. 6:1–2). Dispensational pretribulationists have consistently and almost universally interpreted the emergence of this horse and rider to represent the Antichrist who will at first conquer by deception (Matt. 24:5; Rev. 6:2). If the second, third, and fourth seals are attributed to God, so also must the first one be. If the seals are God's wrath, then God alone must take direct responsibility for a counterfeit religious system and the emergence of the Antichrist, for that is precisely what the first seal depicts.

To attribute the emergence of the Antichrist to God is obviously preposterous. It is to have a divided house—to have God opposing Himself—and a house divided cannot stand. The emergence of the Antichrist will signal movement toward the ultimate rebellion against God: the deification of man by men at the Tribulation temple on Mount Moriah at Jerusalem. To attempt to achieve his satanic ambition, the Antichrist will plunge the world into war (the second seal, the red horse and rider); the resultant devastation of war will cause famine (the third seal, the black horse and rider); and the predictable unsanitary conditions which, like a waiting scavenger, always follow war and famine will result in pestilence (the fourth seal, the pale horse and rider). That has been the historic *pretribulational,* premillennial interpretation of the first four seals. To suggest that the first four seals are God's wrath is totally unfounded. It strains reason to think that once God begins His Day of the Lord wrath, the Antichrist is able to assume control of the world.

But what of the fifth seal? It cannot be omitted from this discussion. When the fifth seal is opened, it depicts the martyrdom of a believing remnant who have not bowed to the Antichrist. These faithful saints are heard to be crying "with a loud voice, saying, How long, O Lord, holy and true, dost thou not judge and avenge our blood on them that dwell on the earth?" (Rev. 6:10; cf. Matt. 24:9–26). If the seals are God's wrath, then He is responsible for the martyrdom of His own faithful children, those who refuse to give their allegiance to the Antichrist and thereby forfeit their lives. Impossible, you say. That is correct. The very testimony of the martyrs settles the matter. They pleaded for divine retribution against their persecutors. That is another reason why the seals cannot be God's wrath, and the Day of the Lord cannot begin at the beginning of the Tribulation period.

Third, pretribulationism suggests that in the book of Revelation it is the Lamb of God who takes the scroll out of the right hand of Him who sits upon the throne (Rev. 5:6–7). The scroll, as it is opened, brings to fruition the seventieth week of Daniel. Since it is the Lamb alone who has the right to open the scroll and loose the seals thereof (Rev. 5:9), the entire tribulation period is the outpouring of His wrath.

It strains reason to think that once God begins His Day of the Lord wrath, the Antichrist is able to assume control of the world.

This argument totally ignores the distinction between God's active will and permissive will, both of which are equally under His sovereign control. Further, it rests on an inadequate understanding of the purpose of the seventieth week of Daniel. God the Son is clearly depicted in Revelation as the sovereign Lord who is bringing history to a consonant ending. He is in command, and all things will proceed according to His preordained path. But there are a number of different purposes God is accomplishing during the seventieth week. Those purposes relate to the distinctive significance of the seals, trumpets, and bowls of the book of Revelation.

The seal, in the Roman world and in the Bible, indicates ownership and protection. The seal for the believer is the Holy Spirit Himself (Eph. 1:13; see also Rev. 5:1, 5; 7:3). His indwelling presence in the believer is the absolute guarantee that his eternal salvation is secure, that what God has begun in His child He will bring to consummation, and that nothing can thwart the divine purpose for His redeemed ones.

How comforting for believers is the realization that when going through the period of man's greatest inhumanity to man, when the Antichrist is demanding that men bow to him or perish—the Son, who is opening the seals, is in complete, sovereign control; nothing can happen to the child of God, even during the Great Tribulation, except that which his sovereign Lord permits. Concerning that period, the Lord warned, "Then shall they deliver you up to be afflicted, and shall kill you" (Matt. 24:9). And John wrote, "And when he had opened the fifth seal, I saw under the altar the souls of them that were slain for the word of God, and for the testimony which they held" (Rev. 6:9). Here is the epitome of the truth found right in the context of the seventieth week: "And fear not them who kill the body, but are not able to kill the soul; but rather fear him who is able to destroy both soul and body in hell" (Matt. 10:28).

"All of the things which occur under the first five seals are brought about and engineered by men who instigate and carry forward these events as indicated in Rev. 6:1–11."

Even Walvoord, commenting on the seals, has written, "The judgments of war, famine, and death, and the martyrdom of the saints [the fifth seal] have largely originated in human decisions and in the evil heart of men."[7]

Leon Morris has written, "The first four seals form a unity. They show us the self-defeating character of sin. When the spirit of self-aggrandizement and conquest is abroad all God need do is let events take their course and sinners will inevitably be punished."[8]

Commenting on the fifth seal, William Newell wrote, "This fifth seal exhibits especially three things; . . . Third, the utter wickedness of the earth which is plainly expected to go on martyring the full complement of God's saints."[9]

The significance of the Lord Jesus Christ opening the seals is, among other things, the assurance of eternal security for those believers who may be martyred for Christ's sake. The Antichrist, under the permissive hand of the sovereign Lord, can touch their bodies—but not their eternal souls. The seals are not God's wrath; they are God's promise of eternal protection during *man's* wrath, a wrath precipitated by the Antichrist who is empowered by Satan (Rev. 13:4). Here is the ultimate manifestation of the principle, "Surely the wrath of man shall praise thee" (Ps. 76:10). That the Lord is in sovereign control during the opening of the seals is underscored in the strongest possible way. The impact of the first four seals is restricted by Him to one-fourth of the earth (Rev. 6:8).

Gary Cohen, in a discussion of the seals, has written, "The first five seals are seen to contain providential-type judgments. Such judgments are those which God, in His holy and wise control of all things in the world, permits to rise up out of natural causes."[10]

David Cooper, staunch defender of pretribulation rapturism and a prolific writer on prophetic truth, has stated,

> At the breaking of each of the first four seals, there appears upon the earth a rider upon a certain colored horse. These horse men are symbols of movements and events of that period. This movement brings the Antichrist into power. . . . A martyrdom of Tribulation saints occurs at the breaking of the fifth seal. *All of the things* which occur under the first five seals are brought about and engineered by men who instigate and carry forward these events as indicated in Rev. 6:1–11.[11]

Nothing can happen to God's sons and daughters except that which He permits. He is sovereign, a fact elegantly attested by the truth that He opens the seals, trumpets, and bowls. But to suggest that the first five seals are God's wrath goes against the evidence of Scripture and the testimony of the overwhelming majority of commentators on the book of Revelation. It must also be noted that the first five seals are mentioned by the Lord Himself as signs of His coming. Nowhere does He say that they are His wrath.

Concerning the trumpet judgments, in ancient Israel the trumpet had two specific purposes. First, it was used to call a solemn assembly of the people; that is, to gather them to the presence of the Lord (Lev. 23:24–25; Num. 10:2–3, 7, 10; Ps. 81:3). Second, the trumpet was used to sound an alarm for war and judgment (Num. 10:9; Jer. 4:19; Joel 2:1). The trumpet judgments will be precisely that. The church will be raptured to God's presence;

then God's eschatological Day of the Lord judgment upon an unrepentant world will occur. It will fall on both Jews (Ezek. 20:30–38) and Gentiles (Isa. 2:12–22; 24:20–23).

The bowl judgments also have a unique and limited purpose. The Greek word translated *bowl* refers to a wide, shallow dish. A righteous Jew would cleanse himself by washing his hands before the Sabbath or for a variety of religious observances in just such a vessel. When finished, he could discard the dirty water in one quick swish because the bowl was wide and shallow. The rapid pouring out of that which was dirty and useless became the descriptive language by the Jews for the divine judgment upon the Gentile nations. The psalmist wrote, "Pour out thy wrath upon the nations that have not known thee, and upon the kingdoms that have not called upon thy name. For they have devoured Jacob, and laid waste his dwelling place" (Ps. 79:6–7). And the prophet Jeremiah wrote, "Pour out thy fury upon the nations that know thee not, and upon the families that call not on thy name; for they have eaten up Jacob, and devoured him, and consumed him, and have made his habitation desolate" (Jer. 10:25; cf. Zeph. 3:8). Both texts speak of (1) the pouring out of judgment; (2) that it will be on the nations, and (3) that it will be based upon their treatment of Jacob (Israel). That judgment on the nations will begin at the end of the seventieth week. Christ will literally return to assume His kingdom at the seventh trumpet (Rev. 11:15–17). It will be the occasion of Israel's national Day of Atonement (Zech. 12:10). At that time the judgment on the nations will be poured out (Rev. 11:18). The prophet wrote, "And it shall come to pass, in that day, that I will seek to destroy all the nations that come against Jerusalem" (Zech. 12:9). That poured-out judgment will be swift, encompassing the thirty days beyond the last three and one-half years of the seventieth week (Dan. 12:11). The chart below illustrates the relationship of the seals, trumpets, and bowls.

Permit one further word at this time concerning attempts to start the Day of the Lord at the beginning of the seventieth week. Even a cursory examination of the Day of the Lord texts indicates it is a period of unprecedented, awesome judgment from the hand of God. The arm of omnipotence is depicted unleashing righteous wrath upon an unrepentant and unrighteous world.

This planet and its inhabitants will reel under its impact. The proposition that after the Day of the Lord judgment begins, the Antichrist will emerge, expand his power, erect an image of himself in Israel, ask men to bow to his authority, kill multitudes who

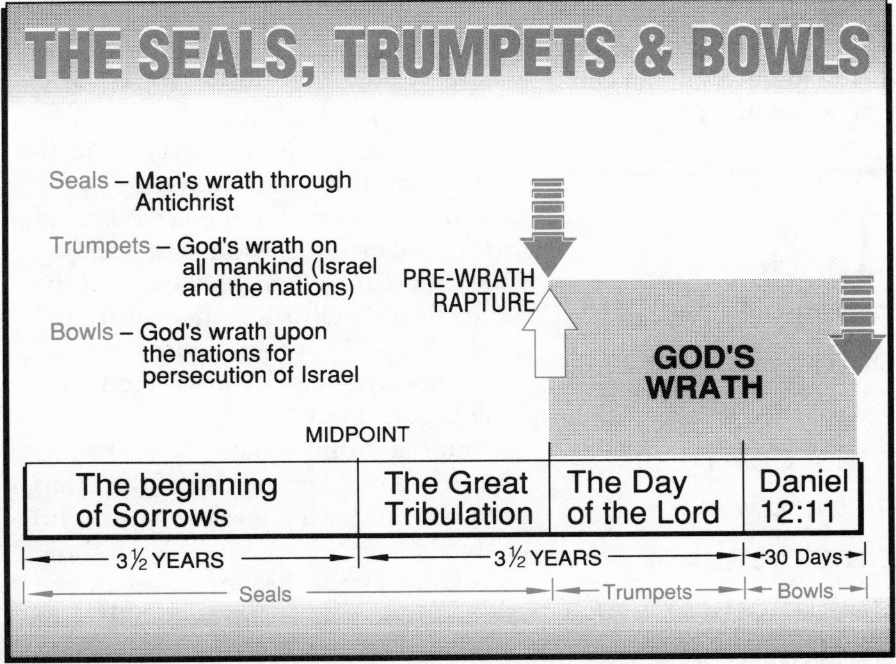


refuse, and eventually become a world ruler (Rev. 13:1–8)—all of this over a period of time extending more than three and one-half years into the Day of the Lord judgment—cannot be seriously entertained in the light of biblical characteristics of the Day of the Lord. Isaiah 2 says the Lord alone will be exalted in that day and *all* the proud brought low.

Not only does starting the Day of the Lord at the beginning of the Tribulation have its own insurmountable exegetical problems, it compounds its error by standing in opposition to the clear teaching that the Day of the Lord starts with the opening of the seventh seal.

Evidence that the Day of the Lord starts with the opening of the seventh seal follows.

The clear and repeated teaching of the Word of God is that there must be a *cosmic disturbance* of considerable magnitude before the Day of the Lord begins. The prophet Isaiah wrote, "Behold, the day of the LORD cometh, cruel both with wrath and fierce anger, to lay the land desolate; and he shall destroy the sinners out of it. For the stars of heaven and the constellations thereof shall not give their light; the sun shall be darkened in its going forth, and the moon shall not cause its light to shine" (Isa. 13:9–10). Clearly, cosmic disturbances are associated with the Day of the Lord.

The clear and repeated teaching of the Word of God is that there must be a *cosmic disturbance* of considerable magnitude before the Day of the Lord begins.

The prophet Joel wrote, "Multitudes, multitudes in the valley of decision; for the day of the LORD is near in the valley of decision. The sun and the moon shall be darkened, and the stars shall withdraw their shining" (Joel 3:14–15). Once again, cosmic disturbance is clearly associated with the Day of the Lord.

But the prophet is not done; he has more to say: "For the day of the LORD is great and very terrible, and who can abide it? . . . And I will show wonders in the heavens and in the earth: blood, and fire and pillars of smoke. The sun shall be turned into darkness, and the moon into blood, before the great and the terrible day of the LORD come" (Joel 2:11, 30–31). Once again, cosmic disturbance is clearly associated with the Day of the Lord. But one must not allow the precision to go unnoticed. "The sun shall be turned into darkness, and the moon into blood, *before* the great and terrible day of the LORD come." Not only will there be cosmic disturbance, but it will occur *before* the Day of the Lord begins.

On this point there can be no question. If the Day of the Lord starts at the beginning of the seventieth week, as pretribulation rapturists normally insist, then the cosmic disturbance must precede the seventieth week, for it appears before the Day of the Lord begins. There is no legitimate biblical alternative. But that, once again, poses an insurmountable problem for pretribulation rapturism. A major facet of pretribulation rapturism is the concept of imminence. Imminence is the belief that no prophesied events must occur before the Rapture of the church. Walvoord calls im-

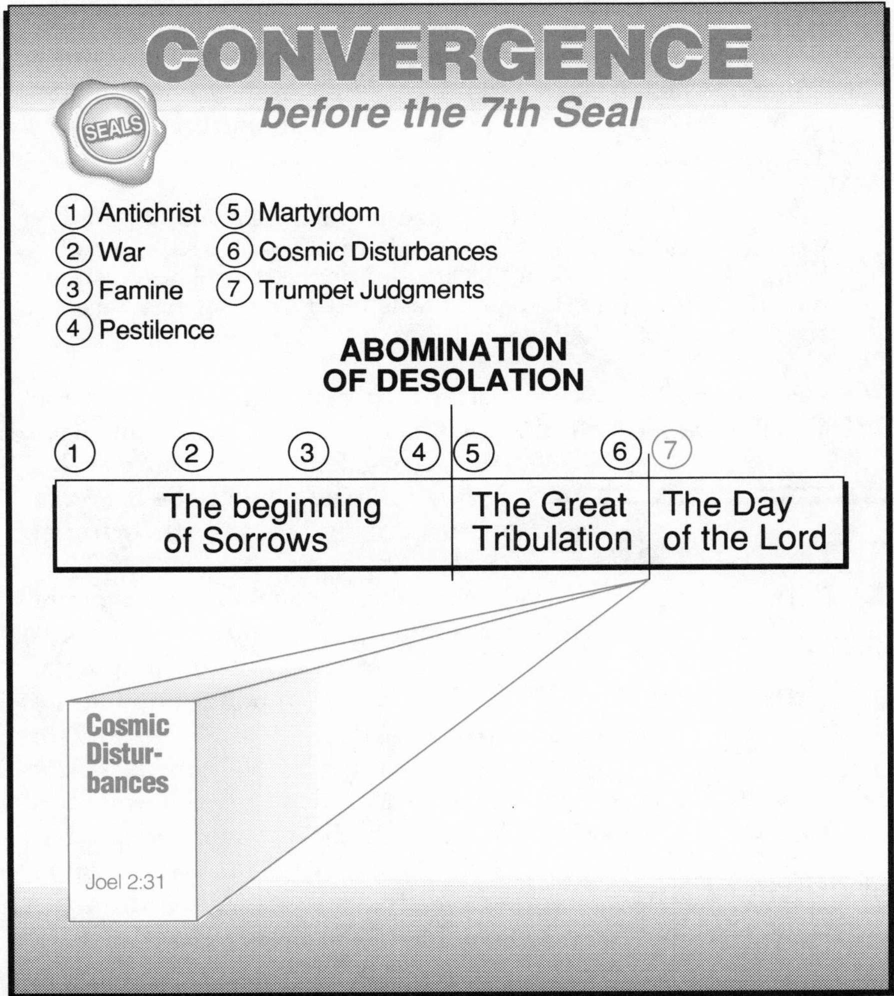


minence the "heart of Pretribulationism,"[12] and the majority of pretribulation rapturists have followed suit. However, if the Day of the Lord starts at the beginning of the seventieth week, and the prophesied cosmic disturbance must occur first, then the cosmic disturbance must occur before the seventieth week begins. *Pretribulation rapturism is, therefore, faced with the enigma that the doctrine of imminence, a major pillar of pretribulation rapturism, is untenable. That is a crucial, clear, unassailable truth that cannot be dismissed by those making careful inquiry.*

A new question must now be raised. Is it possible to know when the cosmic disturbance—precursor to the Day of the Lord—will begin? The journey need not be long. Credulity need not be stretched. A container to fit need not be manufactured.

The apostle John wrote,

> And I beheld, when he had opened the sixth seal and, lo, there was a great earthquake, and the sun became black as sackcloth of hair, and the moon became like blood; And the stars of heaven fell unto the earth, even as a fig tree casteth her untimely figs, when she is shaken of a mighty wind. (Rev. 6:12–13)

Here is specific cosmic disturbance that occurs inside of the Tribulation period with the opening of the sixth seal. Some have tried to negate the significance of this fact by confusing it with the heavenly disturbance of the fourth trumpet (Rev. 8:12).

Here is specific cosmic disturbance that occurs inside of the Tribulation period with the opening of the sixth seal.

First, there is no parallel of thought or language. Second, six passages of Scripture converge in language, thought, and common ground at the sixth seal (Isa. 13:10; Ezek. 32:7–8; Joel 2:31; Matt. 24:29; Mark 13:24–25; Luke 21:25). Third, it conforms perfectly with the chronology of Matthew 24. But how far inside of the seventieth week of Daniel does the opening of the sixth seal occur?

Many scholars have called attention to the similarity of the Lord's comments in Matthew (Matt. 24:5–8) and the four horses and riders of the Apocalypse (Rev. 6:1–8). That similarity is here demonstrated.

| THE LORD'S DESCRIPTION OF THE 70TH WEEK | | THE APOSTLE JOHN'S DESCRIPTION OF THE 70TH WEEK |
|---|---|---|
| "For many shall come in my name, saying, I am Christ; and shall deceive many" (Matt. 24:5). | ⟷ | THE FIRST SEAL is the white horse and rider. He is understood to be false religion personified in the Antichrist who conquers by deception (Rev. 6:1–2). |
| "And ye shall hear of wars and rumors of wars; see that ye be not troubled; for all these things must come to pass, but the end is not yet. For nation shall rise against nation, and kingdom against kingdom" (Matt. 24:6–7a). | ⟷ | THE SECOND SEAL is the red horse and rider. He is given a sword and has power to conquer through war (Rev. 6:3–4). |
| "And there shall be famines" (Matt. 24:7b). | ⟷ | THE THIRD SEAL is the black horse and rider. He is given a scale to measure the food supply. He will bring famine (Rev. 6:5–6). |
| "And pestilences, and earthquakes in various places. All these are the beginning of sorrows" (Matt. 24:7c–8). | ⟷ | THE FOURTH SEAL is the pale horse and rider. He represents death and pestilence. He kills with sword, hunger, and beasts of the earth (Rev. 6:7–8). |

Unfortunately, many commentators who touch on the subject conclude the comparison at that point. The Word of God, however, continues the comparison.

<table>
<tr>
<td>"Then shall they deliver you up to be afflicted, and shall kill you; and ye shall be hated of all nations for my name's sake" (Matt. 24:9).</td>
<td>↔</td>
<td>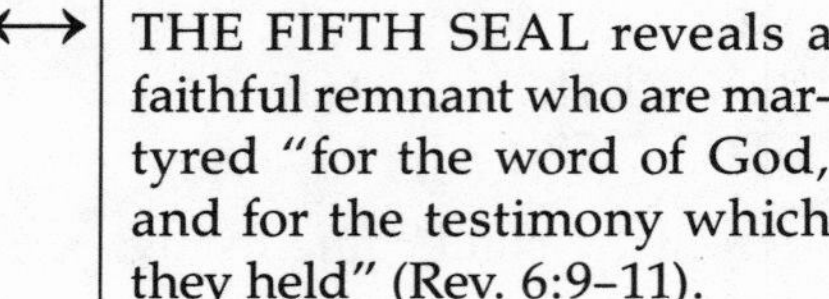
THE FIFTH SEAL reveals a faithful remnant who are martyred "for the word of God, and for the testimony which they held" (Rev. 6:9–11).</td>
</tr>
<tr>
<td>"Immediately after the tribulation of those days shall the sun be darkened, and the moon shall not give its light, and the stars shall fall from heaven, and the powers of the heavens shall be shaken" (Matt. 24:29).<br><br>And again, "But in those days, after that tribulation, the sun shall be darkened, and the moon shall not give its light, And the stars of heaven shall fall, and the powers that are in the heavens shall be shaken" (Mark 13:24–25).<br><br>And one more time, "And there shall be signs in the sun, and in the moon, and in the stars; and upon the earth distress of nations, with perplexity; the sea and the waves roaring" (Luke 21:25).</td>
<td>↔</td>
<td>THE SIXTH SEAL reveals cosmic disturbance: "And I beheld, when he had opened the sixth seal and, lo, there was a great earthquake, and the sun became black as sackcloth of hair, and the moon became like blood; And the stars of heaven fell unto the earth, even as a fig tree casteth her untimely figs, when she is shaken of a mighty wind" (Rev. 6:12–13).</td>
</tr>
</table>

If the Bible is the verbal, plenary, inspired Word of God, if it is to be interpreted literally and normally, if men can comprehend it, then this is patently clear: cosmic disturbance precedes the Day of the Lord. And that cosmic disturbance occurs with the opening of the sixth seal. To deny or ignore that fact is to force the Scriptures to conform to a pre-conceived pretribulation rapture mold. Two points are of great significance. First, the sixth seal is opened after the Great Tribulation. And the Great Tribulation is cut short and ends before the end of the seventieth week (Matt. 24:29; Mark 13:24; Luke 21:23–25; see also Rev. 6:12, where cosmic disturbance occurs after the martyrdom associated with the Great Tribulation).

Second, the sign of the appearing of the Son of man in heaven will be manifested following the opening of the sixth seal (Matt. 24:30; Mark 13:26; Luke 21:27). This occurs after the Great Tribulation but long before the end of the seventieth week. The seven trumpet judgments must be poured out before the seventieth week ends (Rev. 11:15). The fifth trumpet judgment alone is said to last five months (Rev. 9:1, 5). This appearance of the Son of man in heaven before the opening of the seventh seal is related to the rapturing of the church before the Day of the Lord's wrath begins. God does not exempt His people from *man's* wrath; He does exempt them from *His* wrath (Lot was told to flee Sodom and Noah to get into the ark before God's wrath fell). God's wrath begins with the opening of the seventh seal, for out of the seventh seal the seven trumpet judgments will emerge.

The cosmic disturbance introduced with the opening of the sixth seal is the prelude of the Rapture of the church and the Day of the Lord wrath.

# 11

# Elijah Must Appear First

Momentum will now accelerate. Biblical evidence that the Day of the Lord begins with the opening of the seventh seal will now increase. Arguments that converge at the seventh seal will each, on their own merit, be strong. Collectively I believe they will be impregnable.

Moses and Elijah are premier personalities of the Old Testament Scriptures. Dispensational premillennialists have frequently equated these two men with the two witnesses who will appear during the Tribulation period (Rev. 11:3–19).[1] An impressive number of reasons have given rise to that identification.

First, Moses is viewed as the great lawgiver and Elijah as the premier prophet. This is borne out in the Old Testament Scriptures and Jewish theology. Together, Moses and Elijah represent the whole of the Law and the prophets, and they are found in tandem in many prophetic texts (see e.g., Mal. 4:4–5; Matt. 17:3).

Second, mystery surrounds the death of Moses. He was buried by God "in a valley in the land of Moab" (Deut. 34:6). The Bible tells of conflict over the body of Moses. Jude wrote, "Yet Michael, the archangel, when contending with the devil he disputed about the body of Moses, dared not bring against him a railing accusation, but said, The Lord rebuke thee" (Jude 9). And in the case of Elijah, the Word of God records that he was caught up into heaven: "And it came to pass, as they still went on, and talked, that, behold, there appeared a chariot of fire, and horses of fire, and separated them, and Elijah went up by a whirlwind into heaven" (2 Kings 2:11).

Third, the Lord told His disciples that some of them would see Him coming in His glory before they died (Matt. 16:28). These privileged disciples (three of them in number: Peter, James, and John) would get a *preview of coming attractions;* that is, they would see Christ with the glory which He will manifest at His second coming, but they would see it in advance of that event. These three disciples were taken up to a high mountain, and Jesus was transfigured before them (Matt. 17:2). Dispensational premillennialists acknowledge that this scene portrays a preview of Christ's coming glory. And concerning that preview of divine glory it is written, "And, behold, there appeared unto them Moses and Elijah talking with him" (Matt. 17:3). Moses and Elijah were present at the *preview showing* of God's future glory.

Peter, James, and John would get a *preview of coming attractions;* that is, they would see Christ with the glory which He will manifest at His second coming.

Fourth, the two witnesses of the Apocalypse are said to have miraculous power. John wrote, "These have power to shut heaven, that it rain not in the days of their prophecy; and have power over waters to turn them to blood, and to smite the earth with all plagues, as often as they will" (Rev. 11:6). Power to shut heaven—that is precisely what Elijah did (1 Kings 17:1; 18:41–45; 2 Kings 1:10–12). Power to perform plagues—that is precisely what Moses did to Pharaoh down in Egypt (Ex. 7:20; 8:1–12:29).

Some have argued, with little basis, that the two witnesses are Elijah and Enoch. Enoch, like Elijah, was caught up into heaven (Gen. 5:24), and so he is sometimes identified as one of the two witnesses.

However, in either motif, Moses and Elijah or Enoch and Elijah, the latter is viewed as one of the two witnesses ministering during the seventieth week. The specific duration of the ministry of the two witnesses is three and one-half years. The Word of God is precise on that point: "And I will give power unto my two witnesses, and they shall prophesy a thousand two hundred and threescore days [forty-two months or three and one-half years], clothed in sackcloth" (Rev. 11:3).

The large majority of premillennial expositors have located the ministry of these two witnesses during the last half of the seventieth week, and with that view this author strongly concurs. Some commentators have placed their ministry during the first three and one-half years. In either case, Elijah is seen to be ministering inside and during the seventieth week.

But how does all of this bear on the starting point of the Day of the Lord and the time of the Rapture?

The last writing prophet of the Old Testament is Malachi, and in the very last verses of his prophecy concerning end-time events, he penned these words: "Behold, I will send you Elijah, the prophet, *before* the coming of the great and terrible day of the LORD; And he shall turn the heart of the fathers to the children, and the heart of the children to their fathers, lest I come and smite the earth with a curse" (Mal. 4:5–6).

These verses of Scripture have been a cornerstone of Jewish theology for unnumbered centuries. Year after year, beginning on the fourteenth day of the Jewish month Nisan (corresponding to March/April), Jewish people the world over celebrate the feast of Passover. During the dinner (called the Seder) on the first evening of the feast, the story of the Egyptian Exodus is recounted. The prophet Elijah plays a prominent role in the festivities. A place setting is set for the prophet Elijah. A chair is kept vacant. A cup larger and more ornate than the others, called the "cup of Elijah," is placed before his setting. At one point in the ceremony, a youngster is sent to open the door with the great expectancy that Elijah will enter, sit down, drink from the cup, and announce that the Messiah is coming.

Simply stated, this observance is based on the ancient rabbis' understanding of the words of the prophet, "Behold, I will send you Elijah, the prophet, before the coming of the great and terrible day of the LORD." Jewish theology is replete with teaching that Elijah must appear to herald the coming of the Messiah. That same theology is brought over into the New Testament. After a group of Jewish leaders were told by John the Baptist that he was "not the Christ" (John 1:20), their follow-up question to John was, "Art thou Elijah? And he saith, I am not" (John 1:21). They clearly understood that the prophet Elijah was to announce the coming of the Christ.

The prophet Joel declared that the cosmic disturbance is to occur *before* the Day of the Lord commences (Joel 2:31). Now the prophet Malachi proclaims that Elijah will appear *before* the Day of the Lord commences (Mal. 4:5). According to Mosaic law a matter was settled in the mouth of two witnesses (Num. 35:30; Deut. 17:6; 19:15). Will not, then, the consistent witness of the inspired prophets Joel and Malachi do? Was not a prophet to be stoned to death if he erred in his prophetic utterance (Deut. 13:1–10)?

Once again, pretribulational rapturism has an unsolvable problem with imminence. They can resolve their problem only if they accept *all* of the following:

- Elijah is not one of the two witnesses (Rev. 11:3).
- There is not another who comes in the power and spirit of Elijah, if not Elijah himself.
- Malachi was in error when he said that Elijah must come before the Day of the Lord commences.
- Elijah appears before the seventieth week begins. In this case, if Elijah appears before the seventieth week begins, that becomes a prophesied event that must occur in this age, before the seventieth week commences, and the doctrine of imminence is once again destroyed. Additionally, one is also faced with the considerable problem that the two witnesses minister for precisely three and one-half years (Rev. 11:3). Such a precise time period argues strongly for one-half of the seventieth week of Daniel. Whether the first half or the second is immaterial in this regard.

One leading pretribulation rapturist, understanding the difficulty this poses for his view, tries to resolve the problem by suggesting that the Day of the Lord is not a comprehensive whole; it is a series of mini-Days of the Lord, and somehow Elijah is to get sandwiched in between a couple of them—thus allowing it to be said that Elijah appears before the Day of the Lord but inside of the seventieth week of Daniel.[2] Such reasoning is not only without biblical merit, it is contrary to the clear biblical teaching of a comprehensive, singular, eschatological Day of the Lord.

Another leading pretribulation rapturist sought to minimize the problem. He wrote, "The problem of Elijah is not so overpowering, at least to this reviewer." His bottom-line solution? "On the basis of the Lord's words it is concluded that Elijah personally need not appear, although one will come to fulfill this ministry."[3] Such teaching goes directly against the clear, uncompromising voice of Scripture: "I will send you Elijah, the prophet, before the coming of the great and terrible day of the LORD" (Mal. 4:5).

Furthermore, it does not resolve the problem. Whether it is Elijah himself or one who comes in his spirit or likeness, the basic difficulty remains for pretribulationism. The precursor of one coming (whether Elijah or another) before the Day of the Lord remains in place. And if the Day of the Lord begins at the beginning of the seventieth week, imminence is destroyed.

A final word in this chapter. Sensing the problem of precursors (like cosmic disturbance and Elijah) to the Day of the Lord for pretribulation rapturism, some have attempted to separate the Rapture of the church from the beginning of the seventieth week. The Rapture, they suggest, could occur sometime before the seventieth week begins. This would allow for the cosmic disturbance and the coming of Elijah before the Day of the Lord commences. But such attempts do not resolve the problem. First, there is absolutely no biblical evidence for separating the Rapture from the Day of the Lord. It is simply an assumption without any biblical evidence. Second, the cosmic disturbance is clearly revealed to begin with the sixth seal *inside* the seventieth week—not before it commences. Third, Elijah (or one like him) is to minister for precisely three and one-half years, which almost certainly relates to one-half of the seventieth week (Rev. 11:3). This negates any attempt to place Elijah's appearance between the Rapture and the making of a covenant with the Antichrist. Fourth, Scripture has been cited to demonstrate that the Rapture and the Day of the Lord are intimately connected, and no significant period of time between these two events can possibly be established. Fifth, pretribulationists cannot have it both ways. Walvoord represents the majority when he wrote, "The pretribulational interpretation regards the coming of the Lord and the translation [Rapture] of the church as preceding *immediately* the fulfillment of Daniel's prophecy of a final seven-year period before the second advent."[4] Only because the problem of precursors for pretribulationism has been pointed out in relatively recent years have later defenders, in the opinion of this author, impotently appealed to a period of time between the Rapture and the seventieth week.

The fact that godly men make such a weak defense against the problem of precursors for pretribulationism only serves to underscore the inherent impossibility of placing the Day of the Lord at the beginning of the seventieth week.

> The fact is that neither posttribulationism nor pretribulationism is an explicit teaching of Scripture. The Bible does not, in so many words, state either.

Pretribulation rapturism is exegetically indefensible. Some of the best theological minds of the twentieth century have not been able to exegetically defend it. If that statement sounds exaggerated, then listen to the admission of Walvoord: "The fact is that neither Posttribulationism nor Pretribulationism is an explicit teaching of Scripture. The Bible does not, in so many words, state either."[5] If pretribulationism is not explicitly taught, then it must be based on inference. And if, from the mouths of its own adherents, such is the case, it should not be dogma. And if not dogma, it should not be divisive.

Pretribulationism has often simply been seen as a less problematic position than mid- and posttribulationism.

This chart illustrates the precursor of Elijah's coming before the Day of the Lord.

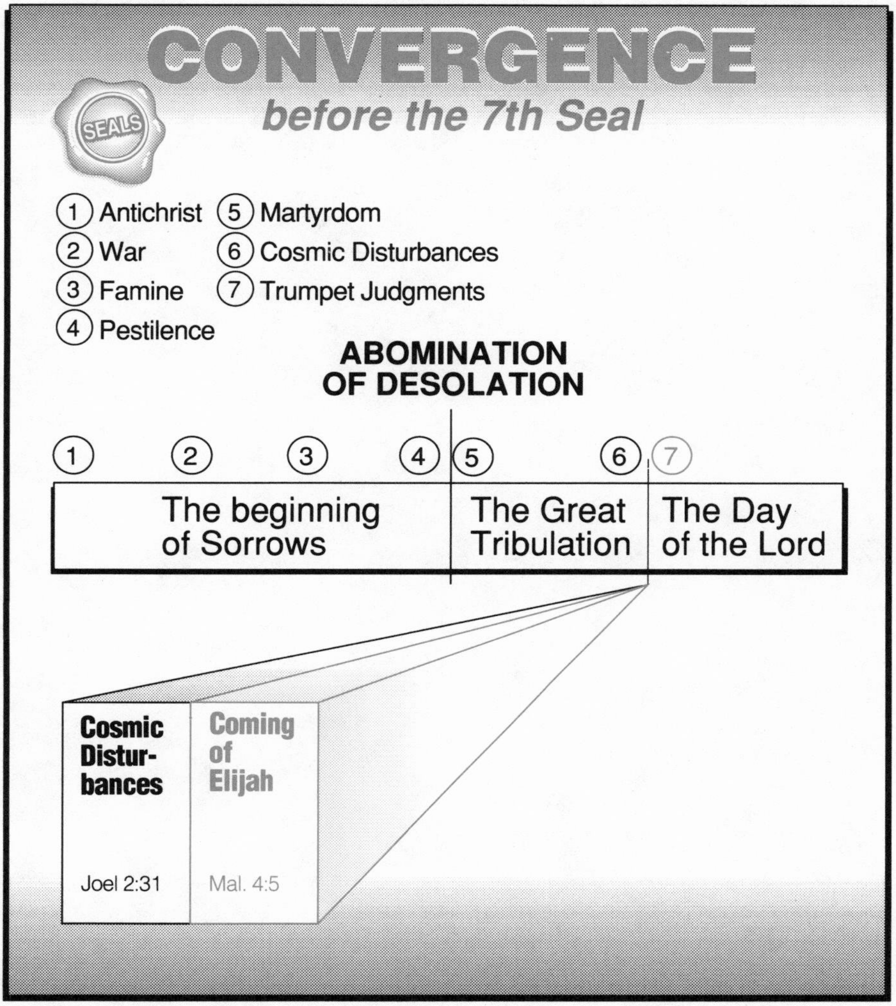

CONVERGENCE
before the 7th Seal

SEALS

(1) Antichrist
(2) War
(3) Famine
(4) Pestilence
(5) Martyrdom
(6) Cosmic Disturbances
(7) Trumpet Judgments

ABOMINATION OF DESOLATION

(1) (2) (3) (4) (5) (6) (7)

| The beginning of Sorrows | The Great Tribulation | The Day of the Lord |
|---|---|---|

| Cosmic Distur-bances | Coming of Elijah |
|---|---|
| Joel 2:31 | Mal. 4:5 |

# 12

# The Day of His Wrath

One of the qualities properly assigned to God is the attribute of being long-suffering. In a prophetic context, the apostle Peter wrote, "The Lord is not slack concerning his promise, as some men count slackness, but is long-suffering toward us, not willing that any should perish, but that all should come to repentance" (2 Peter 3:9). God sometimes waits, holds back His judgment, and gives men time to repent.

Personhood has been defined as the ability to think, feel, and act; or, put another way, that which can think, feel, and act possesses personhood. By that criteria, God has personhood. He thinks—He has intellect; He feels—He exhibits emotion; He acts—He exercises volition.

Another attribute of God is His wrath. Writing to the church in Rome, the apostle Paul said, "For the wrath of God is revealed from heaven against all ungodliness and unrighteousness of men, who hold the truth in unrighteousness" (Rom. 1:18). God's wrath is an expression of hatred and abhorrence against ungodliness (a mental attitude that lacks reverence for God) and unrighteousness (the committing of acts that do not conform to God's character). Men first think wrong concerning God, and then they act wrong toward God. That is always the process.

The final wrath of God (against man's ungodliness and unrighteousness) will result in divine judgment during *the Day of the Lord*. When that occurs, God's long-suffering will have come to an end. His wrath will result in the act of righteous judgment on a godless, unrepentant world.

The starting time for the outpouring of God's wrath, as has been indicated, is controversial. Pretribulationists want to start it at the beginning of the seventieth week. Midtribulationists want to start it at the middle of the seventieth week. Posttribulationists want to start it near or at the end of the seventieth week. It should not be, and it need not be, controversial. The Scriptures are both clear and precise. Immediately following the opening of the sixth seal, there will be cosmic disturbance (Rev. 6:12–14). In that connection it is written,

> The kings of the earth, and the great men, and the rich men, and the chief captains, and the mighty men, and every slave, and every free man, hid themselves in the dens and in the rocks of the mountains, and said to the mountains and rocks, Fall on us, and hide us from the face of him that sitteth on the throne, and from the *wrath* of the Lamb. (Rev. 6:15–16)

The cosmic disturbance associated with the opening of the sixth seal will indicate to men of all stations of life (kings, great men, rich men, captains, mighty men, slaves, and free men) that they should flee to the caves of mountains for protection. The reason is given and confirms what the Old Testament prophets had foretold concerning this event: "For the great day of his *wrath* is come, and who shall be able to stand?" (Rev. 6:17).

Once again, pretribulation rapturism has a big problem. In reality, it is larger than big—it is mountainous and unscalable. The clear teaching of Scripture is that God's wrath is about to begin following the opening of the sixth seal and in anticipation of the opening of the seventh. To attempt to negate this problematic obstacle to pretribulationism, which normally and historically places the Day of the Lord at the beginning of the seventieth week, some Bible teachers point out that the Greek verb translated *is come* in the phrase "For the great day of his wrath is come" is in the aorist tense. As such, they argue, it must be interpreted as referring to an event which has already occurred and which includes the five seals that preceded it. Thus, when it says, "his wrath is come" (Rev. 6:17), it is covering a period of substantially more than three and one-half years and includes all of the events of the seventieth week to that point in time. In contemporary language, they want to "grandfather clause" the previous six seals and thus include them in the statement "the great day of his wrath is come." But such exegesis is strained and unjustified. It is true that the verb *is come* is in the aorist tense. It is *not* true that it must be made retroactive to include all six seal judgments and, therefore, the entire Tribulation period.

The aorist tense of the Greek language is frequently thought to refer to a once-and-for-all past action. But that is not necessarily the case. In a discussion of the Greek verb translated *is come* in Revelation 6:17, John Sproule, former head of the Greek department at Grace Seminary and present dean of Capital Seminary, wrote, "If the verb is taken as a constative, then it speaks of past action and includes the preceding seals. If, however, it is a dramatic aorist, the tense of the verb is indecisive."[1] In other words, it can refer to either a past action or an event still future.

Paul Feinberg of Trinity Evangelical Seminary, while interacting with Robert Gundry on the Rapture issue, wrote, "The verb wrath in Revelation 6:17 can be an ingressive aorist expressing a condition 'just entered' or a dramatic aorist which functions like a future tense—that the wrath is about to begin."[2]

D. A. Carson, in his excellent book *Grammatical Fallacies,* makes this observation:

> More than a decade ago, Frank Stagg wrote an article about 'The Abused Aorist.' The problem as he saw it was that competent scholars were deducing from the presence of an aorist verb that the action in question was "once for all" or "completed." The problem arises in part because the aorist is often described as the punctiliar tense. Careful grammarians, of course, understand and explain that this does not mean the aorist could be used only for point actions. The aorist, after all, is well-named: it is a-orist (that is, without a place, undefined). It simply refers to the action itself without specifying whether the action is unique, repeated, ingressive, instantaneous, past, or accomplished.[3]

All these men are clearly indicating that an aorist tense can be used to express either a past action or an event that is about to occur.

In this regard, the comment by Gary Cohen, a Greek scholar

and a staunch pretribulation rapturist, on a parallel passage in the book of Revelation is important. He wrote,

> The announcement . . . "for the marriage of the Lamb is come" (Rev. 19:7), is made after the Great Harlot is said to have been judged, and shows that the marriage is now imminent. The fact that the verb translated 'is come' is in the aorist cannot be allowed to push the marriage itself back into the past. The expression *elthen ho gamos* . . . , "the marriage . . . is come" (v. 7) is parallel to *elthen he hora,* "the hour is come" (Mark 14:41). This latter saying is made by Christ speaking at Gethsemane of His impending *future* crucifixion. Thus the aorist tense of the verb *erchomai,* lit. "has come," is sometimes used in the third person to tell of an overhanging event about to occur. Its significance is precisely this here in Revelation 19:7 and it conveys the thought that the time of the marriage has now at last arrived.[4]

In Mark 14:41 the phrase "the hour is come [aorist tense]" spoken by the Lord in the Garden of Gethsemane is incontrovertibly referring to His impending crucifixion. It was about to happen; it had not yet occurred. In Revelation 19:7 the equivalent phrase "the marriage of the Lamb is come [aorist]" refers to the impending wedding of the Lamb. It is about to happen; it has not yet occurred. In Revelation 6:17 again the equivalent phrase "For the great day of his wrath is come [aorist]" can be demonstrated to have but one meaning: God's Day of the Lord wrath is impending. It is about to happen; it has not yet occurred. There is no legitimate way that the phrase "the great day of his wrath is come" in the context of Revelation 6:17 can be made retroactive to include the first six seals.

Since the verb *is come* in Revelation 6:17 tells of the action but not the time of the action, the context must be appealed to for that determination. When that is done, the evidence that the phrase "the great day of his wrath is come" refers to an event which is about to occur is both substantial and compelling. Nonetheless, in an attempt to defend pretribulationism, some have vainly attempted to deny that compelling evidence. The reason for that attempt is clear: If, as the overwhelming majority of pretribulationists contend, the Day of the Lord commences with the seventieth week, how does one explain the fact that God's wrath does not begin until the seventh seal, a considerable period of time beyond the starting point of the seventieth week?

It is important to now examine those contextual arguments which demonstrate that the phrase "the great day of his wrath is come" refers, not to a past event, but to an event about to occur, and that in concert with the opening of the seventh seal.

> **In Revelation 6:17 again the equivalent phrase "For the great day of his wrath is come" can be demonstrated to have but one meaning: God's Day of the Lord wrath is impending. It is about to happen; it has not yet occurred.**

First, Revelation 6 gives a clear, progressive, chronological sequence of events. The first seal is opened, and certain events are said to unfold (vv. 1–2). The second seal is opened, and more events unfold (vv. 3–4). The same thing is true for the third (vv. 5–6), fourth (vv. 7–8), and fifth (vv. 9–11) seals. Then it is recorded that the sixth seal is opened (vv. 12–17), and more events occur. Among them, John informs his readers that "the great day of his wrath is come" (v. 17). As has been demonstrated, the aorist tense gives no basis for making that statement refer to a past event. Neither does the context. A normative reading of Revelation 6 simply indicates a logical progression of events. Seals are opened and events occur. Only after the sixth seal is opened does John declare that "the great day of his wrath is come." There is no exegetical basis for making the sixth seal retroactive. The author consulted forty commentaries on the book of Revelation. Not one suggested that the sixth seal was retroactive and encompassed the events of the first five seals. Attempts to suggest otherwise are new in origin and vainly attempt to resolve this glaring problem for pretribulation rapturism.

Second, in connection with the opening of the sixth seal, John describes cosmic disturbance. He wrote,

> And I beheld, when he had opened the sixth seal and, lo, there was a great earthquake, and the sun became black as sackcloth of hair, and the moon became like blood; And the stars of heaven fell

> unto the earth, even as a fig tree casteth her untimely figs when she is shaken of a mighty wind. And the heaven departed as a scroll when it is rolled together; and every mountain and island were moved out of their places. (Rev. 6:12–14)

This cosmic disturbance, which is clearly said to follow the opening of the sixth seal, is precisely the same event which signals the approach of the Day of the Lord and outpouring of God's wrath according to the Old Testament prophets. Joel wrote, "And I will show wonders in the heavens and in the earth: blood, and fire, and pillars of smoke. The sun shall be turned into darkness, and the moon into blood, before the great and the terrible day of the LORD come" (Joel 2:30–31). Joel foretold that there would be cosmic disturbance *before* "the great and the terrible day of the LORD come." That is precisely what occurs with the opening of the sixth seal.

The sun shall be turned into darkness, and the moon into blood, before the great and the terrible day of the LORD come. (Joel 2:31)

Listen to the prophet once more: "Multitudes, multitudes in the valley of decision; for the day of the LORD is near in the valley of decision. The sun and the moon shall be darkened, and the stars shall withdraw their shining" (Joel 3:14–15). And Isaiah wrote,

> Behold, the day of the LORD cometh, cruel both with wrath and fierce anger, to lay the land desolate; and he shall destroy the sinners out of it. For the stars of heaven and the constellations thereof shall not give their light; the sun shall be darkened in its going forth, and the moon shall not cause its light to shine. (Isa. 13:9–10)

Repeatedly, the prophets give the warning of cosmic disturbance immediately prior to the Day of the Lord. The prophetic book of Revelation is teaching the same truth. The sixth seal will be opened, cosmic disturbance will commence, and that will indicate that "the great day of his wrath" is about to begin. How could the Word of God be more precise?

Third, John makes still another clear identification with an Old Testament Day of the Lord Scripture following the opening of the sixth seal. The two parallel texts are placed side by side.

| | |
|---|---|
| And they shall go into the caves of the rocks, and into the holes of the earth, for fear of the LORD, and for the glory of his majesty, when he ariseth to shake terribly the earth. In that day a man shall cast his idols of silver, and his idols of gold, which they made each one for himself to worship, to the moles and to the bats; To go into the clefts of the rocks, and into the tops of the ragged rocks, for fear of the LORD, and for the glory of his majesty, when he ariseth to shake terribly the earth (Isa. 2:19–21). | And the kings of the earth, and the great men, and the rich men, and the chief captains, and the mighty men, and every slave, and every free man, hid themselves in the dens and in the rocks of the mountains, And said to the mountains and rocks, Fall on us, and hide us from the face of him that sitteth on the throne, and from the wrath of the Lamb (Rev. 6:15–16). |

In both passages, men are said to flee to the dens and rocks of mountains. Their reason for fleeing is clearly enunciated. John said that in that day men would cry out to the mountains and rocks to "Fall on us, and hide us from the face of him that sitteth on the throne, and from the wrath of the Lamb. For the great day of his wrath is come" (Rev. 6:16–17). And Isaiah wrote, in an undisputed Day of the Lord context, "And they shall go into the caves of the rocks, and into the holes of the earth, for fear of the LORD, and for the glory of his majesty, when he ariseth to shake terribly the earth" (Isa. 2:19).

It is clear that men flee from God's wrath *after* the sixth seal is opened. If God's wrath begins with the first seal, as pretribulationism normally asserts, why do men not flee from God's wrath until after the sixth seal is opened—a considerable period of time after the wrath begins?

The solution sometimes suggested is that God's wrath started years earlier but that men did not recognize it as God's wrath until after the sixth seal is opened. Such a strained, unsubstantiated view is not to be taken seriously by those who love and honor God's Word. Even a cursory look at the Day of the Lord texts indicates that when God's Day of the Lord wrath begins, the world will know it. There will be no question about it. His wrath will be awesome in its intensity. This planet will be shaken to its very foundations.

After the opening of the sixth seal there is cosmic disturbance, and then men flee to the mountains to attempt to escape from God's wrath. That is precisely what the Old Testament writers said would occur immediately prior to the Day of the Lord.

> Sealing has two basic concepts associated with it. In the Roman world, things were sealed to indicate ownership and to guarantee protection.

Fourth, in the phrase, "the great day of his wrath is come; and who shall be able to stand?," John is undeniably alluding to Malachi 3:2. The prophet Malachi wrote, "But who may abide the day of his coming? And who shall stand when he appeareth?" In Revelation 6:17 what John calls the "great day of his wrath," Malachi calls the "day of his coming" and "when he appeareth." Therefore, the expressions *the day of the Lord, coming,* and *appearance* are tied together and used interchangeably in anticipation of the opening of the seventh seal. Since the "coming" is intimately associated with the Day of the Lord, it is impossible to have the Day of the Lord commence within the seventieth week and the Lord's coming for the church be pretribulational.

Fifth, following the announcement that "the great day of his wrath is come" the question is asked, "and who shall be able to stand?" (Rev. 6:17). Immediately thereafter John wrote of four angels who are about to begin divine judgment on the earth: "And after these things I saw four angels standing on the four corners of the earth, holding the four winds of the earth, that the wind should not blow on the earth, nor on the sea, nor on any tree" (Rev. 7:1). Before they can begin their judgmental work, however, John said,

> And I saw another angel ascending from the east, having the seal of the living God; and he cried with a loud voice to the four

> angels, to whom it was given to hurt the earth and the sea, Saying, Hurt not the earth, neither the sea, nor the trees, till we have sealed the servants of our God in their foreheads." (Rev. 7:2–3)

Sealing has two basic concepts associated with it. In the Roman world, things were sealed to indicate ownership and to guarantee protection. Commenting on the *sealing* of believers in Ephesians 1:13, Ryrie wrote, "A seal indicates possession and security."[5] Here in Revelation 7 the 144,000 are sealed in their foreheads as an indication that they belong to God (possession) and will experience His security (protection). Their sealing will be for the purpose of exempting them from God's wrath, which had just been announced and then delayed until they were sealed. Since their sealing occurs after the opening of the sixth seal, they could not possibly have been protected from God's wrath if it had begun earlier. Contextually, therefore, once again God's wrath cannot be understood to include the first six seals.

Sixth, John notes that with the opening of the seventh seal there is silence in heaven: "And when he had opened the seventh seal, there was silence in heaven about the space of half an hour" (Rev. 8:1). That silence is immediately and directly associated with seven angels who were entrusted with the seven trumpet judgments (Rev. 8:2).[6] Why this silence in heaven immediately prior to the trumpet judgments? Simply stated, because there is a command for silence associated with the outpouring of God's wrath during the Day of the Lord. In this regard, the prophet Zephaniah wrote, "Hold thy peace at the presence of the Lord GOD; for the day of the LORD is at hand; for the LORD hath prepared a sacrifice, he hath bid his guests" (Zeph. 1:7). The world is called upon to be silent with the awareness that the Day of the Lord has arrived—that divine judgment is about to fall.

Seventh, the wrath of God is a major topic in the book of Revelation. No less than eight times the word *wrath* is used. The first occasions are in Revelation 6:16–17 in anticipation of the opening of the seventh seal. It is significant to note that not once is the word *wrath* used before Revelation 6:16–17 or in describing the six seals. Only with the opening of the seventh seal and beyond is the word *wrath* mentioned in the book of Revelation. It can rightly be insisted, therefore, that the use of the word *wrath* is restricted to the events of the trumpets and bowls and, therefore, exempts the first six seals. And since the seals constitute more than half of the seventieth week (the fifth seal begins the Great Tribulation), the divine wrath is restricted to the latter part of the seventieth week, specifically the Day of the Lord period. The wrath passages now follow in chronological sequence.

> And said to the mountains and rocks, Fall on us, and hide us from the face of him that sitteth on the throne, and from the *wrath* of the Lamb. For the great day of his *wrath* is come, and who shall be able to stand? (Rev. 6:16–17)
>
> And nations were angry, and thy *wrath* is come, and the time of the dead, that they should be judged, and that thou shouldest give reward unto thy servants, the prophets, and to the saints, and them that fear thy name, small and great, and shouldest destroy them who destroy the earth. (Rev. 11:18)
>
> The same shall drink of the wine of the *wrath* of God, which is poured out without mixture into the cup of his indignation; and he shall be tormented with fire and brimstone in the presence of the holy angels, and in the presence of the Lamb. (Rev. 14:10)
>
> And I saw another sign in heaven, great and marvelous, seven angels having the seven last plagues; for in them is filled up the *wrath* of God. (Rev. 15:1)
>
> And one of the four living creatures gave unto the seven angels seven golden bowls full of the *wrath* of God, who liveth forever and ever. (Rev. 15:7)
>
> And I heard a great voice out of the temple saying to the seven angels, Go your ways, and pour out the bowls of the *wrath* of God upon the earth. (Rev. 16:1)
>
> And the great city was divided into three parts, and the cities of the nations fell; and great Babylon came in remembrance before God, to give unto her the cup of the wine of the fierceness of his *wrath*. (Rev. 16:19)

The use of the word *wrath* in Revelation does not occur until the Day of the Lord wrath begins (Rev. 6:17), not with the beginning of the seventieth week. The reason is clear: God's wrath does not start until the opening of the seventh seal.

Eighth, the concept of cosmic disturbance followed immediately by the *wrath* of God is exactly what Christ was referring to in His Olivet Discourse.

> And there shall be signs in the sun, and in the moon, and in the stars; and upon the earth distress of nations, with perplexity; the

> sea and the waves roaring; men's hearts failing them for fear, and for looking after those things which are coming on the earth; for the powers of heaven shall be shaken. (Luke 21:25–26)

The expectation of *wrath* in verse 26 anticipates what is to follow, not an event which had occurred earlier.

Ninth, when the seventh seal is opened, God's wrath will begin. Each and every one of the trumpet and bowl judgments that follow will be executed through God's angelic servants. In marked contrast, none of the seals are angelically induced. The reason is clear: the seals are not God's wrath.

Two further matters are germane to a consideration of the starting point of the Day of the Lord.

First, in Matthew 24:5–7 the Lord described the first three and one-half years of the seventieth week. That description parallels the four horses and riders of the Apocalypse (Rev. 6:1–8). He characterized that period of time with these words: "All these are the beginning of sorrows" (Matt. 24:8). Literally, the Greek text says, "All these are the beginning of birth pangs." The Lord's description of the first half of the seventieth week, then, is of a woman in the early stages of labor ("the beginning of birth pangs"). In marked contrast, when Paul describes the period immediately prior to the Day of the Lord, he uses the imagery of a woman, not in beginning birth pangs, but in hard labor, about to deliver (Paul's contrast is between "sudden destruction" and "travail upon a woman with child"). The apostle wrote, "For yourselves know perfectly that the day of the Lord so cometh as a thief in the night. For when they shall say, Peace and safety, then sudden destruction cometh upon them, as travail upon a woman with child, and they shall not escape" (1 Thess. 5:2–3). And the prophet Isaiah wrote, "Wail; for the day of the LORD is at hand; it shall come as a destruction from the Almighty. . . . And they shall be afraid. Pangs and sorrows shall take hold of them; they shall be in pain like a woman that travaileth" (Isa. 13:6, 8).

What becomes abundantly clear is this: The time immediately prior to the Day of the Lord is likened to a woman in travail (hard labor), but the first part of the seventieth week is likened to a woman with beginning birth pangs. If the seventieth week of Daniel begins with the Day of the Lord, the indisputable fact is that the hard labor must precede the beginning birth pangs.

That's impossible! And so, too, is the proposition that the Day of the Lord starts with the seventieth week.

Second, Paul not only likened the period before the Day of the Lord to a woman in hard labor, he also characterized that time as a period when men would be deluded by the expectation of peace and safety. He wrote, "For when they shall say, Peace and safety, then sudden destruction cometh upon them [the Day of the Lord], as travail upon a woman with child, and they shall not escape" (1 Thess. 5:3).

When does this call for peace and safety occur? If the peace and safety is placed inside the seventieth week, the Day of the Lord cannot begin at the beginning of the seventieth week. That statement is based on the fact that, according to Paul, the Day of the Lord follows the cry of peace and safety. If the call of peace and safety is placed before the seventieth week, then a prophesied event must precede the seventieth week, and the pretribulational pillar of imminence once again crumbles. Is there a solution—a proper time placement for the call of peace and safety? There certainly is. And once more, it fits perfectly and unstrained with a prewrath rapture of the church.

At the middle of the seventieth week the Antichrist will make his capital the city of Jerusalem (Dan. 11:42–45). He will seek to become a world ruler, ruthlessly destroying men and nations as he moves to consolidate his power. His greatest fury will be unleashed against the Jewish nation. For that reason, this period of time is called "the time of Jacob's trouble." It will be a time of such severity that except those days were shortened, no flesh (in context, Jewish) would live. But for the elect's sake, those days will be shortened. At that moment cosmic disturbance will signal the approach of the Day of the Lord. Jews being persecuted by the Antichrist will view this as divine intervention on their behalf in the nick of time. They will proclaim "peace and safety," but their cry will be premature—an expression of short-lived duration: "For when they shall say, Peace and safety, then sudden destruction cometh upon them" (1 Thess. 5:3). That destruction will be the Day of the Lord wrath unleashed with the opening of the seventh seal. What miscalculation! In that day the Jewish people will think that the Day of the Lord will bring deliverance and national atonement. They will not heed their prophet's warning:

> Woe unto you that desire the day of the LORD! To what end is it for you? The day of the LORD is darkness, and not light, As a man did flee from a lion, and a bear met him; or went into the house, and leaned his hand on the wall, and a serpent bit him. Shall not the day of the LORD be darkness, and not light? Even very dark, and no brightness in it?

Israel's expectation of peace and safety (deliverance) will not occur during the Day of the Lord. That day will be a period for chastening and purifying. Her national Day of Atonement will await Christ's physical return to the earth.

Unlike those who will not escape the Day of the Lord wrath, Paul says to believers, "But ye [in contrast to those who say 'Peace and safety'], brethren, are not in darkness, that that day should overtake you as a thief. Ye are all sons of light, and sons of the day; we are not of the night, nor of darkness" (1 Thess. 5:4–5). But (and this is so important) if the Rapture is pretribulational and signless, *that day* would, in fact, overtake believers as a thief in the night. Once again, in a context of cosmic disturbance and men's hearts failing them, the Lord promises His children both a sign (Luke 21:25), so they would not be caught off guard, and deliverance from His wrath (v. 28).

To recapitulate the major points of this chapter:

1. In Revelation 6 the first six seals are opened in chronological sequence. After each seal is opened, certain events occur. After the sixth seal is opened, John states that "the great day of his wrath is come." There is no justification for making God's wrath retroactive and thus to include the first six seals.
2. The verb in the statement "the great day of his wrath is come" is in the aorist tense. The use of the aorist tense gives no hint of when the action occurs. But since it occurs following the opening of the sixth seal, it is normal to understand that that is when the action occurs.
3. Men are said to flee to the dens and caves of the mountains to escape the wrath of the Lamb. This follows the opening of the sixth seal. The prophet Isaiah said men would flee to the caves of the mountains immediately before the Day of the Lord.
4. In Luke 21:26, Christ foretells in the Olivet Discourse that

men will faint in fear over the expectation of what follows the cosmic disturbance of the sixth seal.

5. The 144,000 Jews, 12,000 from each of the 12 tribes of Israel, are sealed to be protected from God's wrath. This sealing follows the opening of the sixth seal. They could not be sealed from God's wrath if it began with the first seal.

6. The Bible says there is silence in heaven at the start of the Day of the Lord (Zeph. 1:7). Silence is said to occur with the opening of the seventh seal (Rev. 8:1).

7. The word *wrath* occurs eight times in the book of Revelation. All eight occurrences follow the opening of the sixth seal. The word *wrath* is never used in connection with the first five seals.

8. Angels initiate all of the trumpet and bowl judgments of God; however, they play no part in the seals because the seals do not encompass God's wrath.

David Cooper's classic "Golden Rule of Interpretation" is appropriate to heed.

> When the plain sense of Scripture makes common sense, seek no other sense; therefore, take every word at its primary, ordinary, usual, literal meaning unless the facts of the immediate context, studied in the light of related passages and axiomatic and fundamental truths, indicate clearly otherwise.[7]

Pre-, mid-, and posttribulation scholars are correct in this regard. The starting point of the Day of the Lord is a watershed issue in the Rapture debate, for the Rapture of the church is an integral part (in fact, the immediately preceding event) of the Day of the Lord. That day starts with the opening of the seventh seal (not with the beginning of the seventieth week of Daniel), as the chart below indicates.

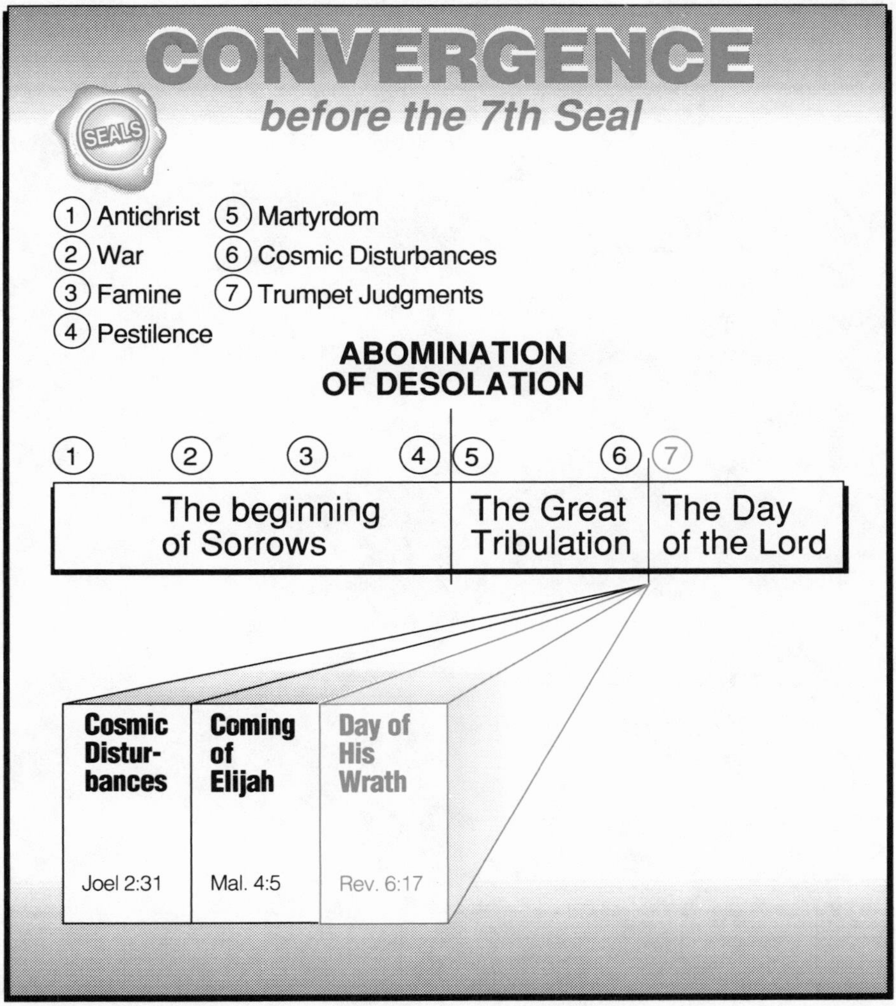

# CONVERGENCE
## before the 7th Seal

SEALS

(1) Antichrist
(2) War
(3) Famine
(4) Pestilence
(5) Martyrdom
(6) Cosmic Disturbances
(7) Trumpet Judgments

**ABOMINATION OF DESOLATION**

(1) (2) (3) (4) (5) (6) (7)

| The beginning of Sorrows | The Great Tribulation | The Day of the Lord |
|---|---|---|

| Cosmic Distur-bances | Coming of Elijah | Day of His Wrath |
|---|---|---|
| Joel 2:31 | Mal. 4:5 | Rev. 6:17 |

# 13

# The 144,000 and a Great Multitude No Man Could Number

The sixth chapter of Revelation describes the seventieth week of Daniel from its inception until the Day of the Lord is about to begin. It chronicles the "beginning" birth pangs (the first three and one-half years) through the opening of the first four seals (Rev. 6:1–8). With the opening of the fifth seal, the Great Tribulation commences (Rev. 6:9–11). It is initiated in the middle of the seventieth week by what the Lord called "the abomination of desolation" (Matt. 24:15). It is in connection with that event that the faithful martyrs who were slain because they would not bow to the Antichrist are heard proclaiming, "How long, O Lord, holy and true, dost thou not judge and avenge our blood on them that dwell on the earth?" (Rev. 6:10). At the opening of the sixth seal, the cosmic disturbance, prelude to the Day of the Lord, occurs (Rev. 6:12–14). When that happens, men of every station of life will scurry to the caves and mountains to hide from the wrath of the Lamb (Rev. 6:15–16). The reason for their consternation is then given: "For the great day of his wrath is come [it will begin with the opening of the seventh seal out of which the seven trumpets emerge], and who shall be able to stand?" (Rev. 6:17).

In Revelation 8 that seventh seal is opened: "And when he had opened the seventh seal, there was silence in heaven about the space of half an hour. And I saw the seven angels who stood before God, and to them were given seven trumpets" (Rev. 8:1–2). The reason for the "silence" in heaven at the opening of the seventh seal is most solemn. It signals the start of the Day of the Lord's wrath on the earth. It will be so awesome that heaven can only observe in silence. Again, hear the prophet Zephaniah speak to this point:

> Hold thy peace at the presence of the Lord GOD; for the day of the LORD is at hand; for the LORD hath prepared a sacrifice, he hath bidden his guests. . . . The great day of the LORD is near, it is near, and hasteneth greatly, even the voice of the day of the LORD; the mighty man shall cry there bitterly. That day is a day of wrath, a day of trouble and distress, a day of waste and desolation, a day of darkness and gloominess, a day of clouds and thick darkness. (Zeph. 1:7, 14–15)

The prophet speaks of silence because the Day of the Lord is at hand and because He has prepared a sacrifice. Concerning what that sacrifice is, men are not left in doubt. The Word of God is precise. It is God's judgment of the nations. In a clear Day of the Lord text, the prophet Isaiah wrote,

> Come near, ye nations, to hear; and hearken, ye peoples: let the earth hear, and all that is therein; the world, and all things that come forth from it. For the indignation of the LORD is upon all nations, and his fury upon all their armies; he hath utterly destroyed them, he hath delivered them to the slaughter [for sacrifice]. . . . The sword of the LORD is filled with blood; it is made fat with fatness, and with the blood of lambs and goats, with the fat of the kidneys of rams; for the LORD hath a sacrifice in Bozrah, and a great slaughter in the land of Edom . . . For it is the day of the LORD's vengeance, and the year of recompenses for the controversy of Zion. (Isa. 34:1–2, 6, 8; cf. Rom. 2:3–10)

Here then are two irrefutable parameters. In Revelation 6, with the opening of the sixth seal and the attendant cosmic disturbance, God's wrath "is come"—it is about to occur. In Revelation 8, with the opening of the seventh seal, the trumpet judgments of God's wrath are beginning to be poured out. Between the warning that God's wrath is about to be poured out in chapter 6 and the actual pouring out of that wrath in chapter 8 lies Revelation 7.

In that chapter, two events of paramount importance occur. The first is the sealing of 144,000 Jews, 12,000 from each of the 12 tribes of Israel (Rev. 7:1–8). The second is the appearing in heaven of a great multitude which no man could number (Rev. 7:9–17). Who are these two distinct groups? What do they represent? And why do they appear at this precise time?

The message is clear, urgent, precise, and given as a command: *Do not begin pouring out God's wrath until the remnant of 144,000 Jews are first sealed for protection from that wrath.*

Following the opening of the six seals and the impending outpouring of divine wrath, the scene dramatically changes. What the apostle John beholds is important for an understanding of prophetic events and the timing of the Rapture. He sees four angels standing on the four corners of the earth empowered to hold back the wind on the earth, "that the wind should not blow on the earth, nor on the sea, nor on any tree" (Rev. 7:1). Angels are God's servants. Since it is God's wrath which is about to be poured out, angels will be employed (2 Thess. 1:7–8). Again, the first five seals represent the ultimate rebellion of man under the Antichrist, who is empowered by Satan. Thus, no angelic beings were involved. Now John beholds another angel ascending from the East. He probably is to be identified as the archangel Michael, who has a specific guardian relationship to Israel (Dan. 12:1), and the 144,000 are Jews: "And he cried with a loud voice to the four angels, to whom it was given to hurt the earth and the sea, saying, Hurt not the earth, neither the sea, nor the trees, till we have sealed the servants of our God in their foreheads" (Rev. 7:2–3).

The message is clear, urgent, precise, and given as a command: *Do not begin pouring out God's wrath until the remnant of 144,000 Jews are first sealed for protection from that wrath*. It cannot be demonstrated that this is a parenthesis looking back to an earlier event for it is not the seals which hurt the earth, sea, and trees, but the trumpet judgments which follow (Rev. 8:7–11). Later, in chapter 14, this group of 144,000 are said to have the "Father's name written in their foreheads" (Rev. 14:1). They are sealed to indicate ownership and protection. This is in contrast to those who receive the mark of the beast "in their right hand, or in their foreheads" (Rev. 13:16), an indication of ownership and protection by one (the Antichrist) who himself will one day be defeated. The 144,000 are said to have been "redeemed from the earth" (Rev. 14:3). They are "not defiled with women; for they are virgins" (Rev. 14:4). This reference to their being virgins may mean that they never married or perhaps that they purposely remained celibate in their separation unto God (2 Cor. 11:2). Perhaps, however, it reflects the fact that they did not submit to the spiritual seduction of the Antichrist and his enticements (Rev. 13:15; cf. Isa. 57:3, 4, 8). The kingdom over which he ruled is referred to as,

> the great harlot that sitteth upon many waters; With whom the kings of the earth have committed fornication, and the inhabitants of the earth have been made drunk with the wine of her fornication. . . . And the woman was arrayed in purple and scarlet color, and bedecked with gold and precious stones and pearls, having a golden cup in her hand, full of abominations and filthiness of her fornication; And upon her forehead was a name written, MYSTERY, BABYLON THE GREAT, THE MOTHER OF HARLOTS AND ABOMINATIONS OF THE EARTH. (Rev. 17:1–2, 4–5)

The 144,000 are also said to be "the firstfruits unto God and to the Lamb" (Rev. 14:4). They are the forerunner of a host of Jewish people who will survive the Day of the Lord and come to the Savior at the end of the seventieth week. Nowhere in the Bible are they called evangelists, as has been popularly proclaimed. And whether they are regenerated (saved) at the time of their sealing (Rev. 7:4) or sealed for physical protection and later regenerated (Rev. 14:4) is a matter of speculation. What is abundantly clear and was obviously important to the angel is the fact that 144,000 Jews must be sealed before the Day of the Lord wrath begins. Details may be debated; but that central fact cannot be.

A second significant event is now brought into clear focus. John wrote, "After this I beheld, and, lo, a great multitude, which no man could number, of all nations, and kindreds, and peoples, and tongues, stood before the throne, and before the Lamb, clothed with white robes, and palms in their hands" (Rev. 7:9). The identification of this great multitude in heaven is of importance.

One well-known expositor reflects the traditional view of pretribulationism with these words: "Chapter 7 does not advance the narrative but directs attention to two major groups of saints in the tribulation. The opening portion of the chapter pictures the 144,000 representative of the godly remnant of Israel on earth in the great tribulation. The latter part of the chapter describes a great multitude of martyred dead in heaven, those who died as a testimony to their faith from every kindred, tongue and nation."[1] This commentator, along with many others, is anxious to get this great multitude "dead"—through martyrdom. However, nowhere in the considerable description of this group (Rev. 7:9–17) is it ever said they are martyred. In the previous chapter, a group of martyrs is seen. Their martyrdom occurred with the opening of the fifth seal, at the beginning of the Great Tribulation: "And when he had opened the fifth seal, I saw under the altar the souls of them that were slain for the word of God, and for the testimony which they held" (Rev. 6:9). They are heard to be crying out to God that their blood be avenged on "them that dwell on the earth" (Rev. 6:10). They are given white robes and told to "rest yet for a little season, until their fellow servants also and their brethren, that should be killed as they were, should be fulfilled" (Rev. 6:11). These martyrs are to be resurrected and given bodies on the first day of the Millennium (Rev. 20:4).

This great multitude in chapter 7 is clearly a different group from those described in chapter 6. The contrasting and additional truth is significant.

First, they are so numerous that John is told no man could number them. This is in marked and direct contrast to the immediately previous group who are said to number 144,000; therefore, this has to be a tremendously large number. Further, this great multitude of chapter 7 is international in scope, representing all nations, kindreds, peoples, and tongues (v. 9). Those mentioned after the fifth seal are clearly said to be martyrs. This new group is seen after the opening of the sixth seal, of necessity only a short time later. If they are also martyrs, then one must postulate that a universal multitude, of such great magnitude that they could not be numbered, were saved, became witnesses (for that is what a martyr is), were slain, and are now seen before the throne of God—all of this in a very brief time span (probably a matter of months and during the sixth seal when men are fleeing to the caves and dens to escape the impending wrath of God). Even if credulity were stretched to allow for such a thing to occur, there is never a hint in the Bible of that kind of evangelistic success during the Great Tribulation. According to pretribulation rapturism, the church is gone, the 144,000 have just been sealed, there is no indicator that the two witnesses have met with success (Rev. 11:3–10), and the gospel angel has not yet been sent forth (Rev. 14:6). If these are martyrs, how does such a multitude (from every kindred, tongue, and tribe) get saved so quickly, particularly during a time pretribulationists say God is dealing primarily with Israel?

Second, the martyrs in Revelation 6 are souls under the altar asking God to avenge their blood (Rev. 6:9–10). The great multitude in Revelation 7, in contrast, are before the throne proclaiming with a loud voice, "Salvation to our God who sitteth upon the throne, and unto the Lamb" (Rev. 7:10).

Third, in Revelation 6 the multitude is said to be souls "under the altar" (Rev. 6:9). In Revelation 7 the multitude is said to be standing "before the throne, and before the Lamb, clothed with white robes,, and palms in their hands" (Rev. 7:9). The former group are *souls*—the latter group have *bodies*.

Fourth, in Revelation 6 John immediately recognizes the martyrs as those who "were slain for the word of God, and for the testimony which they held" (v. 9). In Revelation 7 it is clear that John does not recognize who this great multitude is. To the question directly proposed to John, "Who are these . . . ?" (v. 13), he gives this response: "Sir, thou knowest" (v. 14), a clear admission that he did not recognize them.

If this great multitude—which suddenly appears in heaven, which no man can number, and which has universal representation—are not martyrs, who are they?

This great multitude, innumerable, universal, and suddenly

appearing in heaven with white robes (purified) and palm branches (triumphant), is the raptured church. This event occurs immediately prior to the opening of the seventh seal and the outpouring of the Day of the Lord wrath (Rev. 8:1): "For God hath not appointed us to wrath, but to obtain salvation [this is precisely what the multitude was proclaiming] by our Lord Jesus Christ" (1 Thess. 5:9).

John is asked two questions about that great multitude by one of the elders: (1) "Who are these who are arrayed in white robes?" and (2) "From where did they come?" (Rev. 7:13). John does not have an answer. The small struggling church of his day had now become an innumerable host—the triumphant body of Christ. And so, the elder gives the answer to John. Regarding who they are, he is told they are those who "have washed their robes, and made them white in the blood of the Lamb." In answer to the question, "from where [whence] did they come?" he is told, "These are they who came out of the great tribulation" (Rev. 7:14).

John wrote: "And all the angels stood round about the throne, and about the elders and the four living creatures, and fell before the throne on their faces, and worshiped God" (Rev. 7:11). A host of different groups are present to greet this great multitude. This host does not include the church, which is conspicuous by its absence. It is reasonable to expect that the church would have been present if it already had been raptured pretribulationally.

This great multitude represents the true church which goes into the seventieth week of Daniel. They are raptured at the end of the Great Tribulation but before the Day of the Lord begins. They are raptured before God's wrath is poured out but are not exempt from the ultimate rebellion of unregenerate men.[2]

The symmetry, balance, and timing of Revelation 7 should not be missed. With chapter 8, the Day of the Lord will begin. Therefore, in chapter 7 the church is raptured. But immediately prior to the Rapture of the church, the 144,000 Jews are sealed. It is almost like a baton being passed between runners. The 144,000 must be sealed for protection to go through the Day of the Lord before the church can be caught up to the throne in heaven. God will not leave Himself without a people on the earth.

The following chart illustrates the context of this chapter.

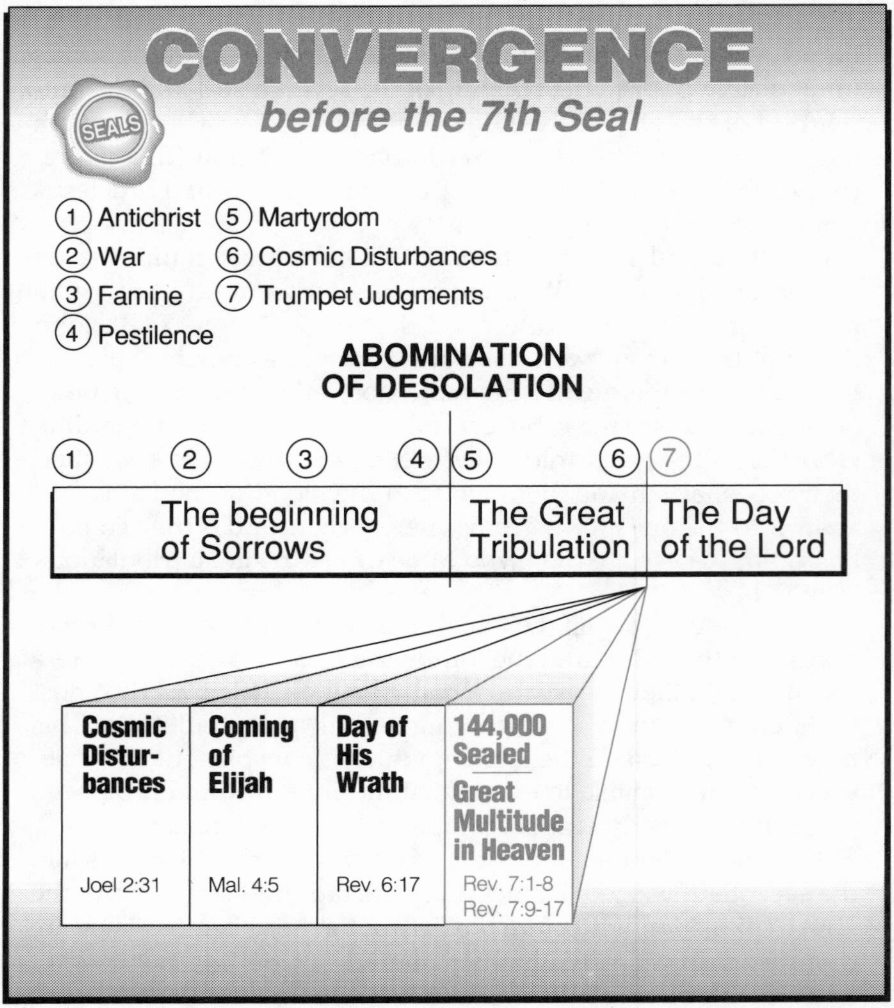

# CONVERGENCE
## before the 7th Seal

SEALS

(1) Antichrist
(2) War
(3) Famine
(4) Pestilence
(5) Martyrdom
(6) Cosmic Disturbances
(7) Trumpet Judgments

ABOMINATION
OF DESOLATION

(1) (2) (3) (4) (5) (6) (7)

| The beginning of Sorrows | The Great Tribulation | The Day of the Lord |
|---|---|---|

| Cosmic Distur- bances | Coming of Elijah | Day of His Wrath | 144,000 Sealed / Great Multitude in Heaven |
|---|---|---|---|
| Joel 2:31 | Mal. 4:5 | Rev. 6:17 | Rev. 7:1-8<br>Rev. 7:9-17 |

# 14

# The Last Trump

Perhaps the clearest text in all the Word of God for determining the timing of the Rapture is found in 1 Corinthians 15. The entire chapter is given over to a consideration of the doctrine of bodily resurrection. In this chapter, Paul first reminded the Corinthians that physical resurrection is an integral part of the gospel and that he had taught them the truth of resurrection on an earlier occasion (1 Cor. 15:1–11).

Second, he dealt with the irrefutable logic that if there is no such thing as general resurrection of the dead, then Christ is not raised; and if Christ is not raised, life itself is futile and hopeless (1 Cor. 15:12–19).

Third, Paul asserted that Christ was resurrected from the grave, and His resurrection is the absolute guarantee that all men will one day be raised from the dead—some to everlasting life and some to everlasting death (1 Cor. 15:55; John 5:25–29). The twin enemies of death and the grave will be defeated at His coming (1 Cor. 15:20–34).

Fourth, Paul gave the most thorough discussion found anywhere in the Bible on the nature of the resurrection body (1 Cor. 15:15–50). The physical body "is sown in dishonor; it is raised in glory. It is sown in weakness; it is raised in power" (1 Cor. 15:43).

Fifth, Paul explained that one generation will receive that glorified, immortal, resurrection body without going through the process of dying (1 Cor. 15:51–58). He wrote to the Corinthians, "Behold, I show you a mystery: We shall not all sleep, but we shall all be changed, in a moment, in the twinkling of an eye, at the last trump; for the trumpet shall sound, and the dead shall be raised incorruptible, and we shall be changed" (1 Cor. 15:51–52).

In Pauline theology, the concept of a biblical *mystery* is very significant. His use of the term *mystery* should not be confused with the contemporary use of the word. Today it is in vogue to speak of a mystery as a who-dun-it. A book or film where the guilty party is not revealed until the end is called a "mystery thriller." A person confronted with a problem he is having difficulty resolving will, with perplexity, declare, "It's a mystery to me."

Biblically, a mystery has three identifiable components. First, a biblical mystery is something that was always part of the divine plan; that is, it is not an afterthought. God does not merely respond to unanticipated circumstances. Second, a biblical mystery is something that God sovereignly chose not to reveal in the Old Testament but which He would reveal later. This is not unlike parents who plan from their children's birth to reveal certain truths to their offspring, but do so at appropriate times in their development. God planned to reveal certain things to mankind but chose not to reveal them during their early developmental (Old Testament) stage. Third, a biblical mystery is a truth that is known only by divine revelation (Eph. 3:5).

Among the significant biblical mysteries are "the mysteries of the kingdom" (Matt. 13:11), the mystery concerning the "blindness" of Israel (Rom. 11:25), the mystery "concerning Christ and the church" (Eph. 5:32), "the mystery of iniquity" (2 Thess. 2:7), and "the mystery of godliness" (1 Tim. 3:16). The three component parts of a biblical mystery are clearly visible in Paul's teaching concerning the "mystery" of the church; that is, that in this age the Jew and Gentile became part of the same body in Christ. To the Ephesians he wrote,

> How that by revelation he made known unto me the mystery (as I wrote before in few words, By which, when ye read, ye may understand my knowledge in the mystery of Christ) Which in other ages was not made known unto the sons of men, as it is now revealed unto his holy apostles and prophets by the Spirit: That the Gentiles should be fellow heirs, and of the same body, and partakers of his promise in Christ by the gospel. (Eph. 3:3–6)

Paul was making three points: (1) the church was always part of God's plan; (2) that truth had not been revealed in past ages; and (3) it was made known to the apostle Paul by direct divine revelation.

The purpose of a biblical mystery has at its core the unveiling of truth never before revealed (see Matt. 13:11; Rom. 11:25; 16:25; 1 Cor. 2:7; 15:51; Eph. 3:3–5; 5:32; 6:19; Col. 1:26–27; 2:2; 4:3; 2 Thess. 2:7; 1 Tim. 3:16; Rev. 1:20; 17:5, 7). To the Corthinians Paul made known a mystery never before revealed: One generation would receive glorified, immortal bodies, not as a result of passing through the valley of death but through the *snatching up* (Rapture) to meet the Lord in the air. The apostle Paul wrote, "We shall not all sleep [die], but we shall all be changed" (1 Cor. 15:51). But Paul has one more important word concerning that mystery. It was not simply that one generation would escape death by rapture. He revealed *when* that rapture would occur, *when* that one privileged generation of believers will receive glorified bodies without dying. Paul declared that it will occur "at the last trump" (1 Cor. 15:52). Those four words, "at the last trump," reveal in the clearest possible way the precise occasion when the Rapture of the church will occur. Men can deny, reject, or ignore that truth; but they cannot change it. The Rapture will occur at the last trump of God. But what is the last trump? And when does it occur?

Traditional posttribulation rapturists consider the seventh trumpet of Revelation 11:15–19 to be "the last trump" and understand it to occur at the end of the seventieth week of Daniel. In their view, since the Rapture must occur, according to Paul, at the last trump, and the last trump occurs at the end of the tribulation period, the Rapture must, of necessity, be posttribulational; that is, at the end of the seventieth week. Therefore, the church must go through the Day of the Lord judgment.

Midtribulation rapturists also appeal to the *time* of the last trump for support of their position. Like posttribulationists, they also believe that the last trump is to be identified as the seventh trumpet. However, unlike posttribulationists, men like J. Oliver Buswell place the blowing of the seventh trumpet at the precise middle of the seventieth week. They therefore conclude, based on their understanding of Paul's writing to the Corinthians (1 Cor. 15:51–52), that the Rapture will occur midtribulationally.

Pretribulation rapturists do not make strong appeal to Paul's statement that the Rapture will occur before the last trump to support their position. Generally speaking, if they mention 1 Corinthians 15 in a Rapture discussion, it is brief and without determinitive significance. The reason is obvious: If the Rapture occurs before the last trump, pretribulation rapturism has no way, exegetically, to associate a pre-seventieth week Rapture with the last trump of God.

But back to an earlier statement. A biblical mystery is the revealing of something that was previously unknown. The mystery which Paul revealed in 1 Corinthians 15 was that one generation would receive glorified bodies without dying (through rapture), and that this event would occur at the last trump of God. Since a biblical mystery was understood by early Christians to be the revealing of a truth that was hitherto unknown, it must be insisted that the Corinthians understood what Paul was teaching.

A biblical mystery is the revealing of something that was previously unknown. The mystery which Paul revealed in 1 Corinthians 15 was that one generation would receive glorified bodies without dying (through rapture).

At this point another major obstacle develops for both post- and midtribulation rapturists. First Corinthians was one of Paul's earlier epistles. It was written in approximately A.D. 55 or 56. By contrast, the apostle John penned the book of Revelation, the last-written document of the New Testament, sometime after A.D. 85. Those dates are not significantly disputed by conservative, Bible-believing scholars. That means that Paul's epistle to the Corinthians was written at least twenty-nine years before the book of Revelation was written. Paul, in unveiling a mystery, was revealing truth to the Corinthians that they could comprehend. Since that truth revolved around the fact that one generation would receive glorified bodies through rapture at the last trump, the Corinthians had to understand the significance of the phrase *at the last trump* without any knowledge of the book of Revelation, which had not yet been written. This clearly means that, in the first instance, the significance of the phrase *at the last trump* must have been understood apart from the book of Revelation if the Corinthians were able to comprehend Paul's teaching. That conclusion cannot be escaped.

The church at Corinth was founded on Paul's second missionary journey. As was his custom, he began his ministry in Corinth in the synagogue where he "reasoned . . . every sabbath, and persuaded the Jews and the Greeks" (Acts 18:4). When he was opposed by many of the Jews, he moved his ministry immediately adjacent to the synagogue (Acts 18:7). His stay in Corinth was lengthy, perhaps as long as eighteen months. Because the church in Corinth was composed of Jews and Gentiles, and because Paul spent a considerable period of time there, it is more than reasonable to assume that his teaching was extensive and included a great deal of truth from the Old Testament Scriptures.

The trumpet played a significant part in the religious ritual of Judaism. Its use began during the wilderness wanderings in the time of Moses and continues until the present hour. When Israeli forces captured Jerusalem in June of 1967, after almost nineteen hundred years of absence from the Promised Land, the first thing the chief rabbi did was blow a ram's horn (trumpet). Symbolically, the rabbi was calling disbursed world Jewry back to Jerusalem.

The trumpet is employed in the observance of Jewish holy days and new months (Num. 10:10). But preeminently, the trumpet was blown by the Jews to call a solemn assembly or to announce a call to war. God commanded Moses,

> Make thee two trumpets of silver; of a whole piece shalt thou make them [on the Arch of Titus in Rome, which celebrated the defeat of Israel and destruction of the Temple, they are pictured as long, straight tubes, flared at the end], that thou mayest use them for the calling of the assembly, and for the journeying of the camps. And when they shall blow with them, all the assembly shall assemble themselves to thee at the door of the tabernacle of the congregation. (Num. 10:2–3)

The Tabernacle was the dwelling place of God. To assemble at the Tabernacle, therefore, was to assemble in God's presence. In a similar way, the trumpet will be blown to call the church of God at the Rapture. Hear Paul's comments to the Thessalonians:

> For the Lord himself shall descend from heaven with a shout, with the voice of the archangel, and with the trump of God; and the dead in Christ shall rise first; then we who are alive and remain shall be caught up together with them in the clouds, to meet the Lord in the air; and so shall we ever be with the Lord. (1 Thess. 4:16–17)

Again to the Corinthians Paul wrote, "Behold, I show you a mystery: We shall not all sleep, but we shall all be changed, in a moment, in the twinkling of an eye, at the last trump; for the trumpet shall sound, and the dead shall be raised incorruptible, and we shall be changed" (1 Cor. 15:51–52).

As noted above, the second major purpose of the trumpet was to call the Israelites to war: "And if ye go to war in your land against the enemy that oppresseth you, then ye shall blow an alarm with the trumpets; and ye shall be remembered before the Lord your God, and ye shall be saved from your enemies" (Num. 10:9).

Joshua was commanded by God to have the priest blow the trumpet in connection with the conquest of Jericho (Josh. 6:4–6, 8–9, 13–16, 20). The judge Ehud blew a trumpet before leading the children of Israel in an attack against the oppressive Moabites (Jud. 3:27–30). Gideon and his band of three hundred blew a trumpet before defeating the Midianites (Judg. 6:34; 7:8–9, 13–16, 20, 22). While they were rebuilding the walls of Jerusalem and were under danger of attack, Nehemiah instructed the Jews with these words: "And I said unto the nobles, and to the rulers, and to the rest of the people, The work is great and large, and we are separated upon the wall, one far from another. In whatever place ye hear the sound of the trumpet, resort ye there unto us. Our God shall fight for us." (Neh. 4:19–20)

When announcing the Day of the Lord, the outpouring of God's wrath, the prophet Joel wrote, "Blow the trumpet in Zion, and sound an alarm in my holy mountain. Let all the inhabitants of the land tremble; for the day of the Lord cometh, for it is near at hand" (Joel 2:1). Once again the language is precise. The trumpet is to be blown *before* the Day of the Lord judgment.

The prophet Zephaniah wrote,

> The great day of the Lord is near, it is near, and hasteneth greatly, even the voice of the day of the Lord; the mighty man shall cry there bitterly. That day is a day of wrath, a day of trouble and distress, a day of waste and desolation, a day of darkness and gloominess, a day of clouds and thick darkness, a day of the trumpet and alarm against the fortified cities, and against the high towers. (Zeph. 1:14–16)

*The last trump will be nothing more, nothing less, and nothing different than the final, climactic, eschatological outpouring of the wrath of God*. The central theme of the prophet Joel is the Day of the Lord. In the clearest possible terms, he teaches that the Day of the Lord will commence with the blowing of a trumpet. "Blow ye the trumpet in Zion, and sound an alarm in my holy mountain: let all the inhabitants of the land tremble: for the day of the Lord cometh, for it is nigh at hand" (Joel 2:1). The prophets repeatedly called that final judgment the Day of the Lord.

The Corinthians to whom Paul wrote could reasonably be expected to have understood that truth after eighteen months under the ministry of Paul.

The mystery which Paul was revealing was clear. One generation would receive glorified bodies without dying, through rapture. That rapture would occur at the last trump—the final, climactic Day of the Lord wrath. Here is confirmation of the truth that the believer is "not appointed . . . to wrath" (1 Thess. 5:9).

Now, back to the trumpet judgments of the book of Revelation. God's Day of the Lord wrath is to be meted out with the opening of the seventh seal (Rev. 6:17). The seventh seal involves no direct judgment of its own, as do the previous six seals. It does, however, contain the seven trumpet judgments, and the seventh trumpet contains the seven bowls. If one were to outline the seals, trumpets, and bowls of the book of Revelation, the trumpets would be indented under the seventh seal, and the bowls would be indented under the seventh trumpet. The seventh seal alone literally contains the trumpet and bowl judgments.

Therefore, as the seventh seal is opened, the seven trumpet and bowl judgments progressively unfold. They are part of a comprehensive whole. Collectively, they are God's Day of the Lord wrath, His final eschatological judgment—the last trump. Since the last trump arises out of the seventh seal, and the Rapture, according to Paul, occurs at the last trump: "We shall all be changed, in a moment, in the twinkling of an eye, at the last trump" (1 Cor. 15:51–52), the Rapture must occur at the opening of the seventh seal and immediately prior to the beginning of God's wrath. That interpretation is unstrained and biblically accurate. The following chart illustrates it.

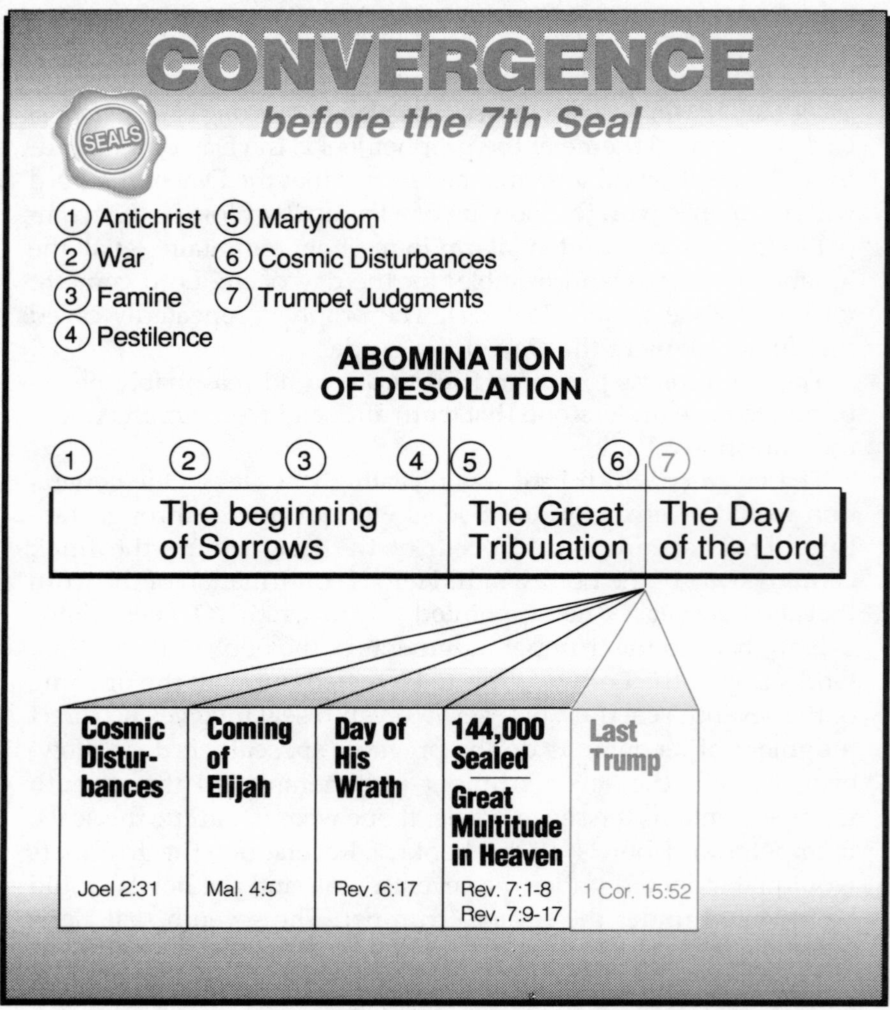

# 15

# The Apostasy and the Man of Sin

Paul's two letters to the church at Thessalonica comprise the fullest treatment on Christ's second coming and the Rapture of the church found anywhere in the Bible. For the Thessalonians, the Rapture was an issue of great importance. But they had a major problem regarding the timing of the Rapture. The issue was already troubling the church and, if left unchecked, would only cause further confusion. In that context, therefore, Paul wrote to the believers at Thessalonica,

> Now we beseech you, brethren, by the coming of our Lord Jesus Christ, and by our gathering together unto him [the Rapture], that ye be not soon shaken in mind, or be troubled, neither by spirit, nor by word, nor by letter as from us, as that the day of the Lord is present. (2 Thess. 2:1–2)

The Thessalonians were greatly disturbed by false teachers who were communicating erroneous doctrine concerning end-time events. This false teaching, according to the apostle, was being propagated in three ways: "by spirit" (prophetic utterance), "by word" (some spoken teaching), and by forged documents attributed to the apostle Paul ("by letter as from us," 2 Thess. 2:2). The core of that false teaching was imbedded in the statement "that the day of the Lord is present."

To correct that error, Paul wrote, "Let no man deceive you by any means; for that day [the Day of the Lord] shall not come, except there come a [literally, the] falling away first [the apostasy], and that man of sin be revealed, the son of perdition" (2 Thess. 2:3). In clear, unmistakable, nondebatable terms, the apostle Paul identified two events which *must* precede the Day of the Lord. First, the great apostasy (the falling away) must occur. And second, the man of sin (the Antichrist) must be revealed. *If, as pretribulation rapturism maintains, the Day of the Lord starts at the beginning of the seventieth week and if, as they normally teach, the Rapture begins the seventieth week, then it must be concluded that these two events (the apostasy and the revealing of the man of sin) occur* before *the Rapture of the church. That reality simply cannot be denied.*

Those difficulties . . . only begin the impossible-to-resolve problems that pretribulation rapturism faces when examined in the light of 2 Thessalonians 2.

Some interpreters, sensing the enormity of the problem, have attempted a solution by again suggesting that perhaps a period of time exists between the Rapture and the starting of the seventieth week—allowing for the apostasy and revealing of the man of sin. However, that suggestion goes against the historic pretribulation view as enunciated by Walvoord: "The pretribulation interpretation regards the coming of the Lord and the translation of the church as preceding immediately the fulfillment of Daniel's prophecy of a final seven-year period before the second advent."[1] Further, the Lord teaches that on the very day that Noah entered the ark, God's judgment fell. In other words, there was deliverance for Noah and his family and judgment on the unregenerate world on the same day. Then the Lord makes this point: "But as the days of Noah were, so shall also the coming of the Son of man be." That is, deliverance of the righteous will be immediately followed by God's Day of the Lord wrath on the wicked. *Biblically, no extended period of time can separate the two events of rapture and wrath.*

One of two things should be conceded: either the doctrine of imminency, which maintains that no prophesied events can precede the Rapture, is invalid; or the proposition that the Day of the Lord starts at the beginning of the seventieth week must be rescinded. There is no legitimate escape from either conclusion.

But those difficulties, as major as they are, only begin the impossible-to-resolve problems that pretribulation rapturism faces when examined in the light of 2 Thessalonians 2. This larger difficulty is related to the following demonstrable facts: (1) The apostasy and revelation of the "man of sin" occur within, not before, the seventieth week of Daniel; (2) the Day of the Lord must, according to Paul, occur after the apostasy and revealing of the man of sin; (3) the Rapture immediately precedes the Day of the Lord; and therefore, (4) the Rapture cannot possibly be pretribulational.

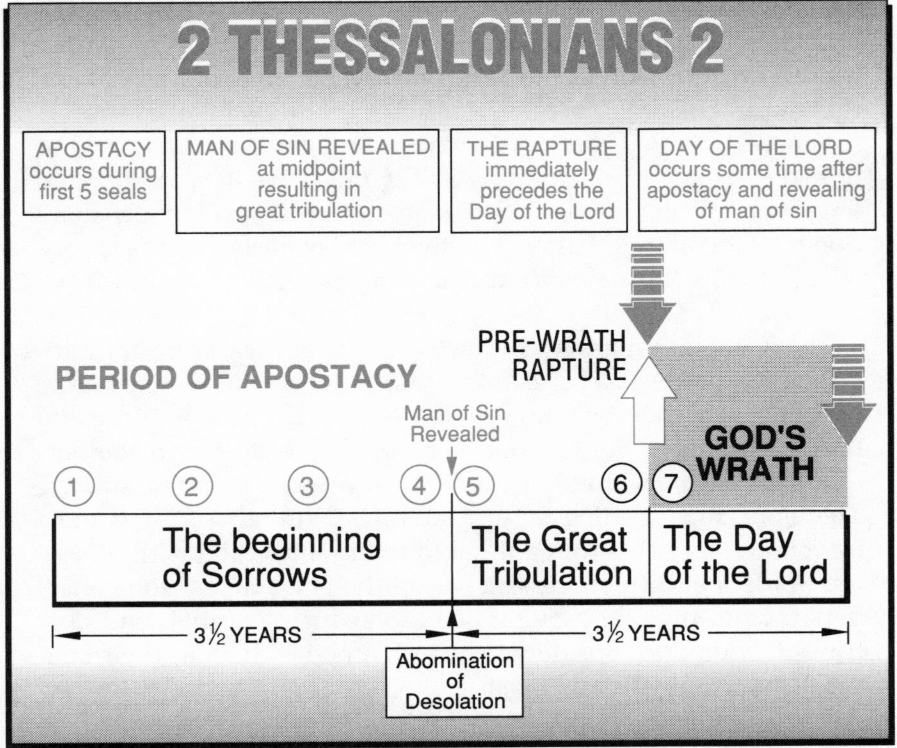


The phrase *falling away* (2 Thess. 2:3) is a translation of the Greek word *apostasia*. It means a *defection, revolt,* or *apostasy*.[2] It signifies a *falling away* or *total abandonment* of something or someone. It is used only twice in the entire Word of God; therefore, how it is used becomes exceedingly important. Dr. Luke used the word *apostasy* in describing an important occasion when the apostle Paul met with the Jewish elders at Jerusalem. Many Jews had accepted Christ, but they continued to adhere to the old covenant and the Mosaic Law (Acts 21:20). They wanted to believe in Jesus, but within Old Testament Judaism. They did not comprehend that Jesus had initiated a new covenant. Speaking of those recent converts, the elders in Jerusalem said to Paul, "And they are informed of thee, that thou teachest all the Jews who are among the Gentiles to forsake [*forsake* is the translation of *apostasia*—to *fall away* or *utterly abandon*] Moses, saying that they ought not to circumcise their children, neither to walk after the customs" (Acts 21:21). Here, then, is one of the only two times the word *apostasy* is used in the Bible. And it is used in the context of the apostle Paul being repudiated for supposedly asking Jews to renounce Moses, circumcision as the basis of convenantal relationship, and the Jewish customs.

When Paul used the word *apostasy* in 2 Thessalonians 2:3, he did so in exactly the same way as Dr. Luke. He was speaking of Jews who, during the seventieth week of Daniel, will totally abandon the God of their fathers and their messianic hope in favor of a false religion (humanism) and a false messiah (the Antichrist, 2 Thess. 2:2–12).

This view is in marked contrast with the general view of pretribulation rapturism. The usual position is that Paul was speaking of believers in this age who will apostatize before the Rapture and the beginning of the seventieth week. Evidence to substantiate that position is lacking but is crucial to pretribulation rapturism. Therefore, in stretching for a proof text, 1 Timothy 4:1–2 is most frequently appealed to. Paul wrote to his son in the faith, "Now the Spirit speaketh expressly that, in the latter times, some shall depart from the faith, giving heed to seducing spirits, and doctrines of demons, Speaking lies in hypocrisy, having their conscience seared with a hot iron."

It must be noted that there are several unsolvable problems associated with that interpretation. First, the word *apostasy,* as it is used in 2 Thessalonians 2, has the definite article; it is speaking of *the* apostasy—a specific, definitive, identifiable event, not some kind of nebulous apostasy at the end of this age. Second, the word *apostasy,* with its very specific and limited meaning, is not used in 1 Timothy 4:1–2 in describing these men. Third, in the context of 1 and 2 Timothy, the troublesome men whom Paul had in view are clearly identified as false teachers. These are men who believed the gospel but then espoused erroneous teaching. They could properly be defined as heretics but never apostates. The terms are not synonymous. Fourth, if a believer in this age can apostatize, by the very definition of the word *apostasy* (a *total abandonment* or *falling away*), the doctrine of the eternal security of the believer in this age must be seriously questioned. And that cannot be allowed to stand.

More importantly, however, there is clear and compelling evidence to identify the apostasy to which Paul referred and precisely when it will occur.

The future ascendancy of the Antichrist is foreshadowed in the Bible by the past emergence of the Syrian leader Antiochus Epiphanes. So important is this personage in history and prophecy that no less than three major passages of the Word of God are given over to his career (Dan. 8:9–25; 11:21–35; Zech. 9:13–17). He is clearly and indisputably set forth in Scripture as an illustration of the Antichrist, and pretribulationists have long taught that concept. The apocryphal book of 1 Maccabees, recognized by conservative scholars as possessing significant historical worth, is primarily given over to a consideration of this man and his insidious career. The first-century historian Josephus is also a major source on the life of this infamous man.

Antiochus sought to defeat surrounding nations through military conquest and then to assimilate them into his kingdom through adoption of the Hellenistic (Greek) culture. He believed that if he could get conquered nations to speak the Greek language, wear Greek clothing, adopt the Greek philosophy of life, and worship the Greek gods, he could quickly and effectively assimilate them into his empire. With that accomplishment, conquered nations would pay tribute to him, serve in his army, be buffers between his empire and enemy nations, and allow his troops to be withdrawn from successfully assimilated nations to fight elsewhere. To achieve that end, in 168 B.C. the troops of Antiochus Epiphanes marched into Israel. On this occasion, history records that they sought to turn the Jewish people from Moses and the Law, from circumcision as an identification of covenant relationship with Jehovah, and from their religious customs (exactly what Paul had been accused of doing [Acts 21:21] and what was described as apostasy). History notes that Antiochus initially met with a great measure of success in Hellenizing the Jewish people. A large segment of the nonreligious Jews entered into a covenant with him and willingly capitulated to his demands. An account of that event, written shortly after it occurred, is recorded in The First Book of the Maccabees.

> In those days [i.e., of Antiochus Epiphanes] lawless men came forth from Israel, and misled many, saying, "Let us go and make a covenant with the Gentiles round about us, for since we separated from them many evils have come upon us." This proposal pleased them, and some of the people eagerly went to the king [Antiochus]. He authorized them to observe the ordinances of the Gentiles. So they built a gymnasium in Jerusalem [for Greek education], according to Gentile custom, and removed the marks of circumcision, and *abandoned* the holy covenant. They joined themselves with the Gentiles and sold themselves to do evil. (1 Macc. 1:11–14)

This falling away or total abandonment of the God of Israel by many of the Jews is specifically called *the apostasy*. First Maccabees continues the account this way: "Then the King's officers who were enforcing the *APOSTASY* came to the city of Modein to make them offer sacrifice" (1 Macc. 2:15). Specifically, this sacrifice was the killing of a pig in the worship of the heathen deity Zeus Olympus. This was an abomination of great magnitude for observant Jews. Under the Mosaic Law, the pig was strictly forbidden (Lev. 11:2, 7; Deut. 13:3, 8). Some of the Jews rebelled against this abomination. Others capitulated to it.

The ancient historian continues the story of Antiochus and the Jews:

> Then the king wrote to his whole kingdom that all should be one people, and that each should give up his customs. All the Gentiles accepted the command of the king. Many even from Israel gladly adopted his religion; they sacrificed to idols and profaned the sabbath. And the king sent letters by messengers to Jerusalem and

> the cities of Judah; he directed them to follow customs strange to the land, to forbid burnt offerings and sacrifices and drink offerings in the sanctuary, to profane sabbaths and feasts, to defile the sanctuary and the priests, to build altars and sacred precincts and shrines for idols, to sacrifice swine and unclean animals, and to leave their sons uncircumcised. They were to make themselves abominable by everything unclean and profane, so that they should forget the law and change all the ordinances. (1 Macc. 1:41–49)

This is a perfect description of apostasy, the total abandonment of Jehovah for a heathen god.

This covenant which many of the Jews entered into with Antiochus Epiphanes prefigures the covenant which many from among Israel will enter into with the Antichrist in a future day. The prophet Daniel spoke of that covenant in this way: "And he shall confirm the covenant with many for one week; and in the midst of the week he shall cause the sacrifice and the oblation to cease" (Dan. 9:27).

This falling away or total abandonment of the God of Israel by many of the Jews is specifically called the apostasy.

The events surrounding Antiochus Epiphanes, his defilement of the temple, and the apostasy of many of the Jewish people is one of the most conspicuous events in Jewish history. It would, therefore, be both appropriate and natural to use the *same term* (apostasy) concerning the *same people* (the Jews) regarding an event to occur at the *same place* (the temple at Jerusalem) in describing a future day when many of the Jews will totally abandon the God of their fathers in the *same way* they did in the days of Antiochus Epiphanes, only to embrace a heathen religion and a false messiah.

The parallels between the historically fulfilled events under Antiochus Epiphanes and the prophetic events awaiting fulfillment under the Antichrist are amazingly similar. There can be no question but that in the Olivet Discourse (Matt. 24–25) the Lord assumed that His hearers were familiar with the events surrounding Antiochus Epiphanes and the Book of the Maccabees. Some of the more conspicuous parallels are these.

1. Both Antiochus and the Antichrist enter into a covenant to protect Israel. Concerning Antiochus it is written, "In those days lawless men came forth from Israel, and misled many, saying, 'Let us go and make a covenant with the Gentiles round about us, for since we separated from them many evils have come upon us.' He [Antiochus] authorized them to observe the ordinances of the Gentiles" (1 Macc. 1:11–12). Of Antichrist it is written, "And he shall confirm the covenant with many for one week" (Dan. (9:27a).

2. Both make their covenants with the *many* within Israel. Although Antiochus Epiphanes and the Antichrist make covenants with Israel, it is of great significance that neither man gets unanimous support. This truth is carefully stressed in both 1 Maccabees and the Bible. The historian wrote, "In those days lawless men came forth from Israel, and misled *many*" (1 Macc. 1:11). And again, "*Many* even from Israel gladly adopted his religion" (1 Macc. 1:43). And once more, "*Many* of the people, every one who forsook the law, joined them, and they did evil in the land" (1 Macc. 1:52). Of the Antichrist it is written, "he shall confirm the covenant with *many*" (Dan. 9:27a). This is the only occasion in the Bible where a covenant is said to be made with *many*.

3. Those Jews who enter into the covenant are, in both instances, said to apostatize. Concerning Antiochus it is written, "Then the king's officers who were enforcing the APOSTASY came to the city of Modein to make them offer sacrifice" (1 Macc. 2:15). Paul wrote of the Antichrist and the future Day of the Lord, "Let no man deceive you by any means; for that day shall not come, except there come the falling away [apostasy] first, and that man of sin [Antichrist] be revealed, the son of perdition" (2 Thess. 2:3).

4. Both Antiochus and the Antichrist break their covenant. "After subduing Egypt, Antiochus returned . . . He went up against Israel and came to Jerusalem with a strong force. He

arrogantly entered the sanctuary and took the golden altar, the lampstand for the light, and all its utensils" (1 Macc. 1:20–21). The Bible describes the same event. Of Antiochus it is written, "And forces shall stand on his part, and they shall pollute the sanctuary of strength, and shall take away the daily sacrifice, and they shall place the abomination that maketh desolate" (Dan. 11:31). Of the Antichrist it is also recorded, "in the midst of the week he shall cause the sacrifice and the oblation to cease" (Dan. 9:27b); that is, he will break the covenant in the midst of the week (cf. Matt. 24:15). Not only do both men, Antiochus and the Antichrist, break their covenants, they break them at the same place—the Temple.

5. Both Antiochus and Antichrist break the covenants by introducing a false god into the temple. Of Antiochus it is said, "He went up against Israel and came to Jerusalem with a strong force. He arrogantly entered the sanctuary [temple]" (1 Macc. 1:20–21). History records that on that occasion he set up an image of his chief deity Zeus Olympus.[3] Significantly, this deity was made in the likeness of a man (humanism). Paul wrote of the Antichrist, "Who opposeth and exalteth himself above all that is called God, or that is worshiped, so that he, as God, sitteth in the temple of God, showing himself that he is God" (2 Thess. 2:4; see also Matt. 24:15; Rev. 13:15).

6. In both instances, some Jews oppose this false religion, and as a result many perish. Of that courageous band it is recorded, "But many in Israel stood firm and were resolved in their hearts not to eat unclean food. They chose to die rather than to be defiled by food or to profane the holy covenant; and they did die" (1 Macc. 1:62–63). Speaking of that future day when the Antichrist will seek to get the Jews to bow to his image and many will refuse, the Lord said, "Then shall they deliver you up to be afflicted, and shall kill you; and ye shall be hated of all nations for my name's sake" (Matt. 24:9).

7. In both instances, religious Jews flee to the mountains (hills) to escape. "Then Mattathias [the righteous priest] cried out in the city with a loud voice, saying: 'Let every one who is zealous for the law and supports the covenant [Mosaic] come

out with me!' And he and his sons fled to the hills and left all that they had in the city. Then many who were seeking righteousness and justice went down to the wilderness to dwell there" (1 Macc. 2:27–29). In the New Testament, in the context of the Tribulation, it is recorded of a righteous remnant, "Then let them who are in Judea flee into the mountains; Let him who is on the housetop not come down to take anything out of his house; Neither let him who is in the field return back to take his clothes. And woe unto those who are with child, and to those who nurse children in those days! But pray that your flight be not in the winter, neither on the sabbath day" (Matt. 24:16–20).

8. In both instances, many of these religious Jews will die because they will not violate the Sabbath. The past historical fact, in the days of Antiochus, graphically and traumatically portrays what will occur in that future day. "Then many who were seeking righteousness and justice went down to the wilderness to dwell there [they were fleeing forced apostasy], they, their sons, their wives, and their cattle, because evils pressed heavily upon them. And it was reported to the king's officers, and to the troops in Jerusalem the city of David, that men who had rejected the king's command had gone down to the hiding places in the wilderness. Many pursued them, and overtook them; they encamped opposite them and prepared for battle against them on the sabbath day. And they said to them, 'Enough of this! Come out and do what the king commands, and you will live.' But they said, 'We will not come out, nor will we do what the king commands and so profane the sabbath day.' Then the enemy hastened to attack them. But they did not answer them or hurl a stone at them or block up their hiding places, for they said, 'Let us all die in our innocence; heaven and earth testify for us that you are killing us unjustly'" (1 Macc. 2:29–37).

The Lord commanded concerning that future day, "But pray that your flight be not . . . on the sabbath day" (Matt. 24:20). Commitment to the Sabbath by religious Jews exceeds fanaticism. To push an elevator button is to break the Sabbath. To drive a car is to break the Sabbath. To enter a restaurant or check into a hotel is to break the Sabbath. The Israeli airline cannot land or take off between Friday sunset and Saturday sunset; to do so is to break the Sabbath. A Sabbath day's journey, according to the rabbis, is two thousand cubits (a little more than half a mile). With the Sabbath fully reinstituted in Israel, religious Jews could neither flee nor fight on the Sabbath. In that light, the Lord's admonition, "But pray that your flight be not . . . on the sabbath day" (Matt. 24:20), takes on added significance, particularly since the Lord's warning relates to getting as far away from Jerusalem as possible, as quickly as possible.

9. In both instances, many women and children will perish. In an attempt to stamp out Judaism and the worship of Jehovah, Antiochus commanded that circumcision (an evidence of covenantal relationship) be abolished. Those who did not comply would die. Of that event the historian wrote, "According to the decree, they put to death the women who had their children circumcised, and their families and those who circumcised them; and they hung the infants from their mothers' necks" (1 Macc. 1:60–61).

Is it any wonder, therefore, that the Lord spoke of that coming time in these terms: "And woe unto those who are with child, and to those who nurse children in those days!" (Matt. 24:19)? Those Jewish women who will not renounce the God of their fathers, as evidenced by the circumcision of their sons, will, with them, be slain. This is reminiscent of Pharaoh's decree to slay all the male children (Exod. 1:15–16); Herod's command to slay all the male children two years of age and under (Matt. 2:16); and, in more recent days, Adolf Hitler's indescribable, systematic murdering of two million Jewish children.

The career of the coming Antichrist and the plight of the Jews are clearly and with divine intention kaleidoscoped in the account of Antiochus Epiphanes and his barbaric treatment of the descendants of Jacob.

In that future day, the apostasizing Jews will believe that the covenant they are making will bring them protection from the surrounding nations. That is precisely what such Jews thought when they made a covenant with Antiochus Epiphanes. In reality, it will be a covenant with death. It will be Israel's great apostasy. Not only will it not bring them the safety and peace they seek; it will, in fact, bring the nation to the very threshold of extinction. The Lord said, "And except those days should be shortened, there should no flesh be saved" (Matt. 24:22). This text is not speaking of universal annihilation. In Matthew 24:15–26 the topic is the abomination of desolation; the location is Israel; the participants are primarily Jews; the occasion is "the time of Jacob's [Israel's] trouble" (Jer. 30:7). It is the Jews in Israel who would perish if the Great Tribulation were not cut short.[4]

The prophet Isaiah, with sarcasm, wrote of that future covenant that Israel will make in this way: "Because ye have said, We have made a covenant with death, and with sheol are we at agreement, when the overflowing scourge shall pass through, it shall not come unto us; for we have made lies our refuge, and under falsehood have we hid ourselves" (Isa. 28:15).

Once again the prophet spoke of that coming apostasy, "And your covenant with death shall be annulled, and your agreement with sheol shall not stand; when the overflowing scourge shall pass through, then ye shall be trampled down by it" (Isa. 28:18).[5] The "overflowing scourge" to which both of these verses ultimately refer and which they will not escape is the Great Tribulation, "the time of Jacob's trouble." This covenant of apostasy into which Israel will enter is spoken of in the imagery of spiritual infidelity and unfaithfulness. How could it be thought otherwise when, in their ultimate day of unfaithfulness, having rejected their true Messiah, they embrace the false messiah?

> Behind the doors also and the doorposts hast thou set up thy remembrance; for thou hast uncovered thyself to another than me, and art gone up; thou hast enlarged thy bed, and made thee a covenant with them; thou lovedst their bed where thou sawest it. And thou wentest to the king with ointment, and didst increase thy perfumes, and didst send thy messengers far off, and didst debase thyself even unto sheol. (Isa. 57:8–9)

All three texts (Isa. 28:15, 18; 57:8–9), in speaking of the covenant Israel will make with the Antichrist (Dan. 9:24–27), refer to it as a covenant with death.

The apostasy, then, to which Paul referred (2 Thess. 2:3–4), will involve Israel, not the church. It will commence when *many* within the nation sign a covenant with the Antichrist (unknown to them, a covenant with death) at the beginning of that seventieth week. The apostasy will encompass a total *abandonment* or *falling away* from renewed covenant relationship (the seventieth week) and from the God of their forefathers and the promised Messiah. They will embrace a counterfeit religion (humanism) and a counterfeit Messiah (the Antichrist) who offers a counterfeit peace and solution to the Middle East dilemma.

In the middle of that seventieth week of Jewish apostasy, the Antichrist will break the covenant with Israel. Having entered the Middle East on the pretext of protecting Israel from her enemies, he will defeat Egypt, Syria, and other nations. Then he will "plant the tabernacles of his palace between the seas [the Mediterranean and Dead Seas] in the glorious holy mountain [Mount Zion]" (Dan. 11:42–45). Only then, in the middle of the seventieth week, with the setting up of his image in the temple, will the Jews realize his true character and real identity and that they have made a covenant with death.

Some commentators, focusing on Paul's statement to the Thessalonians "and that man of sin be revealed, the son of perdition" (2 Thess. 2:3), have placed that event at the signing of the covenant (Dan. 9:24–27) and, therefore, at the beginning of the seventieth week. In doing so they have missed the whole point of Paul's argument. Two facts are of utmost importance: (1) the apostasy must come first (that apostasy can only be understood as the total abandoning by "many" of the Jewish people of their covenantal relationship with the Lord during the first half of the seventieth week); (2) in the middle of the seventieth week the man of sin will be revealed. Paul makes that clear in a most conspicuous way. After stating that the man of sin must be revealed, he does not relate that revelation to the time of the signing of the covenant but to the occasion of the setting up of Antichrist's image. The apostle described the revealing of the wicked one this way: "Who opposeth and exalteth himself above all that is called God, or that is worshiped, so that he, as God, sitteth in the temple of God, showing himself that he is God" (2 Thess. 2:4).

This event, which occurs in the middle of the seventieth week, cannot be divorced from the time the Antichrist is revealed. Paul was not talking about the time when the Antichrist appears on the scene; clearly that was three and one-half years earlier, when the covenant was made. That is not the issue. Paul was speaking of the time when the Antichrist will be *recognized* by the Jews for who he truly is. That recognition will occur when his image is erected in the temple in the middle of the seventieth week (Dan.

9:27; cf. Matt. 24:15). It is then, and only then, that Israel will know she has made a covenant with death. The shock will be indescribable. It will be the worst of nightmares— only it will be real. It will be the worst of horror stories— only it will have substance. No wonder it is called the Great Tribulation (Matt. 24:21) or "the time of Jacob's [Israel's] trouble" (Jer. 30:7).

Paul was speaking of the time when the Antichrist will be *recognized* by the Jews for who he truly is. That recognition will occur when his image is erected in the temple in the middle of the seventieth week.

To understand why Israel will not know who the Antichrist truly is until his image is erected, the following salient facts must be understood.

According to the Word of God, the Antichrist is a man who lived before. He ruled one of the previous seven great empires which directly impacted Israel. The first six were (1) Egypt, (2) Assyria, (3) Babylon, (4) Medo-Persia, (5) Greece, and (6) Rome (Rev. 17:10). The clear identification of the seventh nation awaits further enlightenment. Not only has the Antichrist lived and ruled before, but he will live and rule again. He will literally be raised from the dead. Concerning this raised ruler and his kingdom, the Word of God has much to say. "And I saw one of his heads as though it were wounded to death; and his deadly wound was healed, and all the world wondered after the beast" (Rev. 13:3; cf. 17:9). So astonishing is this fact that more details are provided:

> And I beheld another beast [a false prophet] coming up out of the earth; and he had two horns like a lamb, and he spoke like a dragon [with craft and cruelty]. And he exerciseth all the power of the first beast [the Antichrist] before him, and causeth the earth and them who dwell on it to worship the first beast, whose deadly wound was healed. And he doeth great wonders, so that he maketh fire come down from heaven on the earth in the sight of men [to counterfeit the prophet Elijah, who, according to the Word of

God, is to announce the coming of the true Messiah (Mal. 4:5–6), and who also called down fire from Heaven (see 1 Kings 18:24, 36–38)], And deceiveth them that dwell on the earth by the means of those miracles which he had power to do in the sight of the beast, saying to them that dwell on the earth, that they should make an image to the beast, that had the wound by a sword [military defeat], and did live [again, a reference to his death and restoration to life]. (Rev. 13:11–14)

John has still more to say concerning this coming Antichrist: "And the beast that was, and is not, even he is the eighth, and is of the seven [that is, comes out of the seven], and goeth into perdition" (Rev. 17:11). Once again, the strong implication of the text is that the Antichrist once lived and ruled over a nation, then died, and will be raised to rule over the eighth empire. This should not be surprising. Since the Antichrist will be a counterfeit Christ, he will also perform a counterfeit resurrection. He will be raised, but he will die again and go "into perdition." Jesus was not simply raised; He was resurrected, never to die again.

Concerning the Antichrist, William Newell insightfully observed,

> Thus will lie in the deluded world's inner consciousness "the likeness of an image" of *man*, a wonderful man, who has returned in a manner beyond their knowledge from the unseen realm of the dead . . . One who has been slain with the death-stroke of a sword is "healed"; a killed body stands up! One who has been in the "abyss" he possesses this slain body . . . It might be such a man as Napoleon, for the Fourth Empire is still on until the stone strikes it; but it is more probably one who will rule after the more formal restoration of the Roman Empire. Mussolini, with his ambitions for the restoration of old Rome, his Caesar-ideals, his inflexible will, his undiminishing energy, is a portent of what one of these emperors will be; and also proof how quickly such an one may rise into power! Of course, Mussolini does not begin to fill, the vast picture of the Beast of Revelation 13.[6]

Charles Ryrie, commenting on the Antichrist, wrote,

> One of the heads of the beast was "wounded to death." Literally it reads, "as having been slain to death." This is exactly the same word that was used in 5:6 of the Lamb where it was translated "as it had been slain." If Christ died actually, then it appears that this

> ruler will also actually die. But his wound will be healed, which can only mean restoration to life. In 11:7 he was seen as coming out of the abyss, and that coincides with his restoration to life here. He apparently actually dies, descends to the abyss and returns to life. The world understandably wonders after him.[7]

This worst of all men, the Antichrist, will be directly energized by Satan. Therefore, in bowing to the Antichrist, men will be worshiping Satan. John wrote, "And they worshiped the dragon who gave power unto the beast" (Rev. 13:4a).

The Antichrist will make the covenant with Israel. His former identity (under which he ruled one of the previous seven-beast empires) will become clear to Israel and the world in the middle of the seventieth week when he evidently will be raised from a fatal wound and when the statue of his image is unveiled in the temple. That is precisely the point of Paul's teaching in 2 Thessalonians 2.

The apostasy will occur during the first three and one-half years of Daniel's seventieth week, and then, in the middle of the week, the Antichrist will be revealed to the Jewish people. That event will trigger a period of such severity that unless those days were cut short, no flesh (again in context, Jewish) would live.[8]

The issue at hand, and which to this author is undeniably clear, is that the apostasy and revealing of the man of sin to Israel must occur *inside* the seventieth week, not before it begins. That a remnant of godly believers will recognize the Antichrist when the covenant is made is certainly true and consistent with the teaching of the Lord (Matt. 24:33; cp. vv. 4–28) and the apostle Paul (1 Thess. 5:4–6). But what Paul is teaching is that Israel, the nation with whom the covenant is made, will not recognize the Antichrist until the abomination of desolation occurs in the middle of the week. According to the apostle Paul, the Day of the Lord judgment must take place after those events. Therefore, the Day of the Lord cannot commence at the beginning of the seventieth week, and the Rapture, which occurs at the very outset of the Day of the Lord, cannot possibly be pretribulational.

Pretribulation rapturism is once again mortally wounded, this time by an unstrained, dispensational, premillennial, and literal interpretation of Paul's teaching in 2 Thessalonians 2.

The following chart depicts the two precursors to the Day of the Lord and related truths presented in this chapter.

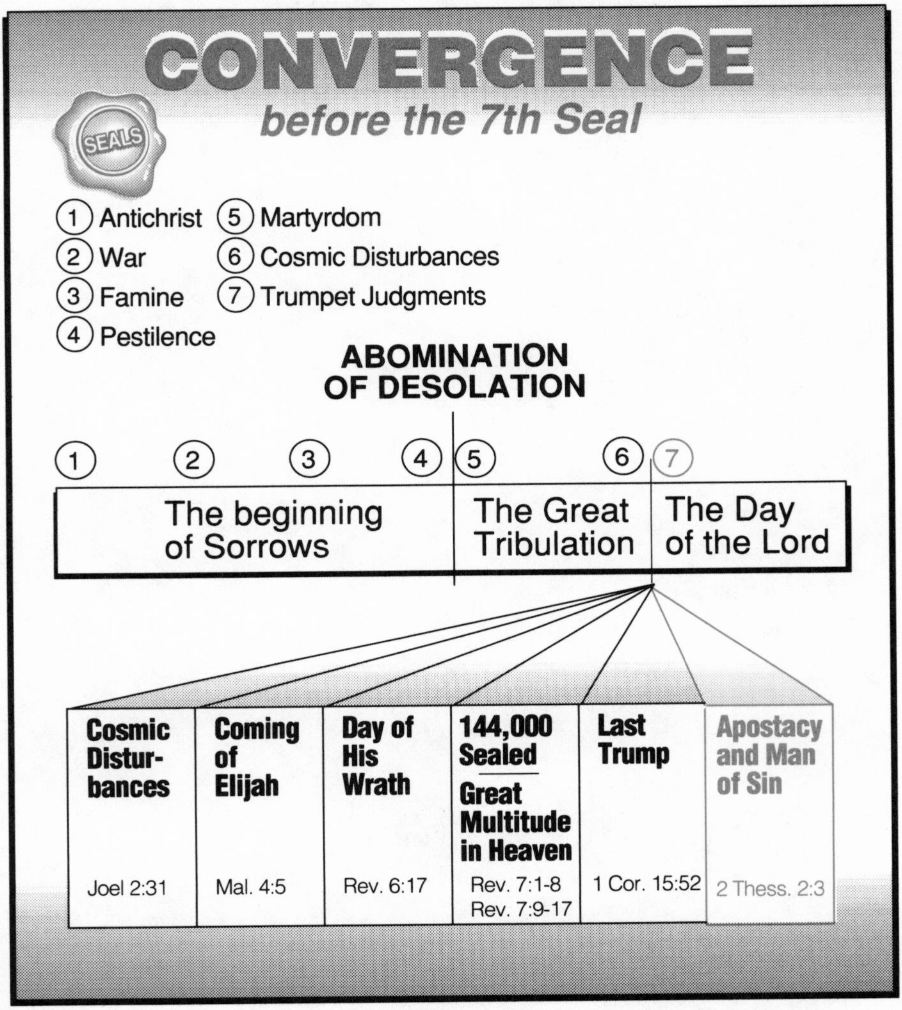

## CONVERGENCE

### before the 7th Seal

SEALS

(1) Antichrist
(2) War
(3) Famine
(4) Pestilence
(5) Martyrdom
(6) Cosmic Disturbances
(7) Trumpet Judgments

ABOMINATION OF DESOLATION

(1) (2) (3) (4) (5) (6) (7)

| The beginning of Sorrows | The Great Tribulation | The Day of the Lord |
|---|---|---|

| Cosmic Distur-bances | Coming of Elijah | Day of His Wrath | 144,000 Sealed / Great Multitude in Heaven | Last Trump | Apostacy and Man of Sin |
|---|---|---|---|---|---|
| Joel 2:31 | Mal. 4:5 | Rev. 6:17 | Rev. 7:1-8<br>Rev. 7:9-17 | 1 Cor. 15:52 | 2 Thess. 2:3 |

# PART III

## THE PREWRATH RAPTURE

# 16

# The Coming and the End

In this chapter two terms will be defined, and their relationship to the timing of the Rapture will be examined. Both terms are crucial, and both are found in a question which the disciples asked of the Lord. They were on the Mount of Olives. The mood was tense. Major conflict between the Jewish leadership and Jesus had reached its apex. Now Jesus was leaving. His nation would not see Him again until they were ready to say, "Blessed is he that cometh in the name of the Lord" (Matt. 23:39b). The disciples were dismayed and stunned. "And as he sat upon the Mount of Olives, the disciples came unto him privately, saying, Tell us, when shall these things be? And what shall be the sign of thy coming, and of the end of the age?" (Matt. 24:3).

The first word to be considered is *coming*. It is the translation of the Greek word *parousia* and is pronounced *pa-ROO-zee-a*. That examination will not be tedious. It is important. That will become clear.

The word *parousia* (coming) occurs twenty-four times in the New Testament. It is used in nine books: Matthew, 1 and 2 Corinthians, Philippians, 1 and 2 Thessalonians, James, 2 Peter, and 1 John; and by five authors: Matthew, Paul, James, Peter, and John. Additionally, Matthew attributes its use to the disciples (Matt. 24:3) and to the Lord Himself (Matt. 24:27, 37).

Three other words are also employed to speak of the return of Christ. One of them is the Greek word *erchomai,* simply translated *coming*. It is used, for instance, in these words of the Lord: "Verily I say unto you, There are some standing here, who shall not taste of death, till they see the Son of man coming [*erchomai*] in his kingdom" (Matt. 16:28).

A second word that enters into the discussion of the Rapture is the word *apokalypsis,* usually translated *coming* or *revelation*. Its basic meaning is "to disclose or bring to light." In the Word of God there is a disclosure bringing light of the Lord Jesus by men who were under the controlling influence of the Holy Spirit. At His coming *(apokalypsis),* He will reveal Himself, or bring Himself to light. The apostle Paul wrote to the Corinthians, "So that ye come behind in no gift, waiting for the coming [*apokalypsis*], or self-disclosure, of our Lord Jesus Christ" (1 Cor. 1:7).

The final word is *epiphaneia,* most often translated *appearing*. Concerning Christ's *epiphaneia* (appearing), Lawrence Richards has written in his *Expository Dictionary of Bible Words:* "As a religious term, it indicates a visible manifestation of a hidden deity, either in person or by some great act through which his presence is revealed. Jesus will come in a starburst of power, burning his image on the retinas of faithless, blinded humanity."[1] Writing to young Timothy, Paul said, "I charge thee, therefore, before God, and the Lord Jesus Christ, who shall judge the living and the dead at his appearing [*epiphaneia*] and his kingdom" (2 Tim. 4:1).

On the basis of these different words employed in connection with Christ's return and the different emphases which they make, some have attempted to prove two separate comings. One coming, it is suggested, is for the purpose of rapturing the church, and the other refers to His return in glory. Paul Feinberg writes, "Both pretribulationists and midtribulationists have pointed out differences between the Rapture and the Second Coming. The central passages dealing with each event reveal these differences."[2] Feinberg's logic, and that of those who follow in his train, is unproven. The Greek words *erchomai* (coming), *apokalypsis* (coming or revelation), and *epiphaneia* (appearing) are not describing two comings, first to rapture the church and then to return in glory seven years later. They are words employed to describe different aspects of Christ's singular coming.

The word *parousia* (coming) is much broader in significance than the other words employed in Second Coming texts, and that significance must be clearly understood. *Parousia* (coming) is derived from two Greek words, *para* meaning *with* and *ousia* meaning *being*. *Parousia,* then, denotes two things: an arrival and a consequent presence with. The Greek scholar W. E. Vine illustrates this by referring to a papyrus letter in which a lady speaks of the necessity of her *parousia* in a place in order to attend to matters relating to her property (a coming and continued presence in order to accomplish certain matters).[3] On at least two occasions, the apostle Paul uses the word *parousia* in the sense of his presence. Quoting what others had said about him, he wrote, "For his letters, say they, are weighty and powerful, but his bodily presence [*parousia*] is weak, and his speech contemptible" (2 Cor. 10:10). And again, "Wherefore, my beloved, as ye have always obeyed, not as in my presence [*parousia*] only but now much more in my absence, work out your own salvation with fear and trembling" (Phil. 2:12). In this verse his *parousia* (presence) is contrasted to his absence.

And of the Antichrist Paul wrote, "whose coming [*parousia*] is after the working of Satan with all power and signs and lying wonders" (2 Thess. 2:9). The coming *(parousia)* of the Antichrist includes his continuing presence to perform his satanic work of false signs and lying wonders. The coming *(parousia)* of Christ will include His continuing presence to rapture the church and His Day of the Lord judgment of the wicked. The other words employed to describe His coming or revelation focus on one aspect of His coming, whereas *parousia* is speaking of the totality of that glorious *series* of events. Christ's coming *(parousia)* will be seen in the heavens (that is, His glory—not His bodily form), and there will be a continuous presence for the purpose of rapturing the Church and judging the wicked. When men today speak of Christ's first coming, it is not restricted to His birth alone. Rather, it includes the annunciation to Mary, the incarnation, Jesus' reasoning at the temple at age twelve, His growth before men and God, His public ministry, His crucifixion, resurrection, and ascension. All of this comprises His first com-

*Parousia* is speaking of the totality of that glorious *series* of events.

ing. In a similar way, His second coming will include the Rapture of the church, the Day of the Lord judgment, and His return in glory. Summing up the significance of the words used to describe Christ's return, the *Expository Dictionary of Bible Words* states, "The second coming of Jesus is a rich and complex NT theme. Like Jesus' first coming, it does not take place as a single act but stretches over a span of time as God's many purposes are worked out at time's end."[4]

From an examination of the verses in which the word *parousia* occurs, the following observations can be made.

First, in the *King James Version* of the Bible, the word *parousia* is translated *coming* twenty-two times, and two times it is translated *presence* (2 Cor. 10:10; Phil. 2:12).

Second, of the twenty-four times *parousia* is used in the New Testament, eighteen of those times it is used prophetically. Seventeen times it is used of the coming of the Lord Jesus and once of the coming of the Antichrist (2 Thess. 2:9).

Third, the Rapture of the church is one of a number of matters directly associated with His coming. Paul wrote these words to the Thessalonians: "To the end he may establish your hearts unblamable in holiness before God, even our Father, at the coming [*parousia*] of our Lord Jesus Christ with all his saints" (1 Thess. 3:13). "Saints" in this verse is an unfortunate and inappropriate translation. "Saints" in this verse does not refer to believers. The Greek word *hagios* should be translated *holy ones* and is a reference to angelic beings. These angelic beings will accompany Christ at His coming *(parousia)* [cf. Matt. 25:31; 2 Thess. 1:7–8; Rev. 19:14]. In no sense, then, can 1 Thessalonians 3:13 be used to support the teaching that the Lord comes *for* the church at the beginning of the seventieth week and then *with* the church at its end, as some contend.

Concerning the intimate association between Christ's coming *(parousia)* and the Rapture, hear Paul once again: "For this we say unto you by the word of the Lord, that we who are alive and remain unto the coming [*parousia*] of the Lord shall not precede [go before] them who are asleep" (1 Thess. 4:15). The *parousia* (coming) and Rapture are intimately associated. Listen to Paul one final time in this regard: "And the very God of peace sanctify you wholly; and I pray God your whole spirit and soul and body be preserved blameless unto the coming [*parousia*] of our Lord Jesus Christ" (1 Thess. 5:23). Paul's audience was comprised of believers, and they will be united with Christ at His *parousia* (coming). Of necessity, therefore, the coming and the Rapture are, once again, intimately associated.

This fact destroys the attempt by some to start the Day of the Lord in the middle of the seventieth week or later but have a pretribulation rapture at least three and one-half years earlier. The Rapture and Day of the Lord are both intimately related to His coming *(parousia)*. Paul makes this association in his second letter to the Thessalonians, "Now we beseech you, brethren, by the coming of our Lord Jesus Christ, and by our gathering together unto him, That ye be not soon shaken in mind, or be troubled, neither by spirit, nor by word, nor by letter as from us, as that the day of the Lord is present" (2 Thess 2:1–2).

Fourth, the coming of Christ will initiate the Rapture and then be immediately followed by the Day of the Lord judgment. To the Corinthians Paul wrote, "But every man in his own order: Christ the first fruits; afterward they that are Christ's at his coming [*parousia*]" (1 Cor. 15:23). The chronology following Christ's coming is then presented by the apostle: "Then cometh the end, when he shall have delivered up the kingdom to God, even the Father, when he shall have put down all rule and all authority and power" (1 Cor. 15:24). The end to which Paul referred is the final Day of the Lord judgement. The church will be raptured, and then the end—God's wrath—will fall upon an unrepentant world.

In the context of a discussion of His coming, the Lord taught, "But as the days of Noah were, so shall also the coming [*parousia*] of the Son of man be" (Matt. 24:37). And then the Lord described what the days of Noah were like: "For as in the days that were before the flood they were eating and drinking, marrying and giving in marriage, until the day that Noah entered into the ark" (Matt. 24:38). That the days before the flood were wicked is beyond debate (Gen. 6:5–7). But that is not the Lord's point. What the Lord was teaching is that men will be going about their normal activities (eating, drinking, marrying, and giving in marriage—the most basic things of life) with no sense of impending judgment, with no awareness that deity is about to visit humanity in judgment. According to the Lord, they "knew not until the flood came [but then it was too late], and took them all away [they were slain], so shall also the coming [*parousia*] of the Son of man be" (Matt. 24:39). As the flood began on the same day as

Noah entered the ark, so the Lord taught that the Rapture would occur on the same day as the Day of the Lord begins (Luke 17:26–27, 30).

At Christ's coming there will be those inside the ark, as it were through faith in Christ, and those outside the ark, because of having rejected Christ. The Lord illustrated that truth: "Then shall two be in the field; the one shall be taken [in rapture], and the other left [for judgment]. Two women shall be grinding at the mill; the one shall be taken [in rapture], and the other left [for judgment]" (Matt. 24:40–41).[5] This coming inside of the seventieth week has always been a text that has troubled pretribulation rapturism. And many expositors who have attempted to teach Matthew 24 *know* that to be true.

The coming *(parousia)* initiates two things: first, the rapture of the righteous; and second, the end—the Day of the Lord judgment of the wicked.

Fifth, no one will know the day or the hour of Christ's coming *(parousia)*. The Lord taught, "But of that day and hour knoweth no man, no, not the angels of heaven, but my Father only" (Matt. 24:36). The emphasis is on knowing *the day or hour* of Christ's return. That specific detail is unknown.

Sixth, in contrast, spiritually discerning believers will know the approximate time of His coming *(parousia)*. Hear the words of the Savior: "Now learn a parable of the fig tree: When its branch is yet tender, and putteth forth leaves, ye know that summer is near; So likewise, ye, when ye shall see all these things, know that it [in context, "it" refers to His coming] is near, even at the doors" (Matt. 24:32–33). The Lord's teaching is unmistakably clear. The fig tree was a time indicator. When its branches became soft and it put forth leaves, the Jewish people knew that summer was near (getting close), but they did not know the exact time. The fig tree was a sign of approximation. Likewise, when the events described in Matthew 24:4–28 occur, men will know that Christ's coming *(parousia)* is near. Like the fig tree, those events will be a sign of approximation. Men of faith will know the general period of Christ's coming *(parousia)*, but they will not know the hour or the day; therefore, the admonition to watchfulness (Matt. 24:42). This is parallel to the teaching of both Paul and Peter.

Paul wrote,

> But ye, brethren, are not in darkness, that that day should overtake you as a thief. (1 Thess. 5:4)

And Peter warned,

> Looking for and hasting unto the coming of the day of God, in which the heavens, being on fire, shall be dissolved, and the elements shall melt with fervent heat? (2 Pet. 3:12)

Both, like the Lord, teach watchfulness before the *parousia*. Again, if this were describing a coming at the end of the seventieth week, as pretribulationists are forced to interpret it, men would, in fact, know the exact day. There will be precisely 1,260 days from the time the Antichrist sets up his image at the temple, and seven years from the day Israel signs the covenant with him.

Seventh, there will be a sign to indicate Christ's coming *(parousia)*. The disciples inquired, "What shall be the sign of thy coming [*parousia*]?" (Matt. 24:3b). That sign (singular, not plural) will be the manifestation of the glory of God (cf. Matt. 24:30; 25:31). Again the natural light will be turned off and the supernatural light (God's glory) will be turned on. That glory will dispel the darkness associated with the opening of the sixth seal ("the sun shall be darkened, and the moon shall not give its light, and the stars shall fall from heaven" [Matt. 24:29; cf. Rev. 6:12–14]).

Eighth, in the Olivet Discourse, the coming *(parousia)* of Christ is clearly placed *after* the middle of the seventieth week. That becomes obvious in light of the fact that the coming occurs after the setting up of the image of the Antichrist in the middle of the seventieth week (Matt. 24:15–22; cf. Dan. 9:27) and the attempt by false prophets to get Jews out of the caves to which they have fled following the erection of the image of the Antichrist (Matt. 24:23–26). The Lord described His coming following those events this way: "For as the lightning cometh out of the east, and shineth even unto the west, so shall also the coming [*parousia*] of the Son of man be" (Matt. 24:27). His coming will be sudden, unannounced, and unexpected (like lightning) by the unsaved world—exactly like the flood in the days of Noah. They "knew not until the flood came" (Matt. 24:39)—but then it was too late.

From these observations some clear conclusions can be drawn.

In the first place, *the Lord's coming* (parousia) *is a comprehensive whole*. There is only *one* Second Coming. It includes the Rapture of the church, the outpouring of God's wrath during the Day of the Lord, and Christ's physical return in glory. The meaning of the word *coming (parousia)* demonstrates that fact. It means a coming and continuing presence. That would be contradicted by the concept of a coming at the beginning of the seventieth week and another at its end, as pretribulationism has often taught.

The Lord's coming is consistently portrayed as a singular event. The Bible is repetitively consistent on that fact: "And what shall be the sign of thy *coming?"* (Matt. 24:3); "so shall also the *coming* of the Son of man be" (Matt. 24:27, 37, 39); "afterward they that are Christ's at his *coming*" (1 Cor. 15:23); "in the presence of our Lord Jesus Christ at his *coming*" (1 Thess. 2:19); "at the *coming* of our Lord Jesus Christ" (1 Thess. 3:13); "we who are alive and remain unto the *coming* of the Lord" (1 Thess. 4:15); "and I pray God your whole spirit and soul and body be preserved blameless unto the *coming* of our Lord Jesus Christ" (1 Thess. 5:23); "Now we beseech you, brethren, by the *coming* of our Lord Jesus Christ" (1 Thess. 2:1); "whom the Lord shall consume with the spirit of his mouth, and shall destroy with the brightness of his *coming*" (2 Thess. 2:8); "Be patient therefore, brethren, unto the *coming* of the Lord" (James 5:7); "the *coming* of the Lord draweth near" (James 5:8); "when we made known unto you the power and *coming* of our Lord Jesus Christ" (2 Pet. 1:16); "Where is the promise of his *coming?"* (2 Pet. 3:4); "Looking for and hasting unto the *coming* of the day of God" (2 Pet. 3:12); "we may have confidence and not be ashamed before him at his *coming*" (1 John 2:28).

The Lord's coming is consistently portrayed as a singular event. The Bible is repetitively consistent on that fact: "And what shall be the sign of thy *coming . . . ?*"

In each and every instance, the word *coming (parousia)* is either modified by the personal pronoun *his* or *thy* or, most frequently, with the definite article *the*. And in every case, His return is in the singular; not *comings* but *coming*. There is not even a hint—anywhere—of two separate comings. That is simple, unadorned, biblical fact. The often-heard suggestion that Christ will come first *for* His church and then return to the earth a second time seven years later *with* His church is an assumption with no biblical evidence to substantiate it. The argument that verses which speak of His coming sometimes refer to the Rapture and other times to Christ's return in glory, and therefore, that there must be two comings, is without basis. This argument totally ignores the fact that Christ's coming *(parousia)* includes both His coming and consequent presence to accomplish His purposes. Some texts which speak of Christ's coming are emphasizing the Rapture and the Day of the Lord; others His return in power and glory. But these events are part of one composite whole—the Second Coming.

There is clear evidence that there is a coming *(parousia)* of Christ some time after the middle of the seventieth week (cf. Matt. 24:3, 15, 27). For pretribulation rapturism to stand, among other things, two points must be demonstrated: First, that there are two comings; and second, that one of them occurs before the seventieth week begins.

Here a genuine and, by intent, gracious invitation is extended to friends of pretribulational persuasion: Demonstrate (and by that it is meant by careful exegesis of *any* biblical text) that there are two future comings of Christ (because such must be the case for pretribulationism to stand), and this author will publicly, and with deep and humble apology, repudiate the major thesis of this book. That invitation is genuine. But if that cannot be done, the thesis of this book is greatly enhanced.

Furthermore, *since the Rapture is directly related to the coming* (parousia, *1 Thess. 3:13; 5:23; 2 Thess. 4:5), and the demonstrable coming* (parousia) *occurs after the middle of the seventieth week (specifically before the opening of the seventh seal, Matt. 24:27; Rev. 6:12–17), so too the Rapture must occur beyond the middle of the seventieth week*. Once again, this negates any attempt to place the Rapture at the beginning of the seventieth week and the Day of the Lord at the middle or later. Some teachers have attempted to do that because they acknowledge that the Day of the Lord starts beyond the middle of the seventieth week, but they still want to hold to pretribulationism.

In addition, *no one can know the day or the hour of Christ's coming* (parousia). That is clearly taught by the Lord Himself (Matt. 24:36–37). However, men are to know the *general* time period of

Christ's coming. That is also taught by the Lord (Matt. 24:32–33). The apostle Paul warned the Thessalonians that the Lord's coming *(parousia)* would be as "a thief in the night" (1 Thess. 5:2). Then he explained the response of both the saved and the unsaved to the Lord's coming. Concerning the unsaved he wrote, "For when they shall say, Peace and safety, then sudden destruction cometh upon them, as travail upon a woman with child, and they shall not escape" (1 Thess. 5:3). The picture Paul portrayed is of an unsaved world caught completely off guard and unprepared for Christ's return. But of the saved he wrote regarding Christ's coming *(parousia)*, "But ye, brethren, are not in darkness, that that day should overtake you as a thief. Ye are all sons of light, and sons of the day; we are not of the night, nor of darkness. Therefore, let us not sleep, as do others, but let us watch and be soberminded" (1 Thess. 5:4–6; see also 2 Pet. 3:12).

No amount of rationalizing can explain away the fact that if the coming of the Lord is imminent and pretribulational, He will, of an absolute necessity, return as "a thief in the night" even for the believers. The Pauline admonition to *watchfulness* for an event which has no prophesied events to precede it would be the ultimate exercise in futility. If, on the other hand, Christ's coming and the Rapture occur after the events of Matthew 24:4–28, as the thesis of this book contends (immediately prior to the opening of the seventh seal), then the Lord's words make perfect sense. "So likewise ye, when ye shall see all these things [the events portrayed in the first five seals], know that it [His coming *(parousia)*] is near, even at the doors" (Matt. 24:33; cf. Luke 21:28). That day need not overtake a believer like "a thief in the night" precisely because events of the seventieth week will announce its approach—not the very hour, but the general time period—exactly as the Lord taught.

Finally, *in the clearest possible way, if there is only one coming, the doctrine of imminency is destroyed by the question posed by the disciples.* They inquired, "What shall be the sign of thy coming [*parousia*]?" (Matt. 24:3). Signs are miracles or wonders given to authenticate or substantiate important divine truth (Isa. 7:14). In this case, the disciples asked concerning the sign of His coming *(parousia)*. Since the sign must precede the coming, and the Rapture is related to the coming, the Rapture cannot be signless. And imminency, which Walvoord has called the central pillar of pretribulation rapturism, is once more discredited.[6]

There is another word to which attention is now drawn. The disciples asked, "What shall be the sign of thy coming, and of the end of the world?" (Matt. 24:3).

The phrase "the end of the world" (as in the *Authorized Version*) is particularly misleading. It is better translated "the end of the age." The Greek word *aion* is not the *world* but a period or era during which events take place. Commenting on this subject, the Greek scholar W. E. Vine noted that the "end of the age" does not denote a termination but the moving of events toward an appointed climax.[7] And there is still more beyond that climax.

When the disciples asked, "What shall be the sign of thy coming [*parousia*], and of the end of the age [*aion*]?" (Matt. 24:3), they realized that Christ's coming would end one era and commence another (the millennial kingdom). A synonym for *the end* or *the end of the age* is the phrase "until the harvest" (Matt. 13:30). This phrase occurs in the Lord's parable of the wheat and the tares.

> Another parable put he forth unto them, saying, The kingdom of heaven is likened unto a man who sowed good seed in his field; But, while men slept, his enemy came and sowed tares among the wheat, and went his way. But when the blade was sprung up, and brought forth fruit, then appeared the tares also. So the servants of the householder came and said unto him, Sir, didst not thou sow good seed in thy field? From where, then, hath it tares? He said unto them, An enemy hath done this. The servants said unto him, Wilt thou, then, that we go and gather them up? But he said, Nay; lest while ye gather up the tares, ye root up also the wheat with them. Let both grow together until the harvest; and in the time of harvest I will say to the reapers, Gather together first the tares, and bind them in bundles to burn them, but gather the wheat into my barn. (Matt. 13:24–30)

Later the disciples asked the Lord to interpret the parable, and He did so:

> He answered and said unto them, He that soweth the good seed is the Son of man; The field is the world; the good seed are the children of the kingdom, but the tares are the children of the wicked one; The enemy that sowed them is the devil; the harvest is the

> end of the age; and the reapers are the angels. As, therefore, the tares are gathered and burned in the fire, so shall it be in the end of this age. (Matt. 13:37–40)

The *earthly story* part of the parable was quite simple. The wheat and the weeds were to grow together. Only at the harvest were they to be separated. The wheat would go into the barn; the weeds would be burned.[8]

The *spiritual truth* of the parable is equally clear. Righteous and unrighteous men are to coexist in the world. Then at "the harvest [which] is the end of the age" (Matt. 13:39), separation will occur. The wicked will be cast into hell (Matt. 13:41–42), and "the righteous [shall] shine forth as the sun in the kingdom of their Father" (Matt. 13:43).

The Lord taught, in the clearest possible way, that the final harvest is the separation of the righteous and unrighteous, and that the final harvest is the end of the age. That absolute identification is made: "the harvest *is* the end of the age" (Matt. 13:39). Speaking of that final harvest, John the Baptist, referring to Christ, said,

> Whose fan is in his hand [a small shovel for tossing grain against the wind and separating the wheat from the chaff], and he will thoroughly purge his floor, and gather his wheat into the granary [through rapture], but he will burn up the chaff with unquenchable fire [through the Day of the Lord judgment]. (Matt. 3:12)

For the Rapture to be pretribulational, "the end" (or the harvest which occurs at Christ's coming) must begin at the beginning of the seventieth week. But once again, the clear, irrefutable fact is "the end of the age" *does not begin* at the beginning of the seventieth week. The evidence for that fact is substantial and convincing.

First, the events of Matthew 24:4 and following are understood by the overwhelming majority of dispensational, pretribulational interpreters to be describing events *within* the seventieth week. The *Ryrie Study Bible* states that view succinctly. Verses 4–14 list characteristics of the first half of the Tribulation period, while verses 15–28 deal with the second half.[9] In verse 6 (which Ryrie properly places within the seventieth week) the Lord teaches, "And ye shall hear of wars and rumors of wars; see that ye be not troubled; for all these things must come to pass, but the *end* is not yet." The final harvest, the separation of the righteous and the unrighteous, had not yet occurred within the seventieth week. Again in verse 13 the Lord taught, "But he that shall endure unto the *end,* the same shall be saved." Even further within the seventieth week, there is still no final harvest—no separation of the wheat and tares. And if, as some suggest, the end occurs at the conclusion of the seventieth week, then what are these people being saved (delivered) from? If, on the other hand, the Rapture occurs, as the thesis of this book contends, immediately prior to the opening of the seventh seal, then those believers who endure to the end (a theme repeated three times: Matt. 10:22; 24:13; Mark 13:13) will be saved (delivered) from the Day of the Lord wrath.

Second, in direct response to the inquiry of the disciples concerning "the end of the age," the Lord taught this truth: "And this gospel of the kingdom shall be preached in all the world for a witness unto all nations; and then shall the end come" (Matt. 24:14). The end had still not yet occurred, although the context is well into the seventieth week. But a new truth is added. The gospel will be preached in all the world *before* the end will come.

Now a new problem arises for pretribulation rapturism; namely, the Great Commission of the church:

> And Jesus came and spoke unto them, saying, All authority is given unto me in heaven and in earth. Go ye, therefore, and teach all nations, baptizing them in the name of the Father, and of the Son, and of the Holy Spirit, teaching them to observe all things whatsoever I have commanded you; and, lo, I am with you always, even unto the end of the age. Amen. (Matt. 28:18–20)

The Lord's promise in the Great Commission included the fact that He would be with them "unto the end of the age" (Matt. 28:20).

In Matthew 24:14 four things are clear: (1) the Lord is speaking to the disciples; (2) the gospel is to be preached to all nations; (3) following the preaching of the gospel in all the world, the end will come; and (4) the end is within the seventieth week. By comparison, in the Great Commission (1) the Lord is speaking to the disciples; (2) they are commanded to preach the gospel throughout the world; (3) the Lord would be with them unto the end of the age; and (4) if "the end" in Matthew 24:14 is inside the seventieth week, then "the end of the age" in Matthew 28:20 must also be inside the seventieth week. The suggestion that the "end" or "end of the age" in these passages do not refer to the same "end" ought not to be taken seriously by those who honor God's Word.

> And ye shall be hated of all men for my name's sake, but he that endureth to *the end* shall be saved. (Matt. 10:22)

> The enemy that sowed them is the devil; the harvest is *the end of the age,* and the reapers are the angels. As, therefore, the tares are gathered and burned in the fire, so shall it be in the *end of this age.* (Matt. 13:39–40)

> And what shall be the sign of thy coming, and of *the end of the age?* . . . And ye shall hear of wars and rumors of wars; see that ye be not troubled; for all these things must come to pass, but *the end* is not yet . . . But he that shall endure unto *the end,* the same shall be saved. And this gospel of the kingdom shall be preached in all the world for a witness unto all nations; and then shall *the end* come. (Matt. 24:3, 6, 13–14)

> Teaching them to observe all things whatsoever I have commanded you, and, lo, I am with you always, even unto *the end of the age.* Amen. (Matt. 28:20)

> Then cometh *the end,* when he shall have delivered up the kingdom to God, even the Father, when he shall have put down all rule and all authority and power. (1 Cor. 15:24)

If the Great Commission of the church is to evangelize the world up to the end, then the church must enter the seventieth week of the book of Daniel in order to fulfill its holy calling, only then to be raptured before the Day of the Lord judgment, because the church, the bride of Christ, is not appointed unto the Bridegroom's wrath, which will fall only on an unrepentant world. The church will be raptured prewrath (at the seventh seal), not pretribulationally (at the beginning of the seventieth week).

In an important text rarely discussed in prophetic debate, the sequence of these events is clearly outlined. Paul wrote to the Corinthians, "So that ye come behind in no gift, waiting for the coming [*parousia*] of our Lord Jesus Christ, Who shall also confirm [guarantee] you unto the end, that ye may be blameless in the day of our Lord Jesus Christ" (1 Cor. 1:7–8). Three distinct truths are in view: (1) the Corinthian believers are waiting for the Lord's coming *(parousia);* (2) He will keep them up to the end (the final harvest when the righteous and unrighteous are separated as wheat and chaff); (3) they will be found blameless and, therefore, escape the Day of the Lord judgment to enter the millennial kingdom.

In summation of this chapter, the following salient facts have been demonstrated:

> If the Great Commission of the church is to evangelize the world up to the end, then the church must enter the seventieth week of the book of Daniel in order to fulfill its holy calling, only then to be raptured before the Day of the Lord judgment.

- The word *coming (parousia)* means a coming and consequent presence.
- Of the seventeen times the word *coming* is used in connection with the return of Christ, it is used only in the singular and always with the definite article or a personal pronoun (i.e., "the coming," "thy coming," or "his coming").
- Not once does the Bible speak of two comings—not even by a hint or implication.
- It can be demonstrated that Christ's coming *(parousia)* occurs after the middle of the seventieth week (Matt. 24:27).
- In no *coming* text can it be demonstrated that the coming occurs pre-seventieth week.
- When the coming *(parousia)* occurs, it will have among its major purposes the Rapture of the righteous and the Day of the Lord judgment of the wicked (1 Cor. 15:20–24). Thus, it is indefensible to argue that the Day of the Lord begins at the middle of Daniel's seventieth week or later and that the church is raptured at least three and one-half years earlier, or before the seventieth week commences.
- The phrase *end of the world* (Matt. 24:3) is more accurately

translated *end of the age* and is speaking of the completion of this era in preparation for entrance into the next (the Millennium). The Day of the Lord will be the transition period from this age to the kingdom age.

- *The end* is clearly identified as the final harvest. Jesus taught, "the harvest is the end of the age" (Matt. 13:39).
- *The final harvest* is the separating of the wheat and the tares. The wheat are the righteous, who are to be harvested into God's barn; the tares are the unrighteous, who are to be harvested and burned (Matt. 13:40–43).
- *The end* is unmistakably identified as occurring *inside* the seventieth week (Matt. 24:3; cf. vv. 6, 13, 14).
- The Great Commission of the church—the task of world evangelism—is to continue *unto the end*. The Lord said, "I am with you always, even unto the end of the age" (Matt. 28:20).

Since the church must continue unto the *end,* and the end is within the seventieth week, a pretribulation rapture is impossible. On the other hand, a prewrath rapture at the seventh seal fits the biblical data unforced and perfectly.

# 17

# Kept From the Hour

Three ancient highways run north and south through Israel. One, on the western side, is located along the shore of the Mediterranean coastline. It is appropriately called the Via Maris, or Way of the Sea. For an ancient pilgrim or army, it was the easiest and normally the best route to follow. The terrain was flat, and water and food were readily available.

There was a second route on the eastern side of the country. It was located in the mountains high above the Syrian-African rift (the longest natural rift in the earth) and includes, as only part of its boundaries, the Sea of Galilee, Jordan Valley, and Dead Sea (the latter being the lowest spot on the earth). This route also had an appropriate name. It was called the King's Highway. Steep and rugged terrain, with less readily available water and food, it was a difficult route, suitable only for a king who had slaves to serve him and an army to protect him.

A third route traversed the center of the land. Climbing steadily from the Sinai Desert, it connected cities like Beersheba, Hebron, Bethlehem, and Jerusalem, where it reached an altitude of twenty-seven hundred feet above sea level. This route, like the Via Maris and the King's Highway, was also appropriately named. It was called the Patriarchal Highway because the patriarchs (fathers) Abraham, Isaac, and Jacob used it in traveling between Beersheba, Hebron, Bethlehem, and Jerusalem. This highway, which divided the land east and west, ascended like a spine through the land of Judah to Jerusalem and then northward.

The rain that fell on the western side of the Patriarchal Highway ran down to the Mediterranean Sea. Rain falling on the eastern side made its way into wadis (narrow ravines or creeks) and, often with thunderous roar and great power, emptied into the Dead Sea. The Patriarchal Highway was a natural watershed, dividing the water flow between east and west.

In a similar manner, for many theologians the watershed in the debate over the timing of the Rapture is one verse of Scripture, which divides the conflicting Rapture views. How this verse is interpreted generally determines whether a Bible teacher is pretribulational, midtribulational, or posttribulational. The apostle John wrote in the Apocalypse, "Because thou hast kept the word of my patience, I also will keep thee from the hour of temptation, which shall come upon all the world, to try them that dwell upon the earth" (Rev. 3:10). Robert Gundry has called Revelation 3:10 the most debated verse in the Rapture discussion.[1] Douglas J. Moo has stated that Revelation 3:10 has always figured prominently in the debate over the timing of the Rapture.[2] Unquestionably, few verses in the New Testament have been as carefully and fully scrutinized by Greek scholars as has been Revelation 3:10. In their scrutiny, they have exhausted the numerous grammars and lexicons, the Septuagint, classical Greek, and the Bible itself to arrive at an understanding of the phrase "I also will keep thee from the hour of temptation" (Rev. 3:10).

The nature of the "temptation" is indicated by the Greek word *ek* translated in the *Authorized Version* as *from*. Pretribulation rapturists generally understand *ek* to mean *removal* from the temptation. Therefore, in their scenario the church is caught up before the seventieth week begins. Posttribulation rapturists interpret *ek* to mean *protection from* what they perceive to be a real and present danger (i.e., the seventieth week). In their view, therefore, the church will be preserved (but not removed) during the Tribulation. Midtribulation rapturists are once again in a mediating position. They believe that during the first three and one-half years, the church is *protected from* the then-present temptation, and that during the last three and one-half years the church will be *removed from* the temptation by rapture. The arguments over the correct interpretation of the Greek text are complex and technical. For that reason, they are restricted to those who possess more than a superficial knowledge of the Greek language.

As already noted, the phrase "I also will keep thee from the hour of temptation" (Rev. 3:10) is seen by many to be a determinative issue in the Rapture debate—the watershed verse that divides the different positions.

The reality of the matter, however, is that there simply is no agreement among conservative Greek scholars as how to best interpret the phrase "I also will keep thee from the hour of temptation." Even within the same theological camps, there are varying views. Therefore, it is fair to say that each scholar is inclined to interpret this phrase to substantiate his view of the Rapture. It would be both easy and safe to concur with the pretribulation view that the believer is removed *from* the time of testing, with the understanding that the time of testing is the Day of the Lord, not the entire seventieth week of Daniel. That view would not negatively impact the basic position of this book. However, because commentators have not generally understood that there are *three* sections to the seventieth week—the beginning birth pangs, the Great Tribulation, and the Day of the Lord—they have, in the view of this author, made a fundamental error. The chart that follows illustrates the general positions of pre-, mid-, and posttribulationism on Revelation 3:10.

There simply is no agreement among conservative Greek scholars as how best to interpret the phrase "I also will keep thee from the hour of temptation."

The position presented in this volume takes a completely different approach to the issue. (It is important to note that the pretribulation position which suggests that the phrase "kept from the hour" means *removal* would fit the prewrath view with the understanding that the "hour" begins with the opening of the seventh seal.) It champions the view that Revelation 3:10, which figures so extensively in the debate concerning the timing of the Rapture, in fact has nothing whatever to do with the Rapture, and that the other views concerning the Rapture have been forced by their respective systems to interpret Revelation 3:10 as they have. A pretribulation rapture demands that the phrase "I also will keep thee from the hour of temptation" be interpreted as *removal from* the temptation of the seventieth week. A midtribulation rapture demands *protection from* the temptation during the first three and one-half years and then *removal from* the temptation during the last three and one-half years. The historic posttribulation rapture demands *protection* from the temptation (without removal) throughout the entire seventieth week.

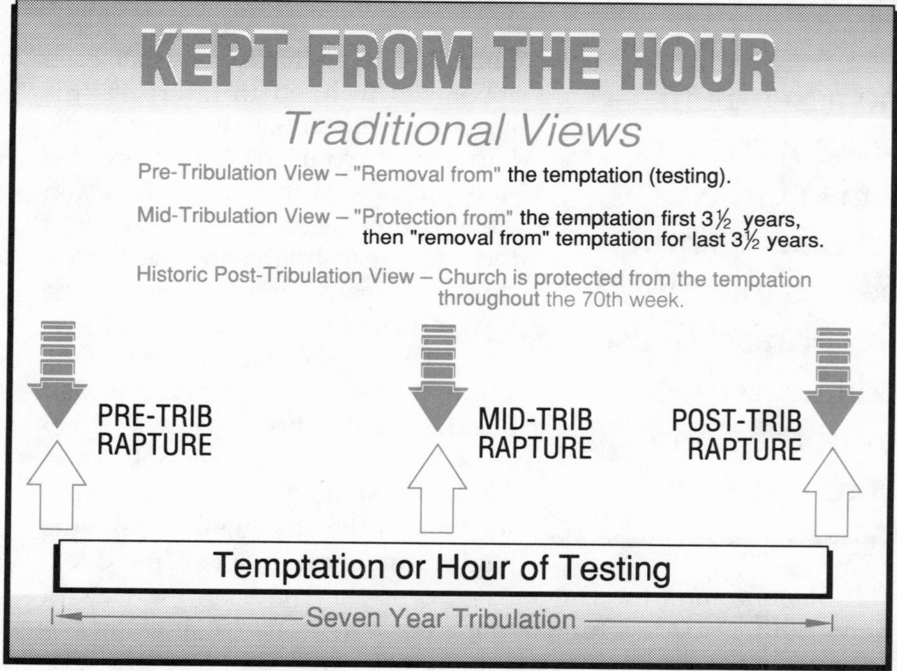


Evidence is here presented that the phrase "I also will keep thee from the hour of temptation" refers to protection from the Great Tribulation, which occurs before the Rapture and the Day of the Lord begins.[3]

The phrase "I also will keep thee from the hour of temptation" must not be segregated from what precedes it. John wrote, "Because thou hast kept the word of my patience, I also will keep thee from the hour of temptation." There is a clearly delineated cause-and-effect relationship. Because faithful believers, for their part, will have kept the word of God's patience, He, for His part, will keep them from the hour of testing. It is crucial, then, to understand the meaning of the phrase "Because thou hast kept the word of my patience."

The word translated *patience* in Revelation 3:10 occurs twenty-eight times in the New Testament. It consistently conveys the idea of *endurance in the midst of adversity*. The *New International Dictionary of New Testament Theology* defines the word *patience* this way: "To overcome difficulties; to persevere, to stand firm, to stand one's ground." The Lord used it in the context of the seventieth week of Daniel. He taught,

> And ye shall be betrayed both by parents, and brethren, and kinsfolk, and friends; and some of you shall they cause to be put to death. And ye shall be hated of all men for my name's sake. But there shall not an hair of your head perish. In your patience [endurance in the midst of adversity] possess ye your souls. (Luke 21:16–19)

Believers are admonished to remain faithful in the midst of adversity. The worst men can do is harm the physical and temporal body; they cannot touch the spiritual and eternal soul. Paul used the word *patience* in the same way in writing to the Thessalonians: "Remembering without ceasing your work of faith, and labor of love, and patience (endurance in the midst of adversity) of hope in our Lord Jesus Christ, . . . And ye became followers of us, and of the Lord, having received the word in much affliction, with joy of the Holy Spirit" (1 Thess. 1:3, 6).

And a second time he wrote to the Thessalonians: "So that we ourselves glory in you in the churches of God for your patience [endurance in the midst of adversity] and faith in all your persecutions and tribulations that ye endure" (2 Thess. 1:4). The apostle John, writing in the context of the abomination of desolation which will occur in the middle of the seventieth week, taught, "He that leadeth into captivity shall go into captivity; he that killeth with the sword must be killed with the sword. Here is the patience [endurance in the midst of adversity] and the faith of the saints" (Rev. 13:10).

Believers will be severely persecuted in that day. Some will be sent into captivity. Others will be slain. But those who perpetrate those deeds will be appropriately punished by God. Those who send others into captivity will themselves be sent into captivity. Those who kill with the sword will themselves be killed by the sword.

God is just, and a living faith will always exhibit patience (Heb. 6:12; 11:13). They (faith and patience) compliment one another like a hand and glove. The believer who has faith will always exhibit patience. He is to endure and abide faithful in the midst of adversity. And the ultimate, humanly instigated adversity will be the Great Tribulation.

John wrote again in the context of the middle of the seventieth week:

> And the third angel followed them, saying with a loud voice, If any man worship the beast and his image, and receive his mark in his forehead, or in his hand, the same shall drink of the wine of the wrath of God, which is poured out without mixture into the cup of his indignation [there will be no dilution of God's wrath]; and he shall be tormented with fire and brimstone in the presence of the holy angels, and in the presence of the Lamb; And the smoke of their torment ascendeth up forever and ever; and they have no rest day nor night, who worship the beast and his image, and whosoever receiveth the mark of his name. Here is the patience [endurance in the midst of adversity] of the saints; here are they that keep the commandments of God, and the faith of Jesus. (Rev. 14:9–12)

In this text, John is contrasting two groups of men. The first group is those who submit to the Antichrist, give him their allegiance, and receive his mark. Their just reward will be to experience the undiluted wrath of God. The second group is those who exhibit patience (endurance in the midst of adversity), some of whom will suffer martyrdom. But of them it is written, "And I heard a voice from heaven saying unto me, Write, Blessed [paradoxically, living] are the dead who die in the Lord [those whose faith is exhibited through patient endurance] from henceforth. Yea, saith the Spirit, that they may rest from their labors, and their words do follow them" (Rev. 14:13).

Patience, then, in its biblical usage, conveys the idea of enduring in the midst of affliction. It is frequently used in the context of the seventieth week of Daniel (Luke 21:19; Rev. 13:10; 14:12). There is a reason for an appeal to patience for believers living during that seventieth week. "For false Christs and false prophets shall rise, and shall show signs and wonders, to *seduce,* if it were possible, even the elect" (Mark 13:22). "And Jesus answered and said unto them, Take heed that no man *deceive* you. For many shall come in my name, saying, I am Christ; and shall *deceive* many" (Matt. 24:4–5). "And many false prophets shall rise, and shall *deceive* many" (Matt. 24:11). "For there shall arise false Christs, and false prophets, and shall show great signs and wonders, insomuch that, if it were possible, they shall *deceive* the very elect" (Matt. 24:24).

A number of salient points must be made. First, God has promised *the church of Philadelphia* that those who keep the word of His patience He will keep from the hour of temptation. (To apply the promise given to the church of Philadelphia to all of Christendom is to interpret the Scriptures nonliterally. It is only the church of Philadelphia which is promised exemption from "the hour of temptation.") Patience is enduring or remaining steadfast in the midst of adversity. It is to overcome difficulties, to persevere, to stand firm, to stand one's ground.

But there is no known or prophesied adversity for the days immediately prior to the seventieth week of Daniel, and if there is, the Rapture cannot be imminent. If the Rapture occurs pretribulationally, there is no sense in which believers can be said to be keeping the word of His patience, to be enduring in the midst of the adversity. There is no reason or logic for that concept.

If, on the other hand, Revelation 3:10 describes an event in the *middle* of the seventieth week, it makes perfect sense. During the first three and one-half years, false Christs and false prophets will emerge; they will do false signs and wonders to seemingly authenticate their false message. Believers will be seduced, hated, and betrayed (Matt. 24:9–10). The love of many for God will grow cold (Matt. 24:12). In that environment, the faith that exhibits patience—that endures in the midst of adversity, that does not reject the true Christ for a false Christ—will be rewarded: "Because thou hast kept the word of my patience, I also will keep thee from the hour of temptation."

A second important term is also encountered. It is the word *temptation*. This word, as found in Revelation 3:10, occurs twenty-one times in the New Testament. It is seen in many familiar verses: "And lead us not into temptation" (Matt. 6:13); "Watch and pray, that ye enter not into temptation" (Matt. 26:41); "And when the devil had ended all the temptation, he departed from him for a season" (Luke 4:13); "There hath no temptation taken you but such as is common to man" (1 Cor. 10:13); "Harden not your hearts, as in the provocation, in the day of temptation in the wilderness" (Heb. 3:8); "I also will keep thee from the hour of temptation" (Rev. 3:10).

The word *temptation* carries with it the explicit idea of a test—a test to prove something. That proof may be good or it may be bad. It is impossible to rightly conclude that to be kept from the hour of temptation is to be raptured before the Day of the Lord commences. The Day of the Lord has no temptation or test associated with it. When all of the Day of the Lord texts are scrutinized, they indicate nothing whatever of testing. The Day of the Lord is a time of divine judgment, of absolute, awesome wrath on a godless and unrepentant world. The Day of the Lord will be the vindication of God's holiness and righteousness through judgment. It will be the natural outcome of God's final testing of man during the Great Tribulation, but it will not be the testing itself. The prophet Isaiah wrote of the Day of the Lord that it would be a time of destruction by the Almighty, a time of wrath and fierce anger, a time when God would punish the world for its evil, a time when He will shake the heavens and the earth—but *not* a time of testing.

The word *temptation* carries with it the explicit idea of a test—a test to prove something. That proof may be good or it may be bad.

> Wail; for the day of the LORD is at hand; it shall come as a destruction from the Almighty. Therefore shall all hands be faint, and every man's heart shall melt; And they shall be afraid. Pangs and sorrows shall take hold of them; they shall be in pain like a woman that travaileth. They shall be amazed one at another; their faces shall be as flames. Behold, the day of the LORD cometh, cruel both

> with wrath and fierce anger, to lay the land desolate; and he shall destroy the sinners out of it. For the stars of heaven and the constellations thereof shall not give their light; the sun shall be darkened in its going forth, and the moon shall not cause its light to shine. And I will punish the world for its evil, and the wicked for their iniquity; and I will cause the arrogancy of the proud to cease, and will lay low the haughtiness of the terrible. I will make a man more rare than fine gold, even a man than the golden wedge of Ophir. Therefore, I will shake the heavens, and the earth shall remove out of its place, in the wrath of the LORD of hosts, and in the day of his fierce anger. (Isa. 13:6–13)

The Great Tribulation, by contrast, *is* a time of testing. Professing believers will have an unprecedented opportunity to prove themselves, to demonstrate by steadfastness in the midst of adversity the genuineness of their faith.

The image of the Antichrist will be erected in the temple. False prophets will abound. Men will be commanded to bow down and worship the Antichrist. Death will be the punishment for those who do not comply. Here is a test with enormous and eternal consequences. In that day, men will either bow to the Antichrist and receive his mark (Rev. 13:15–17) or they will give their allegiance solely to the true Christ and receive His mark (Rev. 14:1).[4]

Now, back to Revelation 3:10. The Lord taught, "Because thou hast kept the word of my patience, I also will keep thee from the hour of temptation, which shall come upon all the world, to try them that dwell upon the earth." Those who keep the word of His patience are those who, under the stress and pressure of the first three and one-half years of the seventieth week, stay steadfast and true in the face of adversity. They will be the overcomers. As a result, they will be kept "from the hour of temptation, which shall come upon all the world, to try them that dwell upon the earth." The "hour of temptation" (a specifically appointed time) is the Great Tribulation. It begins in the middle of the seventieth week but will be "cut short" before the end of the seventieth week. Some men will be kept from that hour in two ways. They will be kept "from the hour" by physical removal (perhaps men of faith and patience who are watchful will flee Jerusalem, as history records a believing remnant did before the Roman destruction of Jerusalem in A.D. 70), and others will be kept "through the hour of temptation" by direct, divine protection. Both concepts, *removal from* and *protection from* the hour of testing, are correct.

An analogy of this promise of exemption from the coming temptation can be illustrated this way: A professor challenges his class with the remark, "If, when we come to the final exam, you have an A average, you will not have to take the test" (that is, if you got an A in all the quizzes, tests, and assignments, you are exempted from the final exam). Only *some* of the students will not have to take the final test—those who have already proven themselves. The promise of exemption from the hour of testing is given by the Lord only to those who, in His words, have "kept the word of my patience" (that is, who have faithfully endured during the adversity of the first three and one-half years). They are exemplified by the church of Philadelphia. Of that church the Lord said,

> I know thy works; behold, I have set before thee an open door, and no man can shut it; for thou hast a little strength, and hast kept my word, and hast not denied my name . . . Because thou hast kept the word of my patience, I also will keep thee from the hour of temptation, which shall come upon all the world, to try them that dwell upon the earth. (Rev. 3:8, 10)

No such exemption is promised to the other six churches.[5] For instance, to the church of Thyatira the Lord said,

> Notwithstanding, I have a few things against thee, because thou allowest that woman, Jezebel, who calleth herself a prophetess, to teach and to seduce my servants to commit fornication, and to eat things sacrificed unto idols. And I gave her space to repent of her fornication, and she repented not. Behold, I will cast her into a bed, and them that commit adultery with her into great tribulation [they will not be "kept from the hour"], except they repent of their deeds. And I will kill her children with death; and all the churches shall know that I am he who searcheth the minds and hearts; and I will give unto every one of you according to your works. (Rev. 2:20–23)

The phrase "I also will keep thee from the hour of temptation" in Revelation 3:10 is *not* a watershed verse to determine the timing of the Rapture. It has nothing whatever to do with the timing of the Rapture. It deals with the Great Tribulation and holds out the promise—the glorious promise—that a remnant who have stayed true to the Lord during the first three and one-half years will be kept from the temptation of the Great Tribulation which will try the souls of men under the barbaric reign of the Antichrist. It is following the Great Tribulation that the Rapture and the Day of the Lord will occur. The chart below illustrates the meaning of the phrase "Because thou hast kept the word of my patience, I also will keep thee from the hour of temptation" as presented in this chapter.

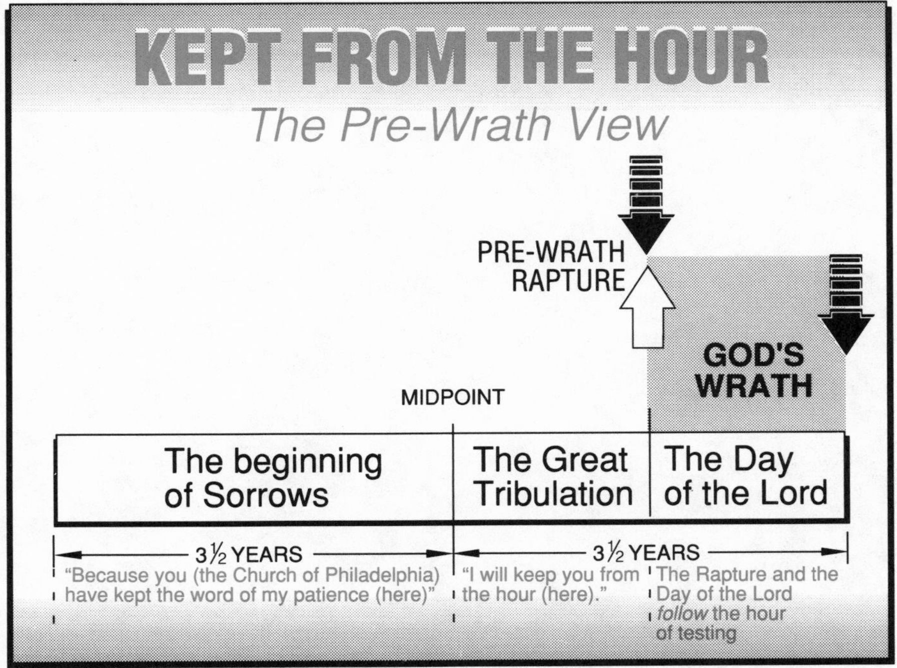

# 18

# Are Pretribulation Rapture Arguments Really Unanswerable?

One need read neither long nor deep in the literature on the Rapture of the church to be confronted with a formidable body of truth in defense of pretribulation rapturism. Men of godly stature, intellectual prowess, and gifted in communicative skills have, in this century, given themselves to that task. Therefore, to make light of pretribulation rapturism, as some have done, is inappropriate, and to reject it without careful examination is foolish. This volume has attempted to avoid both of those pitfalls, acknowledging, as it does, that pretribulationism has more than its share of notables of the faith—choice servants of the Lord—but proclaiming as well that church history is replete with men of distinction who have had blind spots in their theology. Like the noble Bereans, therefore, who "searched the scriptures daily, whether those things were so" (Acts 17:11), this book is a careful attempt to define the timing of Christ's coming in the light of the Scriptures. In pursuit of that end, commonly stated arguments in defense of pretribulation rapturism will be stated and then evaluated. In no sense will this examination be exhaustive. Nor, it must be added, will a straw man be erected and then simplistically dismantled. No intentional misrepresentation has been made of pretribulationism or pretribulationists. In the first chapter, the author acknowledged that he writes as a lover from within the dispensational, premillennial camp, and not as an opponent from without. That attitude has not diminished. Challenging pretribulation rapturism, to me, is an evidence of that love. If it is correct, it will withstand the assault. If it is wrong, men of honor who love God's Word should welcome a change in direction toward the prewrath Rapture.

Now, to those pretribulational rapture arguments.

## ARGUMENT 1

Many pretribulationists point out that the word *church* or *churches* is repeatedly used in the first three chapters of the book of Revelation. Specifically, the word *church* is used seven times in the repeated formula: "Unto the angel [messenger] of the church of [and then the name of the church is given: Ephesus, Smyrna, Pergamum, Thyatira, Sardis, Philadelphia, Laodicea] write . . ." (Rev. 2:1, 8, 12, 18; 3:1, 7, 14). The word *churches* is used elsewhere in the book ten times (Rev. 1:4, 11, 20 [two times]; 2:7, 11, 17, 23, 29; 3:6, 13, 22) for a combined total of nineteen times in the first three chapters of Revelation. But neither the word *church* nor any inference to it appears again until Revelation 22, where in the epilogue it is written, "I, Jesus, have sent mine angel to testify unto you these things in the churches" (Rev. 22:16). It is clear, then, that the church is exceedingly conspicuous in Revelation 1 to 3 (mentioned a total of nineteen times) but not mentioned even once in chapters 4–21, and only referred to again after the return of Christ (Rev. 22:16).[1] This absence of any mention of the church can best be explained by a pretribulation rapture occurring no later than the events recounted in Revelation 4.

## REBUTTAL 1

In response to this argument, the following observations are made. First, for posttribulation rapturism, the conspicuous absence of the church from chapters 4 through 21 creates a significant problem. This is a seven-year period of time during which, according to the posttribulation scenario, the church is being supernaturally protected. Yet in the book of Revelation, which presents the fullest description of that seven-year period, the church is not even mentioned in that description. Posttribulationism has yet to give a satisfactory response to the dilemma which that fact creates for their position.

Second, it will be repeatedly noted that an argument that discredits posttribulation rapturism does not necessarily prove pretribulation rapturism. That obvious fact is important to remember because all too frequently it is ignored.

Third, the pretribulation argument being challenged in this rebuttal not only does not create a problem for the prewrath position espoused in this book, but helps sustain it. In Revelation 1 to 3 the church is repeatedly mentioned (nineteen times). In chapter 4, John was called up to heaven (Rev. 4:1). Chapters 4 and 5 describe a heavenly scene depicting God seated upon His throne. In this heavenly scene, the church would not be expected to be in view. Chapter 6 describes the opening of the first six seals and concludes with the statement that God's wrath "is come" (i.e., is about to occur). It is precisely at this point of time, before the opening of the seventh seal and the commencement of God's wrath, that the church is raptured in chapter 7. Therefore, the fact that the church is not mentioned in chapters 8 through 21 not only is compatible with a prewrath Rapture but gives it essential support.

## ARGUMENT 2

Many pretribulation rapturists argue from the apostle John's statement, "After this I looked and, behold, a door was opened in heaven; and the first voice that I heard was, as it were, of a trumpet talking with me; which said, Come up here, and I will show thee things which must be hereafter" (Rev. 4:1). They take the command to John to "Come up here" to signify the Rapture of the church. Since this occurs in chapter 4, before the opening of the seals, trumpets, and bowls, the Rapture must be pretribulational.

## REBUTTAL 2

In response to this view, the author must acknowledge that this issue was almost omitted from discussion. The argument which suggests that John's being called up to heaven represents the church and determines the timing of the Rapture is fanciful and totally without biblical justification. That kind of interpretation dishonors a literal and grammatical approach to the Scriptures. To make John's being caught up into heaven mean the church is raptured at that time is tantamount to adopting Origen's allegory method of interpretation—an approach premillennarians universally shun in other instances. Because this argument is frequently cited by zealous exponents of pretribulation rapturism, its inclusion here was deemed necessary.

## ARGUMENT 3

Many pretribulation rapturists argue that, because the church is the bride of Christ, it is unthinkable that God would pour out His wrath on His Son's bride. Paul wrote to the Thessalonians, "And to wait for his Son from heaven, whom he raised from the dead, even Jesus, who delivered us from the wrath to come" (1 Thess. 1:10); and he wrote once again, "For God hath not appointed us to wrath but to obtain salvation [deliverance] by our Lord Jesus Christ" (1 Thess. 5:9). Since the church, the bride of Christ, is exempt from God's wrath, and God's wrath is poured out during the seven-year Tribulation period, the church must, therefore, be raptured pretribulationally.

## REBUTTAL 3

In response to this frequently voiced argument that the church is raptured pretribulationally because it is not appointed unto wrath, exception must be taken and its logic challenged. This argument's conclusion (i.e., that the church is raptured pretribulationally) would be valid if it could be demonstrated that its underlying assumptions are correct. To be sure, the church is exempt from the wrath of God. But the matter of *when* that wrath begins is at the very heart of the Rapture debate. The incorrect assumption that the wrath of God commences with the seventieth week cannot be used to validate pretribulation rapturism. It has already been demonstrated (1) that nowhere in the Bible is the seventieth week of Daniel ever called "the Tribulation period"; (2) that the wrath of God is associated with the Day of the Lord; (3) that the Day of the Lord begins inside the seventieth week with the opening of the seventh seal; and (4) therefore the church will enter the seventieth week to be raptured prewrath, before the Day of the Lord begins, not pre-seventieth week—as pretribulationism contends. The true church will be kept from divine wrath, precisely as Paul teaches. The bride (the church) will not experience the Bridegroom's (Christ's) wrath.

## ARGUMENT 4

Pretribulation rapturists contend that the Rapture of the church is the "blessed hope" of believers. Evidence for that belief is embodied in verses like the Pauline instruction to Titus. He wrote, "Teaching us that, denying ungodliness and worldly lusts, we should live soberly, righteously, and godly, in this present age, looking for that blessed hope, and the glorious appearing of the great God and our Savior, Jesus Christ" (Titus 2:12–13). How can it be reasonably asserted that the return of Christ is the "blessed hope" of the church if men must first experience the wrath of the Tribulation period? Only pretribulation rapturism makes sense of the Pauline statement that the Rapture is the blessed hope.

## REBUTTAL 4

In response to this argument, two observations must be noted. First, it does not follow at all that the "blessed hope" is no longer the blessed hope because a period of severe difficulty is to precede it. The blessed hope is the certain prospect of deliverance from God's wrath and of spiritual union between Christ and the church, the Bridegroom and the bride, in spite of all possible obstacles. A strong case can be made for the thesis that the blessed hope is enhanced if a time of difficulty were to precede it (Rom. 5:2–4, 9). The greater the suffering, the more glorious the deliverance. That is precisely what the Rapture is—a glorious deliverance. A blessed hope is literally a living hope, and difficulty and testing does not invalidate that prospect.

But second, and more fundamentally, the objection that the blessed hope is negated if the church enters the seventieth week is raised by those who do not comprehend the nature of the seventieth week. The first five seals relate to man's activity under the controlling influence of Satan. God's wrath has not yet begun; the trumpets and bowls have not yet been opened; Armageddon has not yet commenced. Before God's wrath begins, before the trumpets and bowls are opened, before Armageddon commences, the true church will be raptured to experience spiritual union with Christ, the Bridegroom. That's the blessed (living) hope. And no hope could be better than that. The argument that if the church enters the seventieth week, the blessed hope is invalidated must, therefore, be rejected as resting on theological quicksand.

## ARGUMENT 5

Many pretribulation rapturists argue that if the church is raptured at the end of the seventieth week (posttribulationally), all men would know exactly when it is to occur. The Tribulation is precisely seven years in duration. And the introduction of the image of the Antichrist at the temple ("the abomination that maketh desolate," Dan. 11:31) occurs exactly at the midpoint (Dan. 9:27). Therefore, all that men would have to do is count three and one-half years, or exactly 1,260 days, and they would know the precise time of Christ's return—to the very day. But the Bible teaches that no one knows the hour or day of Christ's return. Therefore, the Rapture must be pretribulational.

## REBUTTAL 5

It is acknowledged that the theology of this argument is correct, and that historic posttribulation rapturism does have a problem in this regard. If the Rapture occurs at the end of the seventieth week, the day of Christ's coming would be known, but the Scriptures make it clear that that day is unknown (Matt. 24:36, 42). However, the *application* of that conclusion is incorrect. The prewrath Rapture occurs immediately before the opening of the seventh seal a considerable period of time before the seventieth week ends, and neither the day nor the hour of that event is known. That is in precise conformity to the Word of God. Once again a recurring error of pretribulation rapturism appears—the assumption that if an argument disproves posttribulation rapturism, pretribulation rapturism is proven.

## ARGUMENT 6

Many pretribulation rapturists argue that Old Testament illustrations teach that God always took believers out of the way before He poured out His wrath upon the wicked. Notable illustrations are Noah, who was told to enter the ark before the flood came, and Lot, who was told to flee Sodom before God judged the city with fire and brimstone. Since the Tribulation period is the time of God's wrath, the church must be taken out before the wrath falls. Thus, pretribulation rapturism is proven.

## REBUTTAL 6

In response to this argument, the following observation is made. The Lord will indeed remove His children before His wrath is poured out; however, His wrath will not begin with the seventieth week of Daniel but with the opening of the seventh seal. And the church will be removed by rapture before that occurs. That is precisely what the Lord taught in Matthew 24:37–39: "But as the days of Noah were, so shall also the coming of the Son of man be. For as in the days that were before the flood they were eating and drinking, marrying and giving in marriage, until the day that Noah entered into the ark, And [the multitudes] knew not until the flood came, and took them all away, so shall also the coming of the Son of man be." Noah and his family got into the ark, and then the flood came. They were delivered before God's wrath. To suggest, within the context of Matthew, that these verses describe events before the seventieth week is simply unsustainable.

## ARGUMENT 7

Many pretribulation rapturists argue that believers are to encourage one another with the prospect of the imminent return of the Lord. Following a classic Rapture text (1 Thess. 4:13–17) in which Paul taught that both the dead in Christ and those who are alive would be caught up at His coming to ever be with the Lord, he admonished believers, "Wherefore, comfort one another with these words" (1 Thess. 4:18). What kind of comfort can be offered if men must first experience the Tribulation period? Therefore, the Rapture must be pretribulational.

## REBUTTAL 7

In response to this argument, two points are made. First, Paul did not teach the Thessalonians that the *Rapture* was imminent. Quite the contrary, he taught that the apostasy must occur first, and that then the man of sin must be revealed (2 Thess. 2:3). Second, for the believer to realize that he will be raptured before the trumpets and bowls of God's wrath are poured out—before Armageddon occurs—is a great and glorious word of comfort. Not only is there comfort in the realization that believers will be spared the wrath of God but also in the fact that those who persecute the believers will be themselves the object of that wrath (see

2 Thess. 1:6; 1 Peter 4:17). That is precisely what the prewrath Rapture teaches.

## ARGUMENT 8

The apostle John wrote, "And round about the throne were four and twenty thrones, and upon the thrones I saw four and twenty elders sitting, clothed in white raiment; and they had on their heads crowns of gold" (Rev. 4:4). Many pretribulationists argue that the twenty-four elders of Revelation 4 represent the church. John Walvoord is representative of this group. He wrote:

> The elders are described as being clothed in white raiment and having on their heads crowns of gold. There are two kinds of crowns in the book of Revelation, involving two different Greek words. One is the crown of a ruler or a sovereign (Gr., *diadem*), which is a crown of governmental authority. The other is the crown of a victor (Gr., *stephanos*), such as was awarded in the Greek games when a person won a race or some contest. This crown was usually made of leaves. The word here is the crown of a victor rather than that of a sovereign. It was made of gold, indicating that the elders had been rewarded for victory accomplished. It is significant that the passage states the twenty-four elders already have their crowns of gold as victors. If this passage is regarded as chronologically before the time of the tribulation which succeeding chapters unfold, it would seem to eliminate the angels, as at this point they have not been judged and rewarded since their judgment seems to come later. For the same reason the elders do not seem to be a proper representation of Israel, for Israel's judgment also seems to come at the end of the tribulation, not before. Only the church which is raptured before chapter four is properly complete in Heaven and eligible for reward at the judgment seat of Christ.[2] In that case, the crowns of gold on the heads of the twenty-four elders would be fitting at this point and would seem to confirm the idea that these may be representative of the church in glory.[3]

Since the church is represented by the twenty-four elders as being in heaven in Revelation 4, the church, of necessity, must be raptured pretribulationally.

## REBUTTAL 8

In response to this argument, a number of observations must be made.

First, there is no agreement on the part of conservative scholars as to the identification of the twenty-four elders. The great scholar Henry Alford believed that the twenty-four elders represent the redeemed of the Old and New Testaments and that the church is comprised of the elect from both economies.[4] Pretribulationist Clarence Larkin took a similar position. He wrote:

> The name Elder is never applied to angels, neither do angels have crowns and sit on thrones. Only redeemed men are promised thrones and crowns (Matt. 19:28; Rev. 3:21; 20:4; 2:10; 1 Pet. 5:2–4; 2 Tim. 4:8). These elders then must be representatives of the Old and New Testament Saints that have been redeemed by the blood of Christ.[5]

In marked contrast, William Newell, whose premillennial, pretribulational commentary on Revelation has remained a standard for years, took a different position. He suggests that the elders of Revelation 4 are angelic beings of some kind, twenty-four in number, and "created and associated by God with His government."[6] It is abundantly clear that conservative scholars, even those of a pretribulational persuasion, are by no means unified in their opinions concerning the identity of the twenty-four elders.

Second, there is significant evidence to suggest that the twenty-four elders do, in fact, represent those redeemed from within Israel and the Old Testament.

The word *elder (presbuteros)*, as used in the book of Revelation, is only used of the twenty-four elders and is used a total of twelve times (Rev. 4:4, 10; 5:5–6, 8, 11, 14; 7:11, 13–14; 11:16–18; 14:3; 19:4). The word *elder* is used in different ways in the Bible. It is used for older men who were tribal leaders. In Egypt, Moses and Aaron called the elders to inform them that Jehovah had sent them (Exod. 4:29–30). Later, seventy elders were set up as a special group to assist Moses (Num. 11:16–17). In the New Testament, the word *elders* was used for the rulers of the synagogues (Matt. 21:23; 26:57) and for the leaders in the early church (Acts 14:23). It was also used in describing the great Old Testament men of faith: "For by it [faith] the elders obtained a good report" (Heb. 11:2).

The significance of the fact that there were twenty-four elders is clarified in the Old Testament. The priesthood of ancient Israel, made up of the house of Aaron, was divided into twenty-four courses or groups of priests (1 Chron. 24). Each group served for two weeks each year on a rotation basis. As the prophet was God's spokesman to the people, so the priest was the people's representative before God. The number twenty-four in connection with the priesthood would speak of complete representation. Each group of priests had one priest who represented it. When these twenty-four priests met together, they represented the entire priesthood and, at the same time, the whole nation of Israel.[7]

These elders were specifically said by John to be "sitting" (Rev. 4:4; 11:16). To any Jewish contemporary of John, that would have been an amazing statement. They knew that the Levitical priests never sat down, because their work was never done. Their work was never done because the sacrifices of animals which they offered could never take away sin—they could only cover sin for a year. But Jesus offered Himself as a sacrifice, a sacrifice that was infinite and eternal and, therefore, never had to be repeated. And so the writer of Hebrews reveals that "when he had by himself purged our sins, [he] sat down on the right hand of the Majesty on high" (Heb. 1:3). These twenty-four elders were seated on thrones around the Heavenly Father because Jesus, the great High Priest, had once and for all opened the way into the *holiest of all*. They represented the redeemed of the Old Testament economy. And what could be more appropriate than to behold the twenty-four elders in the presence of God at the threshold of the seventieth week of Daniel, a time period which will bring to fruitation the ancient promises which God had given Israel? This would be the most conspicuous demonstration of His faithfulness to His covenant.

These elders are said to be "clothed in white raiment" (Rev. 4:4). Again, a Jewish contemporary of John would have immediately understood the significance of the white robes. When the ancient high priest of Israel on Yom Kippur (the Day of Atonement) prepared to enter the Holy of Holies and the presence of God, he discarded his magnificent priestly robes and put on in their place "the holy linen coat" (Lev. 16:4). When he withdrew from the tabernacle, he again put on his traditional priestly garments. "And Aaron shall come into the tabernacle of the congregation, and shall put off the linen garments, which he put on when he went into the holy place, and shall leave them there . . . and put on his garments [the ornate and symbolic priestly garb], and come forth" (Lev. 16:23–24).

In the presence of the people, the magnificent priestly garments were to be worn; in the presence of a holy God who is a consuming fire, a linen robe was deemed more fitting. The "white raiment" in which the elders were clothed speaks elegantly of their entrance "within the veil" in the presence of their God. The same significance is seen in the statement, "He that overcometh, the same shall be clothed in white raiment" (Rev. 3:5). That is, overcomers will enjoy the divine presence forever.

It is said that these twenty-four elders "had on their heads crowns of gold" (Rev. 4:4). As noted in argument 8 in the book of Revelation, there are two distinct crowns. One is the crown of a ruler (Gr., *diadem*). The other is the crown of an overcomer or victor (Gr., *stephanos*). It is this latter crown which the twenty-four elders are wearing. It is this crown that is held out to the church of Smyrna. The Lord said,

> I know the blasphemy of them who say they are Jews, and are not, but are the synagogue of Satan. Fear none of those things which thou shalt suffer. Behold, the devil shall cast some of you into prison, that ye may be tried, and ye shall have tribulation ten days; be thou faithful unto death, and I will give thee a crown [*stephanos*] of life. (Rev. 2:9–10)

The crowns upon the heads of the twenty-four elders suggest that those whom they represent are overcomers and victorious.

These twenty-four elders are seen in their representative priestly ministry—not in sacrifice but in intercession. "And when he had taken the scroll, the four living creatures and four and twenty elders fell down before the Lamb, having every one of them harps, and golden bowls full of incense, which are the prayers of saints" (Rev. 5:8). If these are the prayers being voiced during Daniel's seventieth week, no crystal ball is needed to know the substance of those prayers. As Christ begins the events that lead to His return, the eager prayers of the saints in that day will be, "Thy kingdom come. Thy will be done in earth, as it is in heaven" (Matt. 6:10).

The twenty-four elders are seen in their priestly ministry of praise:

> The four and twenty elders fall down before him that is seated on the throne, and worship him that liveth forever and ever, and

> cast their crowns before the throne, saying, Thou art worthy, O Lord, to receive glory and honor and power; for thou hast created all things, and for thy pleasure they are and were created. (Rev. 4:10–11)

Again they are heard to be singing a new song, saying, "Thou art worthy to take the scroll, and to open its seals; for thou wast slain, and hast redeemed us to God by thy blood out of every kindred, and tongue, and people, and nation; And hast made us unto our God a kingdom of priests, and we shall reign on the earth" (Rev. 5:9–10).

Many of the ancient Greek manuscripts and the consensus of contemporary scholarship favor the omission of the pronoun *us* in verse 9, as in the *Authorized Version*, and change the translation of "And has made *us* unto our God a kingdom of priests, and *we* shall reign on the earth" to "And hast made *them* unto our God a kingdom of priests, and *they* shall reign on the earth" (Rev. 5:10).[8] With the latter translation, the elders are now understood to be praising God for redeeming the church, of which they clearly are not a part.

Here is the ultimate fulfillment of the Abrahamic covenant and the divine promise, "in thee shall all families of the earth be blessed" (Gen. 12:3), and the words of aged Simeon when he lifted the child Jesus into his arms and prophetically proclaimed, "Lord, now lettest thou thy servant depart in peace, according to thy word; For mine eyes have seen thy salvation, which thou hast prepared before the face of all people; A light to lighten the Gentiles, and the glory of thy people, Israel" (Luke 2:29–32).

Evidence suggests that the twenty-four elders represent redeemed Israel. But under any scenario, it is abundantly clear that pretribulationists are in no way agreed regarding the identity of the elders—as to whether they are angels, the church, Old and New Testament saints, or Israel. All those interpretations are suggested by reputable scholars. The presence of twenty-four elders around the throne cannot then, with biblical justification, be used to represent the church in heaven before the seventieth week and, therefore, be used as a valid argument to sustain pretribulation rapturism. John Walvoord, who wants very much to make the twenty-four elders of Revelation 4 represent the raptured church, has nonetheless been forced to admit: "While Stonehouse does as well as anyone could to support the identification of the elders as angels, it is evident that he does not have any final or conclusive proof, and the controversy cannot be resolved. Identification of the twenty-four elders should not be dogmatically held. . . ."[9]

## ARGUMENT 9

Many pretribulation rapturists agree that there is a restraining power in the world today. That restraining power is the Holy Spirit of God Himself. Since the Holy Spirit indwells believers, His restraining power is operative through the presence of believers. At the Rapture, the church is removed from the earth and, with it, the Holy Spirit of God. The removal of the Holy Spirit occurs before the Day of the Lord (2 Thess. 2:3–8). Paul wrote to the Thessalonians,

> Let no man deceive you by any means; for that day shall not come, except there come the falling away first, and that man of sin be revealed, the son of perdition . . . For the mystery of iniquity doth already work; only he who now hindereth will continue to hinder until he be taken out of the way. And then shall that wicked one be revealed, whom the Lord shall consume with the spirit of his mouth, and shall destroy with the brightness of his coming. (2 Thess. 2:3, 7–8)

According to pretribulationism, four facts are considered to be clear: (1) the Holy Spirit is the One who hinders the Antichrist; (2) the Holy Spirit is removed before the Day of the Lord begins; (3) the Day of the Lord begins with the Tribulation period; (4) when the Holy Spirit is removed, the church is removed (or, although it strains the text, the Holy Spirit is removed when the church is removed). Therefore, it is argued the Rapture is pretribulational.

Pentecost spoke of the restrainer this way:

> Explanations as to the person of this Restrainer such as human government, law, the visible church will not suffice, for they will all continue in a measure after the manifestation of this lawless one. While this is essentially an exegetical problem, it would seem that the only One who could do such a restraining ministry would be the Holy Spirit.[10]

## REBUTTAL 9

In answer to this argument frequently raised by pretribulationists, three points will be contested. In fairness, however, it must be noted that Ryrie, along with others, reflects a more moderate position. He states:

> Antichrist is now being held back by a restrainer. Some understand this to be God indwelling His Church by the Holy Spirit, while others see human government as the restraint. According to the former view, the removal will be at the rapture of the church (1 Thess. 4:13–18); according to the latter, at the overthrow of human government by Antichrist.[11]

First, as has been repeatedly pointed out, the Day of the Lord does not commence with the seventieth week of Daniel. Its approach is said to be heralded by cosmic disturbances (the sixth seal, Rev. 6:12–13), and it begins with the opening of the seventh seal.

Second, the hinderer (whoever he may be for the moment) is not removed before the Day of the Lord. He is removed in the middle of the seventieth week with the occurence of the abomination that makes the temple desolate. Paul makes that patently clear. Speaking of the Antichrist, he wrote, "Who opposeth and exalteth himself above all that is called God, or that is worshiped, so that he, as God, sitteth in the temple of God, showing himself that he is God. Remember ye not that, when I was yet with you, I told you these things?" (2 Thess. 2:4–5).

It is in connection with that event which occurs in the middle of the seventieth week, not at its beginning, that Paul teaches concerning the one who hinders (2 Thess. 2:6–9). The hindering is associated with the events of the Great Tribulation, not with the entire seven-year period.

Third, of paramount importance is the identification of the one who restrains or hinders the Antichrist until "he [the restrainer] be taken out of the way." The restrainer is neither the Holy Spirit nor human government. Evidence is strained to support either of those contentions. There is, however, substantial evidence to identify the restrainer. He who restrains until "he be taken out of the way" is the archangel Michael. The following evidence will substantiate that fact.

1. The archangel Michael has long been recognized by both Jewish and Christian scholars as having a special guardian relationship to Israel (Dan. 10:12–13). In relation to Israel, he is called "Michael, your prince" (Dan. 10:21). His name means *Who is like God?* almost as if in contrast to Satan who desires to be "like the Most High" (Isa. 14:14). Daniel is told that Michael is "the great prince who standeth [present continuous tense; that is, he continues to stand] for the children of thy people" (Dan. 12:1).

2. Revelation 12 describes a war that occurs in heaven. The time for that conflict can be pinpointed at precisely the middle of the seventieth week of Daniel (Rev. 12:6, 13–14). It is described this way:

> And there was war in heaven; Michael and his angels fought against the dragon, and the dragon fought and his angels, and [the dragon] prevailed not, neither was their place found any more in heaven . . . And when the dragon saw that he was cast unto the earth, he persecuted the woman who brought forth the male child. (Rev. 12:7–8, 13)

The woman represents Israel, who gave Christ (the male child) to the world (Rev. 12:5) and who will be severely persecuted during the Great Tribulation (Rev. 12:13–17).

3. Speaking of this one who will hinder the Antichrist, Paul said, "only he who now hindereth will continue to hinder until he be taken out of the way" (2 Thess. 2:7). The word *hindereth* means *to hold down,* and the phrase *taken out of the way* means *to step aside*. Therefore, the one who had the job of hindering the Antichrist will step aside; that is, he will no longer be a restraint between the Antichrist and those the Antichrist is persecuting.

4. The Bible is explicit that the archangel Michael is the personage who will *step aside*. Daniel records that event this way: "And at that time shall Michael stand up, the great prince who standeth for the children of thy people, and there shall be a time of trouble, such as never was since there was a nation even to that same time" (Dan. 12:1).

It is important to note *when* this event occurs. The preceding verse says, "And he shall plant the tabernacles of his palace between the seas in the glorious holy mountain" (Dan. 11:45). This can only refer to the Antichrist, who will establish his headquarters between the Dead Sea and the Mediterranean Sea on the glorious mountain—Jerusalem. This occurs in the middle of the seventieth week in connection with his desecration of the temple and erection of a statue of himself.

Further, Daniel has already said that Michael will stand up during "a time of trouble, such as never was since there was a nation even to that same time." The unprecedented time of trouble can only refer to the Great Tribulation. Since Daniel is told that this great trouble relates to his people—and his people are the Jews—this can only be "the time of Jacob's trouble" (Jer. 30:7), which is a synonym for the Great Tribulation. It is at that time that the archangel Michael will stand up.

But what does the Hebrew word for *stand up (amad)* mean? Rashi, one of Israel's greatest scholars and one who had no concern regarding the issue of the timing of the Rapture under discussion in this book, understood *stand up* to literally mean *stand still*.[12] The meaning, according to one of Israel's greatest scholars, would be to *stand aside* or *be inactive*. Michael, the guardian of Israel, had earlier fought for her (Dan. 10:13, 21), but now this one "who standeth for the children of thy [Daniel's] people" would stand still or stand aside. He would not help; he would not restrain; he would not hold down. The Midrash, commenting on this verse, says, "The Holy One, Blessed be He, said to Michael, 'You are silent? You do not defend my children.'"[13]

Other biblical instances of *stand up (amad)* meaning *to be still* or *desist* are "they . . . stood still [desisted], and answered no more" (Job 32:16); and again, "And Ezra opened the book in the sight of all the people (for he was above all the people); and when he opened it, all the people stood up" (Neh. 8:5). Commenting on this verse, Rashi indicates that the people kept quiet (stood still) while Ezra read the Torah.[14]

5. That special guardian relationship which Michael has with Israel is again underscored in a sometimes obscure comment made by Jude, the half brother of the Lord. He wrote, "Yet Michael, the archangel, when contending with the devil he disputed about the body of Moses" (Jude 9).

Further, Moses is thought by many Bible teachers to be one of the two witnesses of Revelation 11. Concerning these two witnesses, God said, "And I will give power unto my two witnesses, and they shall prophesy a thousand two hundred and threescore days [three and one-half years, based on the Jewish calendar of twelve thirty-day months to a year], clothed in sackcloth" (Rev. 11:3). In that light, Michael's conflict with Satan over the body of Moses, as guardian of Israel, once again impacts the precise time of the Great Tribulation and the occasion when the restrainer will step aside.

Some clear facts begin to emerge.

a. The archangel Michael has a special guardian relationship to Israel. He has fought on her behalf in the past (Dan. 10:13, 21; 12:1; Jude 9).

b. In the middle of the seventieth week of Daniel (the Tribulation period), there will be war in heaven. Satan and his fallen angels will be defeated by Michael and the faithful angels (Rev. 12:7–17). Satan will be cast out of heaven to the earth (Rev. 12:13), and, knowing that he has a short period of time (three and one-half years), he will seek to persecute the woman (Israel) who gave physical birth to the man child (Christ, Rev. 12:13). To that end, Satan will personally empower the Antichrist. The Antichrist will erect an image of himself in the temple at Jerusalem and demand that the Jews bow down to this image and worship. That event, three and one-half years into the seventieth week of Daniel, commences "the time of Jacob's trouble," or the Great Tribulation.

c. And what of Michael, the guardian and protector of Israel? What action will he take on this occasion? The apostle Paul is precise in giving an answer, and there can be no doubt that he has Daniel 12 in mind (that is, the Old Testament text which describes the same event Paul is discussing):

> For the mystery of iniquity doth already work (that is, the spirit of Antichrist was already present, cf. 1 John 4:3); only he who now hindereth will continue to hinder (that is, Michael, who restrains the power of Satan in regard to Israel, will continue to do so) until he be taken out of the way. (2 Thess. 2:7)

The archangel Michael will *step aside,* he will *desist* from helping Israel. That is why this period is called "the time of Jacob's [Israel's] trouble." That is what Daniel recorded Michael would do (Dan. 12:1), and that is precisely what Paul affirmed (2 Thess. 2:7). When that occurs, "then shall that wicked one [the Antichrist] be revealed, whom the Lord shall consume with the spirit of his mouth, and shall destroy with the brightness of his coming [*parousia*]" (2 Thess. 2:8). That destruction will occur during the Day of the Lord. The Antichrist's coming, working, and power are detailed by Paul: "Even him whose coming is after the working of Satan [because Satan, expelled from heaven and no longer hindered by Michael, is energizing him] with all power and signs and lying wonders" (2 Thess. 2:9). The explanation for Michael's inactivity on behalf of Israel—his desisting, his stepping aside—is then explained. Since Israel rejected her true Christ and refused God's truth, God will send on them strong delusion so that they will believe the lie (that man is God—humanism) and accept the false Christ. Paul put it this way:

> And with all deceivableness of unrighteousness in them that perish, because they received not the love of the truth, that they might be saved. And for this cause God shall send them strong delusion, that they should believe the lie, that they all might be judged who believed not the truth, but had pleasure in unrighteousness. (2 Thess. 2:10–12)

The strong delusion comes from God. It is His purifying judgment on Israel. That is why Michael will no longer hinder or hold down the wicked one; he will *step aside;* that is, from between Israel and Satan. The strong delusion sent by God is both a punishment for sin and a moral consequence of their rejection of the truth. Ryrie's comment is well-taken, "These verses reflect the Old Testament concept that God is sovereign even in the activities of the powers of evil (cf. Exod. 4:21; Josh. 11:20; 1 Kings 22:19–23; 1 Chron. 21:1; cf. 2 Sam. 24:1)."[15]

It is clear that the restrainer is neither human government nor the blessed Holy Spirit of God. The Word of God teaches that the restrainer is the archangel Michael, a faithful messenger and servant of God.[16] Therefore, the pretribulational contention that the restrainer is removed when the church is raptured cannot stand. The restrainer is not the Spirit. The restrainer is not taken out of the world; he simply ceases restraining. The restrainer does not cease his activity at the beginning of the seventieth week but at the midpoint. All of this activity fits, unstrained and perfectly, into a prewrath rapture of the church. The identification of Michael as the restrainer is by no means a new and novel idea. Michael is mentioned as the restrainer of Satan and the forces of evil as early as the first or second century A.D. in Greek magical papyri.[17]

## ARGUMENT 10

Many pretribulation rapturists argue that a literal interpretation of the Scriptures can only lead to a pretribulational rapture of the church. Pentecost represents that school of thought. He writes,

> Thus we can see that our doctrine of the premillennial return of Christ to institute a literal kingdom is the outcome of the literal method of interpretation of the Old Testament promises and prophecies. It is only natural therefore, that the same basic method of interpretation must be employed in our interpretation of the rapture question. It would be most illogical to build a premillennial system on a literal method and then depart from that method in consideration of the related question. It can easily be seen that the literal method of interpretation demands a pretribulation rapture of the church.[18]

## REBUTTAL 10

In response to that statement by Pentecost and often reflected in pretribulational writings, strong objection must be taken. Robert Gundry is a premillennarian and would argue that his posttribulation rapturism is based on a literal method of interpretation. Gleason Archer is a premillennarian and would argue that his midtribulation rapturism is based on a literal method of interpretation. And the premillennial, prewrath rapture presented in this work has employed a literal method of interpretation. It therefore does not follow at all that "a literal method of interpretation demands a pretribulational rapture of the church." That is like declaring the winner of a debate before the debate begins.

Simply saying that a literal method of interpretation demands a pretribulation rapture does not make it so and does not conform to the facts. Pentecost's statement is true of the millennial issue (a literal interpretation leads to premillennialism). It is *not necessarily true* that a literal interpretation leads to pretribulation rapturism.

## ARGUMENT 11

Many pretribulation rapturists argue that a consistent dispensational approach to the Scriptures leads unerringly to pretribulational rapturism. The logic follows this path: The seventy-week prophecy of the book of Daniel is related to Daniel's people, the Jews (Dan. 9:24). The first sixty-nine weeks end with the crucifixion of Christ. At that point, Israel's prophetic time clock ceases. With the outpouring of the Holy Spirit, the church age begins (Acts 2), and it will run its course until the beginning of the seventieth week of Daniel. At that time, God's program once again reverts back to Israel, and the church is raptured before that seventieth week begins—that is, pretribulationally. Again, Dwight Pentecost presents that view succinctly:

> Since the church did not have its existence until after the death of Christ (Eph. 5:25–26), until after the resurrection of Christ (Rom. 4:25; Col. 3:1–3), until after the ascension (Eph. 1:19–20), and until after the descent of the Holy Spirit at Pentecost with the inception of all His ministries to the believer (Acts 2), the church could not have been in the first sixty-nine weeks of this prophecy. Since it had no part in the first sixty-nine weeks, which are related only to God's program for Israel, it can have no part in the seventieth week, which is again related to God's program for Israel after the mystery program for the church has been completed.[19]

This position can be illustrated as follows:

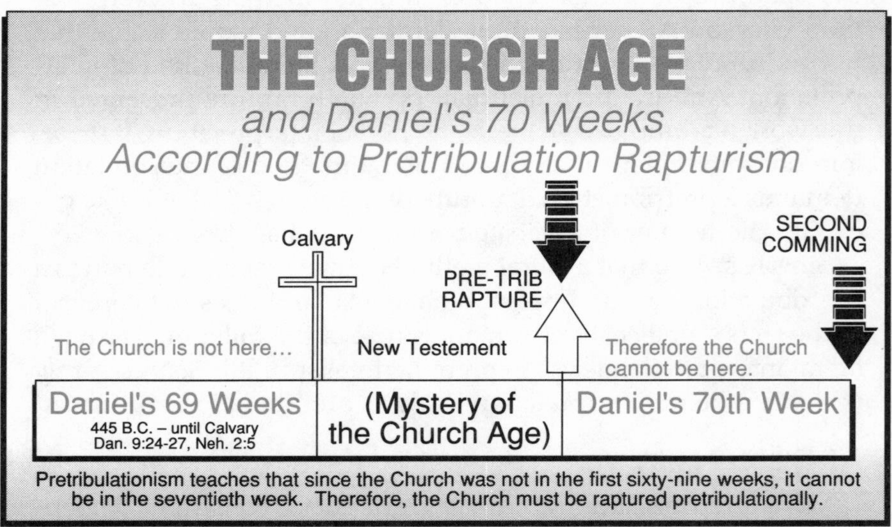

## REBUTTAL 11

In response to this argument, a question must be asked: On what basis can it be argued that since the church was not in the Old Testament, it cannot be in the seventieth week? Certainly not on the basis of the Bible! The church did not exist before the outpouring of the Holy Spirit at Pentecost, so the church could not possibly be in the Old Testament. The church does exist now, however, so it *can* be in the seventieth week. That is precisely what the Word of God teaches.

With the birth of the church at Pentecost (Acts 2), God did not immediately cease His working with Israel. Dispensationalists have always understood the book of Acts to be a book of transition from Israel to the church—from law as an operating system to grace as an operating system. The early Jewish believers continued to go to the Jewish temple for worship (Acts 3:1), and not until as late as Acts 15 did they begin to grasp the truth that believing Jews and Gentiles were one, in the church, the body of Christ (Acts 15:6–18).

Additionally, it would be impossible to defend the position that a Jewish man, living in Jerusalem, who was deemed righteous and acceptable before God under the Old Testament economy the day before Christ died, was, the day after Christ's death, unrighteous and rejected. Further, what of those righteous Jews living throughout the Roman world under the Old Testament Jewish economy who had never even heard of Jesus. The name *Jesus* was not a household word throughout the Roman world in A.D. 30. Would any suggest that they were acceptable before God the day before Christ's death and rejected a day later without ever having heard the gospel of the grace of God? The passing away of the old economy to establish the new necessitated a period of transition where, for a short time, righteous men of both economies co-existed. It may well be that God gave a biblical generation (forty years) for the transition—from Christ's death in A.D. 30 to the destruction of the temple and cessation of the priesthood in A.D. 70. During those years God had no trouble keeping Israel and the church distinct.

That is precisely what will occur when God begins Israel's seventieth week. It will again be a transitional period, in reverse this time, from the church to Israel. As Israel entered the church age, the church will enter Israel's seventieth week to hand off the baton to 144,000 Jews before the Day of the Lord commences (Rev. 7:3–9).

Rightly understood, neither dispensationalism nor premillennialism are infringed upon or injured by the church entering the seventieth week of Daniel to experience a prewrath rapture. It must be added, however, that godly men such as Louis Sperry Chafer, Arno Gabelein, and C. I. Scofield probably gravitated toward pretribulation rapturism because they were engaged in the battle for dispensational premillennialism, and, on the surface, pretribulationism aided and abetted their cause. *This surface defense of premillennialism was doubtless the catalyst for the rapid emergence and quick acceptance of pretribulationism by many early twentieth-century believers.*

# 19

# The Prewrath Rapture: Why This View Now?

Perhaps at this point an important question must be answered. If the thesis of this book is correct; if the church is to be raptured prewrath, at the opening of the seventh seal and, therefore, sometime within the second half of the seventieth week of Daniel, why has this position never been enunciated before? Why, only after more than nineteen hundred years into the church age, does this view appear on the scene? Is it simply a new and fanciful position set forth by an extremist? This is a legitimate issue deserving a satisfactory response.

First, it must be remembered that the evidence of extant historical records indicates that the early church believed that it would enter a period of severe testing before deliverance at Christ's return. In no sense is it claimed that the early church believed in a systematized prewrath Rapture as presented in this book. It is asserted, however, that the prewrath Rapture is consistent with what is factually known of the position of the early church.

Second, when word of the circumstances behind the writing of this book became public, the author received almost two thousand letters within an eight-week period. Hundreds of those letters (written by professors, pastors, missionaries, and Christians from all walks of life) indicated their conviction that the church would enter the seventieth week of Daniel to be raptured before the Day of the Lord begins. Some even pinpointed the starting point of the Day of the Lord with the opening of the seventh seal.

The central thesis of this book, then, is neither new nor novel. It is consistent with early church writings and held by many contemporary believers. The author has simply given a name to this view—the prewrath rapture—and integrated many isolated facts into a comprehensive theological system. In other words, this position's core is old; only its systemization is new.

Third, with regard to its apparent newness, some other important facts must be kept in mind.

To begin with, it must be remembered that no view of the Rapture can be said to be ancient with age and, thus, able to claim antiquity as support of its orthodoxy.

Pretribulation rapturism appeared on the stage of history little more than 150 years ago and arrived on the shores of America as recently as 100 years ago. If proponents of pretribulation rapturism want to explain that phenomenon by saying that prophecy over a period of 1,750 years had not yet developed and systematized, that is acceptable. But the fact remains, it is of recent origin. Therefore, pretribulation rapturism has no longevity to commend it as authentic, although, to be sure, some of its proponents speak as though it began in the early church.

Midtribulation rapturism is even more recent in origin. About fifty years old, it can make no appeal to age for support.

Historic posttribulation rapturism likewise can claim no early roots, although some have tried to root it in antiquity. Gundry's considerable modification of posttribulationism is less than twenty years old. What is clear from early church nonbiblical documents is that they were unclear as to the timing of the Rapture. But the evidence that does exist suggests the church would go through a period of severe testing before Christ's coming.

No Rapture view, then, can legitimately claim support for its position either from the early church or the church during the first seventeen centuries of its existence. Pretribulationists have not convincingly demonstrated the belief in imminency in the early church, even according to some of their own advocates. Posttribulationists have not demonstrated that the early church believed that the generation preceding Christ's return would endure seven years of tribulation. And the midtribulation position claims no early support. All Rapture views are "created equal" in terms of their pedigree based on antiquity, since all are of relatively recent origin. Here is an occasion where it certainly *is not* appropriate to say, "If it was good enough for Paul, it is good enough for me." Therefore, the question of the timing of the Rapture can only be resolved by an appeal to the Word of God—not historical precedent.

But biblical justification for the newness and systematizing of the prewrath Rapture can be demonstrated from the Word of God.

The twelveth chapter of Daniel is of tremendous prophetic significance and is germane to the Rapture issue.[1] The time frame addressed in this chapter can be pinpointed as the last three and one-half years of Daniel's seventieth week. That truth can be substantiated in the following manner: First, the preceding verses (Dan. 11:36–45) describe activity of the Antichrist during the first three and one-half years of the seventieth week, ending at the midway point; that is, at the time when he makes Jerusalem his headquarters. Second, the archangel Michael is said to "stand up [i.e., *stand still* or *desist*]" (v. 1) at a time of great and unprecedented trouble against Daniel's people. That can only have reference to "the time of Jacob's trouble" (Jer. 30:7), which begins in the middle of the seventieth week. Third, Daniel was specifically told that the time involved would be three and one-half years until "all these things shall be finished" (Dan. 12:7); that is, until the seventieth week is completed.

The prewrath Rapture presented in this book is in perfect harmony with Daniel's teaching. First, in chapter 12 Michael, Israel's great prince, shall stand up (desist or stand still) from helping Israel during the time of the Great Tribulation (v. 1a).

Second, following that, Daniel's people will be delivered. But then there is a qualification; that is, "every one that shall be found written in the book [of life]" (v. 1b). The word translated *delivered* (Heb., *yimmalet*) in verse 1 means *to step away* or *escape*. The same word is translated precisely that way in the preceding chapter: "but these shall *escape* [Heb., *yimmalet*] out of his hand" (Dan. 11:41). This escape of Daniel's people whose names are found written in the book of life occurs *after* the Great Tribulation. This escape or slipping away would make no sense if it occurred at the end of the seventieth week, for what would they be escaping from if Christ is present? This slipping away must refer to the Rapture before the Day of the Lord judgment. The Lord taught the same truth in the Olivet Discourse: "But he that shall endure unto the end, the same shall be saved [delivered]" (Matt. 24:13). The same idea of escaping is in view, and once again it would have no significance if it occurred at the end of the seventieth week. At that point in time, there would be no need for deliverance or escape. The deliverance, then, will be by rapture before God pours out His Day of the Lord wrath.

Third, a resurrection of the righteous and unrighteous will be associated with Christ's coming to the earth (v. 2).[2] *The Annotated Study Bible* has a helpful comment at this point:

> After the great tribulation (i.e., [in its view at] the end of the seventieth week) there will be two resurrections, one of the righteous to everlasting life and another of the unrighteous to everlasting contempt. A comparison with Revelation 20:4 shows that these two resurrections are separated by the one thousand year reign of Christ.[3]

The martyrs of Revelation 6 are resurrected at Christ's return; the unrighteous at the end of the Millennium.

Daniel is then told, "And they that be wise shall shine like the brightness of the firmament; and they that turn many to righteousness, as the stars forever and ever" (v. 3). Who are the wise? Who are those who turn many to righteousness? They will be those who will warn their contemporaries that the Antichrist is false; and they will lead many to the Lamb of God. What glory will be theirs—to "shine like the brightness of the firmament" and "as the stars forever and ever." The lovely hymn by William Crushing speaks of that future day.

> When He cometh, when He cometh
> To make up His jewels,
> All His jewels, precious jewels,
> His loved and His own:
> He will gather, He will gather
> The gems for His kingdom;
> All the pure ones, All the bright ones,
> His loved and His own.

Like the stars of the morning,
His bright crown adorning,
They shall shine in their beauty,
Bright gems for His crown.

This scene of glory and reward is not dwelt upon long, for quickly there comes the command, "But thou, O Daniel, shut up the words, and seal the book, even to the time of the end; many shall run to and fro, and knowledge shall be increased" (Dan. 12:4). Ryrie makes the following comment on this verse: "Not that its meaning was to be left unexplained, but that the book was to be kept intact so as to help those living in the future tribulation days."[4] The *New Annotated Study Bible* comes closer to the truth. It comments on the text this way: "It was impossible to understand the significance of these prophecies in Daniel's own day, but God indicated that at the time of the end many would seek to understand these predictions and be able to do so."[5]

*The command to Daniel to "shut up the words" (referring to his book) meant to keep it safe for the appropriate time*. Frank Gaebelein's comments are most helpful:

> In the ancient Near East, important documents such as contracts, promissory notes, and deeds of conveyance were written out in duplicate. The original document was kept in a secure repository, safe ("closed up") from later tampering, in order to conserve the interests and rights of all parties to the transaction.[6]

*The command to "seal the book" provided a second safeguard. It was to authenticate the truth within the book*. The practice of sealing an important document was well-known in the Near East. A recording scribe would write down what his client requested. An attesting scribe would read and confirm that everything was written as requested. The document would then be sealed, attesting to its accuracy. In the case of the prophet Daniel, he was to certify by the sealing of the book of Daniel that it was an accurate transcript of what God had communicated to him. Thus, in commanding Daniel to "shut up the words," God was guaranteeing its preservation; and in commanding him to "seal the book," God was guaranteeing its accuracy. This unusual measure was taken so that those living during the latter days will have God's truth to warn and sustain them.

Daniel was informed that at the time of the end "many shall run to and fro, and knowledge shall be increased." The running to and fro has nothing to do with increased travel and a shrinking world as an indicator of end times, as some have suggested. The running to and fro is speaking of an increased interest in and study of the prophetic word, particularly at the end of the age. One writer, commenting on the phrase "shall run to and fro," suggested that the running to and fro was "mentally with a view to discovering the secrets hidden behind the words which are shut up in the book that is sealed." As a result of that intensified study at the time of the end, "knowledge shall be increased." This increased knowledge is not of a general nature. It is not the accumulated facts of history or a giant step forward in the sciences. It is theological. It is knowledge of the events of the seventieth week as prophesied by Daniel. They will be better comprehended in the latter days. All one need do is look at the myriad of contradictory interpretations of the book of Daniel—often by men of the same theological persuasion, to see this substantiated.

Thus, in commanding Daniel to "shut up the words," God was guaranteeing its preservation; and in commanding him to "seal the book," God was guaranteeing its accuracy.

As Daniel looked, he beheld two angels (Dan. 12:5). They stood, each on the opposite shores of the Tigris River, a wide body of water—which indicated that these angels were far apart. One gets the sense of two choirs singing antiphonally. Between the two angels, a third angel was suspended above the river. Higher in rank than the other two, this angel was the one who was responsible for giving the prophetic vision to Daniel (Dan. 10:1–14). One of the two angels on the riverbank inquired, "How long shall it be to the end of these wonders?" (12:6)—not "How long will it be until these wonders begin?" but "How long will they last once they commence?" The superior angel situated above the water lifted his right hand and his left toward heaven and took a solemn oath (v. 7). Concerning this oath, one commentator has written, "Whereas it was usual to lift one's hand (singular) in taking an oath (Gen. 14:22; Ex. 6:8; Ezek. 20:5), here the heavenly messenger raised both his right hand and his left hand toward heaven, as the more complete guarantee of the truth of what is about to be affirmed."[7]

This majestic angel solemnly swore in the name of the eternal God that the events of the prophecy will last "for a time, times, and an half [time]," or three and one-half years (Dan. 12:7). Daniel was told that this will provide the Antichrist with time for "the breaking up of the power of the holy people." Commenting on this phrase, one writer has said,

> The angel thus revealed the reason for God's permitting the Antichrist to bring his persecution, namely, to break the power of the Jews. As parallel passages indicate, this power and resulting self-sufficiency [of the Jews] will need to be broken so that the Jews will be willing to accept Christ as their own rightful king.[8]

This observation provides perfect logic for the view that on this occasion and for this purpose, Michael will stand still—he will abstain, he will not fight for Israel. This is the precise opposite of what has been normally attributed to Michael on this occasion (i.e., that he stands up to fight for her) and it once again underscores the fact that he, not the Holy Spirit, is the restrainer who steps aside (2 Thess. 2:7).

What is going to happen to my people? How is it all going to end? That was the burden of his heart and the heart of his question.

But Daniel did not fully comprehend the ultimate outcome of the matter. The power of his beloved people would be broken by the Antichrist—but what then? Was that to be the ignominious end of his nation? And so it is recorded of Daniel, "And I heard, but I understood not. Then said I, O my Lord, what shall be the end of these things?" (Dan. 12:8). What is going to happen to my people? How is it all going to end? That was the burden of his heart and the heart of his question. The response was quick in coming from the angel: "And he said, Go thy way, Daniel." The idea is, desist from any further inquiry into the matter. And then the reason is given: "for the words are closed up and sealed till the time of the end" (v. 9). Daniel was reminded again that the words of his prophecy were shut up (locked in the vault of God's omnipotence) and sealed (recorded exactly as God had given them to him) until the time of the end (v. 4). The message would be faithfully preserved for his brethren who will desperately need it during the Great Tribulation. It will become their map and compass—their very lifeline to eternal life. Daniel was not given all the answers he sought. But his beloved people, for whose welfare he was greatly concerned, would have the benefit of the truth which he helped bequeath to them and which is doubtless expanded upon in the book of Revelation.

But the angel's explanation concerning "the time of the end" was not yet complete. He added these words: "Many shall be purified, and made white, and tested, but the wicked shall do wickedly; and none of the wicked shall understand, but the wise shall understand" (v. 10). Here, now, is revealed the ultimate purpose for "the time of Jacob's trouble." Satan will see it as an occasion to annihilate the Jewish race—to destroy the people who gave birth to the Son of God. And God, in infinite wisdom, will permit it for the purging, redeeming, and refining of the Jewish nation. The comment by Leon Wood is to the point:

> The angel was still referring to the events in the tribulation week. Daniel had just asked regarding events which will close this period, and the angel, though having refused the specific request, did add something of a general nature concerning the time. What he said is that during the last half of the seven year period many Jews will experience being "cleansed," "made white," and "refined"; and, since he employed the same verbs as used in 11:35, it is clear that he intentionally paralleled the development with that of Antiochus' day. As many Jews then [in the days of Antiochus Epiphanes] were "cleansed," "made white," and "refined," for a new and more devoted walk before God, so will this be true of Jews in the last days to come. (Zech. 13:8–9)[9]

One cannot help but pause at this point and reflect on the words of the old chorus; "Some through the fire, some through the flood, some through great trials but all through the blood."[10]

At the same time, almost paradoxically, while a remnant is being "cleansed," "made white," and "refined," "the wicked shall do wickedly; and none of the wicked shall understand"; that is, they will be insensitive, oblivious, unprepared for the impending Day of the Lord judgment. The Lord spoke of that occasion this way:

> But as the days of Noah were, so shall also the coming of the Son of man be. For as in the days that were before the flood they were eating and drinking, marrying and giving in marriage, until the day that Noah entered into the ark, and knew not until the flood came, and took them all away, so shall also the coming [*parousia*] of the Son of man be. (Matt. 24:37–39)

In contrast to the wicked who do not understand, Daniel is told, "but the wise shall understand" (Dan. 12:10). The Lord spoke of these two groups in this very same context this way: "They that were foolish took their lamps, and took no oil with them; But the wise took oil in their vessels with their lamps" (Matt. 25:3–4). The wicked are the foolish; the righteous are the wise.

Next Daniel was told of two extensions of time beyond the last three and one-half years of the seventieth week. Commentators have largely ignored this extension of time or have spoken of it in very general terms. Yet, this period of time is crucial to the entire scenario of end-time events and Christ's second coming. It is a crucial concept in the interpretation of the book of Revelation. Daniel was told, "And from the time that the daily sacrifice shall be taken away, and the abomination that maketh desolate set up [that is, in the middle of the seventieth week when the image of the Antichrist is erected], there shall be a thousand two hundred and ninety days" (12:11).

That is an extension of the last three and one-half years (1,260 days) by 30 days to 1,290 days. A second extension of 45 days is then cited: "Blessed is he that waiteth, and cometh to the thousand three hundred and five and thirty days" (v. 12). The last three and one-half years is 1,260 days plus an extension of 30 days equaling 1,290 days, and a final extension of 45 days which makes a total of 1,335 days from the middle of the seventieth week. Why these clearly delineated extensions of time?

At Christ's coming, the Jews who survive the Day of the Lord judgment will be saved. It would appear that one-third of the nation will make it to that point in time. Of that day the prophet Zechariah wrote,

> And it shall come to pass that in all the land, saith the LORD, two parts in it shall be cut off and die; but the third shall be left in it. And I will bring the third part through the fire, and will refine them as silver is refined, and will test them as gold is tested; they shall call on my name, and I will hear them. I will say, It is my people; and they shall say, The LORD is my God. (Zech. 13:8–9)

The phrase *thirty days* has a dual purpose in the Scriptures. It is used as a time of national mourning and as a time for national cleansing. Concerning the death of Moses it is written, "And the children of Israel wept for Moses in the plains of Moab thirty days. So the days of weeping and mourning for Moses were ended" (Deut. 34:8). They also went into national mourning at the death of Aaron: "And when all the congregation saw that Aaron was dead, they mourned for Aaron thirty days, even all the house of Israel" (Num. 20:29). When Israel's national day of atonement occurs at Christ's return, when she realizes that the One she long rejected and despised was none other than her Messiah and Lord, there will be a time of mourning the like of which Israel has never known before. Their own prophet wrote of that day in this way:

The phrase *thirty days* has a dual purpose in the Scriptures. It is used as a time of national mourning and as a time for national cleansing.

> And I will pour upon the house of David, and upon the inhabitants of Jerusalem, the Spirit of grace and of supplications; and they shall look upon me whom they have pierced, and they shall

> mourn for him, as one mourneth for his only son, and shall be in bitterness for him, as one that is in bitterness for his firstborn. In that day shall there be a great mourning in Jerusalem, as the mourning of Hadadrimmon, in the Valley of Megiddon. And the land shall mourn, every family apart; the family of the house of David apart, and their wives apart; the family of the house of Nathan apart, and their wives apart; The family of the house of Levi apart, and their wives apart; the family of Shimei apart, and their wives apart; All the families that remain, every family apart, and their wives apart. (Zech. 12:10–14)

There will be thirty days of national mourning for sin when Israel realizes that Jesus—the One they long rejected, was in truth, their long-awaited Messiah. Those thirty days may also serve as a time for cleansing and preparation. Moses was commanded to provide an alternative time for sacrificing the Passover lamb. This provision was for those who were defiled under Jewish law or who were away on a journey. This alternative date was to occur thirty days after the normal slaying of the Passover lamb. Instead of on the fourteenth day of the first month, it was to be offered on the fourteenth day of the second month—exactly thirty days later (Num. 9:10–11). Concerning that cleansing, the prophet wrote, "In that day there shall be a fountain opened to the house of David and to the inhabitants of Jerusalem for sin and for uncleanness" (Zech. 13:1).

The second extension of time is said to be forty-five days after the thirty days. Daniel was told, "Blessed is he that waiteth, and cometh to the thousand three hundred and five and thirty days" (Dan. 12:12). This is a total of seventy-five days from Christ's physical return and Israel's national day of atonement at the end of the seventieth week.

Bible scholars have long questioned the purpose for the seventy-five-day period. The Jewish calendar provides the answer. From Israel's Day of Atonement (Yom Kippur) to Hanukkah there is always exactly seventy-five days. Hanukkah celebrates the defeat of Antiochus Epiphanes and the cleansing and rededication of the temple. The seventy-five days of the book of Daniel speaks of the period of time between Israel's mourning at the end of the seventieth week when she realizes that Jesus, the One she long rejected, is her Messiah (her national day of atonement), and the cleansing and rededication of the temple, in anticipation of the return of God's glory. For that reason, those who reach that point in time are said to be "blessed" (v. 12).

Finally, Daniel was told, "Go . . . thy way till the end be," and he was given the promise that in the end he will be resurrected to see the fulfillment of this prophecy (the return of God's glory to the temple), "for thou shalt rest, and stand in thy lot at the end of the days" (v. 13).

Within the boundaries of Daniel 11:36 through 12:13, the events of the entire seventieth week plus the extended seventy-five days are brought into clear focus. Once again, the Rapture, as the first aspect of the Second Coming, is seen to occur after the Great Tribulation and before the Day of the Lord. This is illustrated on the chart that follows.

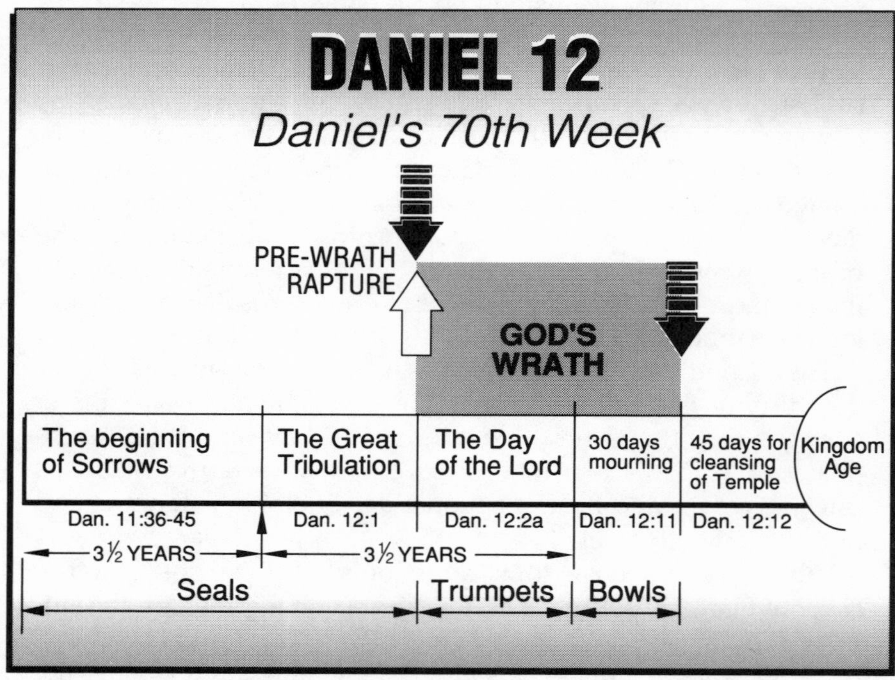


A number of general observations are clear from a consideration of Daniel 12. First, Daniel's prophecy was to be shut up—placed in a safe for security. Second, it was to be sealed by the prophet to authenticate its accuracy. These security measures did not mean that copies were not available for use, but that Daniel's prophecy would remain intact for use at the time of the end. This shutting up and sealing are to be understood in the sense of preserving the truth of the prophecy until the events foretold actually occur.

In the latter days, there will be an increase in the study of Daniel's prophecy. Men will run to and fro in their determination to comprehend prophetic truth. As a result, wisdom will be increased. Men will better understand the events of Daniel's prophecy.

If understanding of the events surrounding the seventieth week will increase in the latter days, as Daniel clearly teaches, then no generation has yet had the last word in the deciphering of prophetic truth. That may be humbling to some—but it is accurate. And it ought to provide a safeguard against division over the understanding of prophecy.

Daniel saw the course of history—of Israel and the nations, of righteous and unrighteous men, of God and His glory—and he wrote of these things before they came to pass.

Daniel wrote the book that bears his name in the sixth century before Christ. As he peered through the corridor of what men call *time,* he was given a glimpse of history before it was actualized. In particular, he saw what is described as the "times of the Gentiles" and the nations' relationship to Israel. He saw the great empires of Babylon, Media-Persia, Greece, and Rome. He saw the death of Christ, the destruction of Jerusalem, the sacking of the Herodian Temple, and the scattering of the Jewish people in A.D. 70. He saw the future emergence of the Antichrist, his covenant with Israel, his breaking of that covenant, and the desecration of the Great Tribulation temple. But in the end, he saw the millennial temple and the glory of God returning to His temple on Mount Moriah at Jerusalem.

Daniel saw the course of history—of Israel and the nations, of righteous and unrighteous men, of God and His glory—and he wrote of these things before they came to pass.

With the passing of time, as more and more of those prophetic utterances became historic events, Daniel's writings became more intelligible.

The miraculous resurrection of Israel from the dead by becoming a nation in 1948, her conquest of Jerusalem in June of 1967, her ongoing fight for survival, the animosity and positioning of her Arab neighbors, the interest and politics of major powers, the emergence of the European Economic Community, the religious and political dissension within Israel herself—all of these events are like pieces of a mosaic shedding light on the prophecy of Daniel's seventieth week. The closer to the seventieth week men come, the greater will be the potential for understanding those events.

Therefore, it is biblical to expect that added insight into prophetic events should increase as history moves unerringly toward the seventieth week of Daniel, the Great Tribulation, and the Day of the Lord.

The Rapture of the church cannot stand alone as an event which precedes the seventieth week of Daniel, a period of time so graphically portrayed in Daniel 11–12. Rather, the Rapture is but one glorious facet in the incomparable gem of the second coming of Christ and the final harvest. The righteous will be raptured; the unrighteous will experience the Day of the Lord wrath.

To recapitulate:

- No Rapture view is ancient and can, therefore, summon antiquity for its support.
- The book of Daniel was to be shut up and sealed unto the time of the end.
- As we approach the end of the age, there will be increased study and insight into prophetic truth, particularly as it relates to the seventieth week of Daniel.
- Finally, it should not be surprising that a new, more detailed, systematic approach to the timing of the Rapture and the events of the seventieth week would be forthcoming.

# 20

# The Prewrath Rapture: Catalyst for Holy Living

There is a spiritual application to the axiom "The same sun that melts the candle hardens the clay." The second coming of Christ will be like that. It will have two distinct effects. For those who have placed their faith in Christ, His coming will bring deliverance, spiritual union, and everlasting life. For those who refused His mercy, rejected His grace, and spurned His love, His coming will bring judgment, separation from God, and everlasting death (see Mal. 4:1–2).

On those crucial points, pretribulation rapturism and prewrath rapturism are in agreement. But significant practical differences do arise out of one's understanding of the timing of Christ's return. If the issue were only academic—a matter for intellectual speculation—this book would not have been written. Such, however, is not the case. It is the burning awareness of the practical implications related to the timing of Christ's return which has been the driving force for the completion of this book.

Not since the opening chapter have personal pronouns referring to the author been employed. Theology does not rest on personal opinion but on divine revelation. "Thus saith the Lord" is always the ultimate authority for the believer. This concluding chapter is not so much a theological defense as it is a personal plea. Therefore, personal pronouns in reference to myself are again employed.

**I plea for** tolerance in discussions related to the timing of Christ's second coming and the Rapture of the church. Godly men of great scholarship are divided on this issue.

In Walvoord's book *The Rapture Question* he has a concluding chapter entitled "Fifty Arguments for pretribulationism."[1] I will not at this point enter into a discussion of the strengths or weaknesses of his arguments. But I will make an important observation. Not once, among the fifty arguments, does this godly Christian leader cite one biblical text that explicitly teaches pretribulation rapturism—not once. This was not an oversight. The reason for the omission of any pretribulation rapture texts is clear. There are none. Walvoord's own comment helps substantiate that fact. He wrote, "It is therefore not too much to say that the rapture question is determined more by ecclesiology [the doctrine of the Church] than eschatology [the doctrine of last things]."[2] In other words, he is saying that verses which deal with the church must be used to prove an issue that relates to the prophecy. There simply is no explicit exegetical evidence for pretribulation rapturism.

Not once, among the fifty arguments, does this godly Christian leader cite one biblical text that explicitly teaches pretribulation rapturism—not once.

Ryrie, in his book *What You Should Know About The Rapture,* after introductory matters, assigns, by conservative estimate, 75 percent of his book to a refutation of posttribulationism. But once again, refuting posttribulationism does not make pretribulationism correct. Why this conspicuous absence of clear, exegetical evidence for pretribulationism by one of our finest scholars? The reason cannot be avoided—the facts are conspicuously clear because pretribulation rapturism is based on circumstantial evidence. By that is meant *inference,* a claimed literal method of interpretation, consistent dispensationalism, and the distinction between Israel and the church—arguments which are subject to convincing refutation. In light of such facts, and with the added reality that the *timing* of Christ's second coming (not the fact of it) is not a fundamental doctrine, the issue, although of considerable practical importance, should never be divisive. It is perfectly appropriate to have a strong personal conviction concerning the timing of Christ's return. I certainly do. But that should not become a badge of orthodoxy or a standard for fellowship.

J. Sidlow Baxter, writing on the timing of the Rapture, lamented, "Ten thousand pities that the glorious future event which is the Church's dearest hope should ever have been allowed to cause acrid heartburning among those who differ, but so it has. Why cannot those who agree on fundamentals disagree lovingly on the incidentals?"[3] And A. W. Tozer wrote, "Here is a doctrine that was not known or taught until the beginning of this century, and it is already causing splits in churches."

**I plea for** the almost Herculean effort required to achieve a measure of objectivity in any consideration of the Second Coming and Rapture issue. We who are theological conservatives say that the Bible is our final authority. In reality, however, our positions are often set in concrete, and we will not be budged, even if significant evidence warrants a possible alternative view. Any suggestion of something contrary to what we hold as correct sets in motion an emotional defense barrier that shuts out truth.

**I plea for** courage on the part of God's people to change their minds and move from the comfort of familiar ground if the burden of biblical evidence justifies such a move. Positions long and strongly held are not easily forsaken.

Now to a consideration of some of those important practical implications.

First, if the prewrath Rapture is correct, the church will enter the seventieth week of Daniel to encounter the difficulties of that period and the Antichrist himself. If it does so, having been taught and convinced of an imminent pretribulation Rapture, the consequences will be calamitous. The church will enter that period unprepared, spiritually naked, vulnerable, and ripe for the Antichrist's deception. The psychological implications will be disastrous. A questioning of the trustworthiness of the Word of God will naturally follow. It will be a spiritual catastrophe—a *Pearl*

*Harbor* of incalculable proportions—a satanically planned sneak attack.

Some will attempt to counter this charge by suggesting that the church is called upon to live holy and righteously at all times, and that, therefore, she should be prepared for any eventuality—even entering the seventieth week of Daniel, if that should occur. Such arguments are idealistic but not realistic. It is impossible to effectively train an army for a major battle if the soldiers are told they will never have to participate. Reservists who see little likelihood that they will ever see combat will never prepare like those knowing they may soon be sent to the front lines.

> The church will enter that period unprepared, spiritually naked, vulnerable, and ripe for the Antichrist's deception. The psychological implications will be disastrous.

Perhaps here is the ultimate error of pretribulation rapturism. It holds out the false hope of *imminent* rapture, instead of the true hope of *expectant* rapture. By *expectant* rapture it is meant that every generation since the first century could have been the generation that entered the seventieth week to experience the Rapture. Only the generation that actually enters the seventieth week will know the general time period. To that generation the Lord says, "So likewise ye, when ye shall see all these things [events of the seventieth week], know that it [His return] is near, even at the doors" (Matt. 24:33). A careful appeal to verses said to teach imminency (no prophesied events must occur before the Rapture) will reveal that what they actually teach is *expectancy*. Note many of the verses frequently cited in reference to Christ's return in the chart that follows.

The student of the Word will search in vain for exegetical evidence to sustain for *imminency*. That men should "wait for," "expect," "look for," "keep awake," "be free from excess," and "be alert," (and similar phrases) do not substantiate the claim that *no prophesied event* must occur before the Rapture. What Scripture does teach is *expectancy*—the belief that any generation could be

| *BASIC MEANING* | *TEXT* |
|---|---|
| Wait for, expect | Luke 12:36<br>Titus 2:13<br>Jude 21 |
| Await eagerly | Romans 8:23, 25<br>1 Corinthians 1:7<br>Galatians 5:5<br>Philippians 3:20<br>Hebrews 9:28 |
| Expect, wait for | James 5:7 |
| Wait for, look for, expect | Matthew 24:50<br>Luke 12:46<br>2 Peter 3:12–14 |
| Be sober, self-controlled | 1 Thessalonians 5:6, 8 |
| Free from excess | 1 Peter 1:13; 4:7 |
| To be awake, to keep awake | Matthew 24:42–43; 25:13<br>Mark 13:34–35, 37<br>Luke 12:37, 39<br>1 Thessalonians 5:6, 10<br>Revelation 16:15; 3:2–3 |
| To keep oneself awake | Mark 13:33 |
| To be on the alert | Luke 21:36 |
| To see, look at | Mark 13:33<br>Hebrews 10:25 |
| To wait for, expect, near | 1 Thessalonians 1:10 |
| At hand | Philippians 4:5<br>James 5:8–9<br>Matthew 24:33 |

called upon to enter the seventieth week of Daniel and there, in the midst of adversity, to remain true. But with the certain hope that those who endure to the end will be delivered by rapture before the Day of the Lord wrath is poured out on the unregenerate world. They will not know the hour or the day, but they *will* know the general time period. They are to be watching, waiting and ready, so that the Day of the Lord does not overtake them as a thief in the night. God never promised His children immunity from the trials of this godless world or the assault of the Antichrist. He did promise, "greater is he [the Holy Spirit] that is in you, than he that is in the world" (1 John 4:4).

Second, a prewrath Rapture which acknowledges that one generation of the church will enter and face the challenge of the seventieth week becomes a catalyst for holy living. That is the proper thrust of Peter's admonition, "Seeing, then, that all these things shall be dissolved [through the Day of the Lord wrath], what manner of persons ought ye to be in all holy living and godliness" (2 Pet. 3:11). A pretribulation Rapture that precludes entering the seventieth week and living right up to the Day of the Lord dilutes that incentive.

A National Football League coach was once asked if he held out incentives to his players, encouraged them, and got them mentally ready and *up* for the game. "Oh no," he responded. "They're pros, they know what they're supposed to do." The next season, with the worst record in the National Football League, the coach was looking for another job. The Word of God is saturated with incentives and warnings—the promise of blessing for obedience or cursing for disobedience, crowns or judgments. Men do not naturally do their best. The Bible is filled with *incentives for righteous living* (Gen. 12:3) *and punishment for unrighteous living* (Rev. 20:15).

Third, a prewrath Rapture of necessity appropriates for the church of every age the warnings of danger during the seventieth week. The pretribulation Rapture, by its insistence that the church will be gone before the seventieth week begins, negates those warnings.

I refer specifically to passages like Matthew 24:42–25:30 and the messages to the seven churches of Revelation 2–3. Concerning the former text, it must be said that this portion of Scripture poses problems for pretribulation expositors. A perusal of pretribulational commentaries will substantiate that fact. It is impossible to place the truth therein described before the Rapture if the Rapture is pretribulational. The chronology of Matthew 24 simply does not permit that. But, on the other hand, it does not make sense if placed immediately before the physical return of Christ at the end of the seventieth week, as pretribulationism normally suggests. They are on the horns of an unsolvable dilemma. The admonition, "Watch, therefore; for ye know not what hour your Lord doth come" (Matt. 24:41–42), makes no sense if this is attributed to Christ's return at the end of the seven-year period. Nor do statements like, "Therefore be ye also ready; for in such an hour as ye think not the Son of man cometh" (Matt. 24:44), or,

> But if that evil servant shall say in his heart, "My lord delayeth his coming"; And shall begin to smite his fellow servants, and to eat and drink with the drunkards, The lord of that servant shall come in a day when he looketh not for him, and in an hour that he is not aware of. (Matt. 24:48–50)

The reason these verses cannot refer to the end of the seventieth week is clear. Christ's physical return is precisely three and one-half years after the clearly established midpoint of the seventieth week. Men will know that Christ is about to return. This entire passage is composed of warnings inside the seventieth week prior to the prewrath rapture and commencement of the Day of the Lord.

These warnings are both sequential and logical. The Lord taught, "Then shall two be in the field; the one shall be taken [in rapture], and the other left. Two women shall be grinding at the mill; the one shall be taken [in rapture], and the other left" (Matt. 24:40–41). And underscore this admonition: "Watch, therefore; for ye know not what hour your Lord doth come" (Matt. 24:42).

The entire series of warnings that follow is directed toward watchfulness (Matt. 24:42–44), faithfulness (Matt. 24:45–51), preparedness (Matt. 25:1–13), and fruitfulness (Matt. 25:14–30). All are in anticipation of the prewrath rapture and Day of the Lord wrath inside of the seventieth week. For this reason, Luke adds, "Watch ye, therefore, and pray always, that ye may be accounted worthy to escape all these things that shall come to pass, and to stand before the Son of man" (Luke 21:36).

By its commitment to rapture before the seventieth week begins, pretribulationism totally negates these God-given warnings to the church.

The same error is made in the pretribulational approach to Revelation 2 and 3. These chapters contain the seven letters to the seven churches of Asia Minor. They were actual churches which existed in the first century. The apostle John was writing to them concerning problems which existed at that time. Technically, John was the scribe, not the author. The last book of the Bible is not, as in some versions, "The Revelation of St. John the Divine," but rather, "The Revelation of Jesus Christ" (Rev. 1:1). He alone is the author; the beloved apostle John served as the amanuensis, or scribe, of the Revelation. This fact sets the book of Revelation apart from other New Testament books. Paul wrote letters; Peter wrote letters; John wrote letters. They are part of the Bible—inspired by God. Only the book of Revelation (Greek, *apokolipse* meaning *unveiling*) is a direct communication from the Lord Jesus Christ.

Since the book of Revelation is a book of eschatology (the doctrine of last things), the letters to the seven churches must have prophetic significance. Otherwise, it would be out of keeping with the rest of the book and its expressed purpose to unveil the Lord Jesus Christ in His coming glory. With that in view, many pretribulational Bible teachers have suggested that the problems exhibited in the seven churches represent the recurring problems which would occur within the church during every age of its history. Ryrie states that position succinctly:

> The seven churches addressed in chapters 2 and 3 were actual churches of John's day. But they also represent types of churches in all generations. This idea is supported by the fact that only seven were selected out of the many that existed and flourished in John's time and by the statement at the close of each letter that the Spirit was speaking to the churches. (vv. 7–11, etc.)[4]

With all due respect to Dr. Ryrie, he appears here to be reaching where there is nothing to grasp. The twin statements that "only seven [churches] were selected out of many" and "the Spirit was speaking to the churches" give no basis for the position that the seven churches are, therefore, representative of the church in each age. That is simply an attempt to create a rationale for inclusion of nonprophetic letters to the seven churches in a book that is admittedly prophetic. The answer for the inclusion of the letters to the churches must be found elsewhere.

Coupled with the above position, many pretribulationists also hold that the seven churches reflect the prophetic character of Christendom during different stages of its history and development. Gary Cohen gives an overview of those stages.[5]

The seven periods are generally given approximately as follows:

> Ephesus—The Apostolic Church (A.D. 30–100)
> Smyrna—The Persecuted Church (A.D. 100–313)
> Pergamos—The State Church (A.D. 313–590)
> Thyatira—The Papal Church (A.D. 590–1517)
> Sardis—The Reformed Church (A.D.1517–1790)
> Philadelphia—The Missionary Church (A.D. 1730–1900)
> Laodicea—The Apostate Church (A.D. 1900–      )

> **There is nothing in the biblical text to even hint that the seven churches represent seven different periods of church history.**

The problem with this position, while held by many competent scholars, is threefold. First, as noted above, there is nothing in the biblical text to even hint that the seven churches represent seven different periods of church history. This is simply an assumption. Second, the view is subjective. Who is to determine when an age represented by one of the churches ends and another begins? Church history is not nearly that clear-cut. Which church historian is to be listened to? What dates accepted? Third, the designations Apostolic church, Persecuted church, State church, Papal church, Reformed church, Missionary church, and Apostate church are stilted and incomplete designations that do not conform to the total content of the letters to the seven churches.

Once again, an attempt is being made to give the letters to the seven churches prophetic significance simply because they appear in a book that is clearly prophetic.

How, then, should the letters to the seven churches be understood? Exactly as other prophetic truth is understood. The Lord Jesus Christ is the author of the book of Revelation. He is, among other things, a prophet. There would be nothing more normal or appropriate than for Him to follow in the train of the Jewish prophets. They frequently took a near contemporary event and used it as a frame of reference to project into the end times, there to discuss an issue of similar nature but greater magnitude. For instance, Daniel the prophet wrote of Antiochus Epiphanes who would persecute the Jews and defile their temple in 168 B.C. (Dan. 11:21–35). Then Daniel moved immediately to the end of the age to describe the Antichrist who will become the ultimate persecutor of the Jews and defiler of their temple (Dan. 11:36–45). The Lord did precisely the same thing. For instance, in Matthew 10, in connection with His first coming, the Lord sent His disciples out to minister throughout the land of Israel. He told them what to preach, the provisions to take, and the kind of response to expect (Matt. 10:1–15). Then, without any noted intervention, the Lord moved in His teaching to the end of the age. Speaking to His servants in that future day, He informed them that He will tell them what to preach, that He will be with them, and what results to expect (Matt. 10:16–42).

The seven churches of Revelation 2 and 3 were chosen from among many churches which then existed to receive letters for two reasons. First, seven is the number of completion and perfection, and, whereas in Genesis God's program is beginning and widening, in Revelation it is narrowing and moving toward consummation. Second, those seven churches perfectly illustrated the full-orbed strengths and weaknesses of Christendom during the seventieth week of Daniel. This commonality allowed the seven churches to be the springboard to give warning to Christendom at the end of the age. Therefore, John was commanded to "Write the things which thou hast seen, and the things which are [the seven churches which exhibit the same characteristics as Christendom in the last days], and the things which shall be hereafter [prophecy]" (Rev. 1:19). Only this view gives logical justification for the inclusion of letters to seven first-century churches in a book that is otherwise wholly prophetic.

Pretribulation rapturism, in its insistence that the church is raptured at the beginning of the seventieth week, cannot allow these churches to represent Christendom during the seventieth week. They are forced to find another way to interpret the letters to the seven churches. More importantly, as in Matthew 24:42–25:30, in so doing they negate the warnings which God gives for the church during the seventieth week.

In considering the status of the seven churches of Asia Minor (modern-day Turkey), a number of important facts should be kept in mind.

First, there is a promise given in common to all seven churches. If they are *overcomers,* they will be rewarded. To the church at Ephesus it is written, "To him that overcometh will I give to eat of the tree of life, which is in the midst of the paradise of God" (Rev. 2:7). To the church of Smyrna it is written, "He that overcometh shall not be hurt of the second death" (Rev. 2:11). To the church at Pergamum it is written, "To him that overcometh will I give to eat of the hidden manna, and will give him a white stone" (Rev. 2:17). A white stone was used in voting for the acquittal of someone on trial. Here the white stone suggests that the overcomer will experience acquittal before God (this occurs at Christ's return). To the church at Thyatira it is written, "And he that overcometh, and keepeth my works unto the end, to him will I give power over the nations" (Rev. 2:26). The phrase "unto the end" can, once again, only have reference to the consummation of this age which occurs with the beginning of the Day of the Lord. That fact is substantiated by the next verse (v. 27) which quotes Psalm 2 and refers to Christ's kingdom reign. Again, the phrase "to him will I give power over the nations" can only refer to events at Christ's return. To the church at Sardis it is written, "He that overcometh, the same shall be clothed in white raiment" (Rev. 3:5). This is an unmistakable reference to the Church, the bride of Christ. Listen to John's words: "Let us be glad and rejoice, and give honor to him; for the marriage of the Lamb is come, and his wife hath made herself ready. And to her was granted that she should be arrayed in fine linen, clean and white; for the fine linen is the righteousness of saints" (Rev. 19:7–8).

To the church at Philadelphia it is written, "Him that overcometh will I make a pillar in the temple of my God" (Rev. 3:12). This has reference to the ancient practice of honoring a magistrate by placing a pillar in his name in a temple, and doubtless, in this context, is referring to the millennial temple. To the church at

Laodicea it is written, "To him that overcometh will I grant to sit with me in my throne" (Rev. 3:21). Once again, a clear allusion to Christ's millennial reign is in view.

To overcome is to vanquish the enemy, to be triumphant over difficulty. The entire context of the seven churches is set in the arena of the seventieth week and the activity of Satan and the Antichrist. Of those who are truly triumphant, John wrote, "And they overcame him by the blood of the Lamb, and by the word of their testimony; and they loved not their lives unto the death" (Rev. 12:11); that is, they were willing to be martyrs, if being an overcomer required it. The only other time the word *overcomer* is used in Revelation is after all of the events of the seventieth week are complete. John wrote: "He that overcometh shall inherit all things, and I will be his God and he shall be my son" (Rev. 21:7).

Second, there is the clear statement to the churches that Christ's return is *at the door*. To the church at Ephesus the Lord wrote, "I will come unto thee quickly" (Rev. 2:5). To the church at Pergamum He wrote, "Repent, or else I will come unto thee quickly" (Rev. 2:16). To the church at Thyatira He wrote, "hold fast till I come" (Rev. 2:25). To the church at Sardis He wrote, "If, therefore, thou shalt not watch, I will come on thee as a thief, and thou shalt not know what hour I will come upon thee" (Rev. 3:3). This is the same exact warning given in Matt. 24:42–44, a clear seventieth week text). To the church at Philadelphia He wrote, "Behold, I come quickly; hold that fast which thou hast, that no man take thy crown" (Rev. 3:11). To the church at Laodicea He wrote, "Behold, I stand at the door, and knock" (Rev. 3:20). If pretribulation rapturism is correct, and the churches represent different periods of history, then the Lord was clearly misleading these churches in His comments of soon return.

The clear, uncluttered, normative understanding of the statements to these churches indicates that they are living at the very threshold of Christ's coming.

Third, to the church at Ephesus it is written, "I know thy works, and thy labor, and thy patience [endurance under affliction]" (Rev. 2:2). To the church at Thyatira it is written, "I know thy works, and love, and service, and faith, and thy patience [endurance under affliction]" (Rev. 2:19). To the church of Philadelphia it is written, "Because thou hast kept the word of my patience [endurance under affliction], I also will keep thee from the hour of temptation, which shall come upon all the world, to try them that dwell upon the earth" (Rev. 3:10). Later, in describing events irrefutably occurring within the seventieth week, it is written, "Here is the patience [endurance under affliction] and the faith of the saints" (Rev. 13:10).

Fourth, to the church of Pergamum the omniscient Lord declares, "I know thy works, and where thou dwellest, even where Satan's throne is" (Rev. 2:13). Pergamum was a center of Roman emperor worship, as well as a center for the worship of the deity Zeus Olympus. This latter "god" was an idol fashioned in the likeness of man. It was this deity which Antiochus Epiphanes evidently attempted to thrust upon the Jews. The phrase "where Satan's throne is" would, therefore, be most appropriate to indicate the worship of Antichrist during the seventieth week, whose human image will be erected in the temple and who will be empowered by Satan.

Fifth, to the church of Thyatira it was said, "Behold, I will cast her into a bed, and them that commit adultery with her into great tribulation" (Rev. 2:22). A reference to the Great Tribulation can be found in five New Testament texts: Matthew 24:21, 29; Mark 13:19, 24; Revelation 7:14. In the five times it is used, it is always used as a description of events that begin in the middle of the seventieth week. It would be logical, therefore, to conclude that the sixth use of the very same designation, the Great Tribulation, in describing events that the church of Thyatira will face would also occur during that same period of time—in the middle of the seventieth week of Daniel.

Sixth, to the church of Sardis it was said,

> And unto the angel of the church in Sardis write: These things sayeth he that hath the seven spirits of God, and the seven stars. I know thy works, that thou hast a name that thou livest, and art dead. Remember, therefore, how thou hast received and heard, and hold fast, and repent. If, therefore, thou shalt not watch, I will come on thee as a thief, and thou shalt not know what hour I will come upon thee. (Rev. 3:1, 3)

The church of Sardis is a dead church, and if it does not wake up, the Day of the Lord will overcome those in it as a thief in the night. This is a parallel to 1 Thessalonians 5:2 and the warning to be prepared: "For yourselves know perfectly that the day of the Lord so cometh as a thief in the night."

*It is highly doubtful that anyone who rightly viewed the book of Revelation as futurist would ever have suggested that the letters to the seven churches were not warnings to Christendom inside the seventieth week—were it not an absolute essential to have the churches removed from that period to sustain pretribulation rapturism.* But, to do so, one must ignore the clear and direct warnings to the churches, avoid the urgent atmosphere that is so prevalent in the letters to the seven churches, and sever chapters 2 and 3 from the seventieth week emphasis of the rest of the book.

If one understands that Christ's second coming is not *imminent* (no prophesied events must occur before Christ's return), as pretribulationism vainly asserts, but *expectant* (the events of the seventieth week, including Christ's return, can occur in any generation), as the weight of biblical evidence teaches, then these warnings become of great significance to every generation of Christians.

It is more than reasonable to expect that a concept as basic and as important as the timing of Christ's return should have clear, explicit, biblical substantiation. Pretribulation rapturism does not. The prewrath Rapture does.

It is more than reasonable to expect that a concept as basic and as important as the timing of Christ's return should have clear, explicit, biblical substantiation. Pretribulation rapturism does not. The prewrath Rapture does.

Men will scrutinize this book. They will search its pages, probing for weakness and vulnerability. That is appropriate, for all commentary must be measured by the Word of God. No inspiration is claimed by the author. Flaws may be found. Some i's may not have been dotted, some t's not crossed; some arguments may appear stronger than others, some flaws detected, and some important areas left untouched. That will be left for other Bible teachers to correct. But I am convinced that the basic tenets found within these pages will not be successfully assaulted. Its gates will not be breached. The prewrath Rapture is not built upon sand. It has the Word of God to sustain it. Winds may blow, rains may descend, and storms may arise—it will not fall. Within two years many men will be teaching the prewrath Rapture. Within five years it will be a recognized position. And, if God pleases, within fifteen years it will become a major position of the believing church—if God gives that many years.

The author strongly affirms the following principles:

1. The Bible teaches that there is a still-future seven-year period to occur. Within that period the Antichrist will arise, the Great Tribulation will occur, the church will be raptured, and the Day of the Lord wrath will commence. That time frame is called the seventieth week of Daniel, never the Tribulation.

2. The Bible teaches that there are three major sections to the seventieth week: the beginning of sorrows (Matt. 24:8), the Great Tribulation (Matt. 24:21), and the Day of the Lord (Matt. 24:30–31).

3. The Bible teaches that the Great Tribulation ("the time of Jacob's trouble") begins in the middle of that seven-year period but does not continue until its end. The Great Tribulation is cut short and followed by cosmic disturbance (Matt. 24:22; Mark 13:24–25).

4. The Bible teaches that Elijah (or one like him, if preferred) must appear before the Day of the Lord commences. If he appears before the seventieth week, there can be no pretribulational doctrine of imminence. If he appears after it begins, the Day of the Lord cannot start at the beginning of the seventieth week, as pretribulationism normally insists.

5. The Bible teaches that the apostasy and revealing of the man of sin must precede the Day of the Lord (2 Thess. 2:1–4). The apostasy and revealing of the man of sin occur within the seventieth week. Therefore, the Day of the Lord cannot begin before the first five seals are broken or at the beginning of the seventieth week.

6. The Bible teaches that a cosmic disturbance immediately precedes the Day of the Lord (Joel 2:31). The cosmic disturbance begins with the opening of the sixth seal. That occurs some time within the second half of the seventieth week.

7. The Bible makes it clear when the Day of the Lord commences. There is no guesswork. It will commence with the opening of the seventh seal. John wrote, "For the great day of his wrath is come" (Rev. 6:17).

8. The Bible teaches that the Day of the Lord is a time of unprecedented judgment upon the whole earth. It will also be a time for purifying Israel.

9. The Bible teaches that there is only *one* second coming of Christ—not one for the Rapture of the church at the beginning of the seventieth week and another seven years later at its end, as pretribulationism sometimes contends.

10. The Bible teaches that the second coming of Christ *(parousia)* speaks of a coming and continuous presence to accomplish a number of divine purposes. It will begin with the Rapture and be followed by the Day of the Lord wrath and the Lord's literal return to the earth.

11. The Bible teaches that the *end* or the *end of the age* is the time of the final harvest (Matt. 13:39). The final harvest is the time of separation between the righteous (wheat) and unrighteous (weeds, or tares).

12. The Bible teaches that the church is to remain on the earth until the *end* (Matt. 28:20). The *end* is always a reference to the end of the age (Matt. 13:39–40). The *end* occurs inside the seventieth week, not immediately prior to its beginning.

13. The Bible teaches that the *end* ("then shall the end come," (Matt. 24:14) commences with the opening of the seventh seal. The righteous (the wheat) are raptured (harvested into God's barn), and then the unrighteous (the weeds) are judged (har-

vested and burned) during the Day of the Lord, concluding with Christ's physical return to the earth.

14. The Bible teaches that at Christ's return, a surviving remnant of Jews will be regathered to Israel and saved. God's covenant promise to Abraham, Isaac, and Jacob will be literally fulfilled (Matt. 24:31; Rom. 11:25–26).

15. The Bible teaches that in connection with Christ's return, the nations will be judged (Matt. 25:32) and Christ's millennial kingdom established.

At the present moment of history, the planet Earth is in grave crises. This celestial ball is on a collision course with its Creator. Man has pushed the self-destruct button. Foundations of godliness have crumbled; things sacred have come unzipped. We have reached the day which the prophet had in mind when he wrote, "Woe unto them who call evil, good, and good, evil" (Isa. 5:20).

The church, which was called to be a royal priesthood, a peculiar people, is, at the present time, neither *royal* nor *peculiar*. Rather, it has stooped in character to commonality with the world and in lifestyle to similarity with the unregenerate.

Many pulpits, even among conservative evangelicals, are weak and vacillating. The fire has all but gone out. "Thus saith the Lord" has become, instead of a thundering voice, an almost inaudible whisper. The pastor, by virtue of his calling, should be the voice heard in the land. More often, it is the scientist, educator, philosopher, sociologist, or politician.

Many who name the name of Christ want the church to provide entertainment, not worship. They want the church to provide a hedged-in, antiseptic, country-club atmosphere, not a "Go out into the highways and hedges, and compel them to come in" philosophy (Luke 14:23). Apart from some notable exceptions, at the present hour the church is splintered, polarized, carnal, materialistic, humanistic, and impotent. The world is *burning*, and the church is *fiddling*.

If there is any hope for the present moment of history, any catalyst that can turn the tide, it is right thinking and correct theology concerning the events of the seventieth week of Daniel, including the emergence of the Antichrist, the Great Tribulation, the Rapture, the Day of the Lord, and Christ's physical return to the earth.

> If there is any hope for the present moment of history, any catalyst that can turn the tide, it is right thinking and correct theology concerning the events of the seventieth week of Daniel.

Pretribulation rapturism provides a false hope, however sincerely proclaimed—an escape before the seventieth week begins. Like sugared water, it may taste good, but it has no medicinal value. Even worse, it will keep the church from what can truly help—the urgent admonition to watchfulness (Matt. 24:42–44; 25:13), faithfulness (Matt. 24:45–47), preparedness (Matt. 25:1–13), and fruitfulness (Matt. 25:14–30). This generation of believers could find itself inside the seventieth week, there to have occasion to resist the Antichrist and stand true to the King of Glory.

The apostle Paul told the Thessalonians that the second coming of Christ is the blessed hope. That hope is based upon two absolutes: First, at His coming the dead in Christ will be resurrected; second, those living in Christ will be raptured, both to meet the Lord in the air and to remain forever with Him. Therefore, Christians are told to "sorrow not, even as others who have no hope" (1 Thess. 4:13).

In the face of death, pagans of Paul's day stood in despair. At best, they met it with grim resignation and bleak hopelessness. Antiquity abounds with testimony to that fact. Aeschylus wrote, "Once a man dies there is no resurrection." Theocritus wrote, "There is hope for those who are alive, but those who have died are without hope." Catullus wrote, "When once our brief light sets, there is one perpetual night through which we must sleep." On their tombstones, grim epitaphs were carved to record for posterity their hopelessness. One man had written, "I was not; I became; I am not; I care not."

Jesus is coming again. That is the blessed (living) hope. At His coming *(parousia),* He will raise the dead and rapture the righteous. Then He will pour out His wrath on the wicked before physically returning to the earth.

*Even so, come, Lord Jesus* (Rev. 22:20).

# Benediction

Sovereign Lord and heavenly Father, in the writing of this book Thy servant has done his best. The journey has been long and difficult—the valleys deep and the mountains high. For the privilege of the journey, I thank Thee.

And now, if it please Thee, Father, breathe upon this volume and give it life. May it cause a renaissance in the study of prophetic truth, a revival in the midst of a cold, vacillating, and worldly church, and a fire in Zion to bring salvation to many sons of Abraham, Isaac, and Jacob *before* the great and terrible Day of the Lord.

For Your glory alone, I ask it.

Amen.

# NOTES

**Chapter 1. The Tension and Anguish Surrounding a Consideration of the Timing of the Rapture**

1. Paul D. Feinberg, *The Rapture: Pre-, Mid-, or Post-Tribulational?* (Grand Rapids: Zondervan Publishing House, 1984), 61.

2. Richard Mahue, *The Prophet's Watchword: The Day of the Lord,* unpublished doctoral thesis (Winona Lake, IN: Grace Theological Seminary, 1981), 93.

3. John F. Walvoord, *The Return of the Lord* (Grand Rapids: Zondervan Publishing House, 1955), 51.

4. In the end, that friend would feel compelled to reverse himself. He became an advocate before the board against my remaining at the Mission.

**Chapter 3. The Options of "When" Laid Out**

1. John F. Walvoord, *The Rapture Question* (Findlay, OH: Dunham Publishing Company, 1957), 115.

2. Pretribulation traced to Margaret MacDonald. See Henry Hudson, *A Second Look at the Second Coming* (Massillon, OH: Calvary Chapel, 3).

3. Walvoord, *The Rapture Question,* 50–54.

4. Robert H. Gundry, *The Church and the Tribulation* (Grand Rapids: Zondervan Publishing House, 1973), 175–183.

5. John A. Sproule, *In Defense of Pretribulationism* (Winona Lake, IN: BMH Books, 1980), 18.

6. J. Barton Payne, *The Imminent Appearing of Christ* (Grand Rapids: Wm. B. Eerdmans, 1962), 90.

[info to come].

7. Sproule, *In Defense of Pretribulationism,* 23.

8. Walvoord, *The Rapture Question,* 9.

9. Such statements are being shared by a large and increasing number of godly pastors and laymen. The author's proposal for reexamination is based on an extensive pulpit ministry, particularly in the area of prophecy, which has given him a unique opportunity to observe this phenomenon.

**Chapter 5. But First the Counterfeit**

1. Had the glory of God still been in the temple, the soldiers of Antiochus would immediately have been divinely slain (see Lev. 16:2). However, the glory of God had left the temple because of Israel's grievous sin prior to the Babylonian captivity (Ezek. 9–12). Seventy years later, the Jewish people returned

from Babylon and rebuilt the modest temple which stood in the time of Antiochus. But nowhere is it recorded in Scripture that the glory returned to the temple.

2. Clarence Larkin, *The Book of Revelation* (Philadelphia: Edwin W. Moyer Co., 1919), 124.

**Chapter 8. And What of the Tribulation Period?**

1. Kenneth S. Wuest, *Wuest's Word Studies in the Greek New Testament,* Vol. 4, "The Exegesis of 2 Peter" (Grand Rapids: Wm. B. Eerdmans Publishing Company, 1966), 71.

2. Louis Sperry Chafer, *Systematic Theology,* Vol. 4 (Dallas: Dallas Seminary Press, 1948), 360.

3. *Ryrie Study Bible,* Charles Caldwell Ryrie, ed. (Chicago: Moody Press, 1976, 1978), 1243. Ryrie calls the entire seven years the Tribulation and the last three and one-half years the Great Tribulation.

**Chapter 9. And Then the Day of the Lord**

1. David L. Cooper, *Future Events Revealed: An Exposition of the Olivet Discourse* (Los Angeles: Biblical Research Society, 1983), 116.

2. *Ibid.,* 86–87.

3. John F. Walvoord, *The Return of the Lord* (Grand Rapids: Zondervan Publishing House, 1955), 51.

4. Zane Hodges, *Walvoord: A Tribute,* chap. 4, "The Rapture in 1 Thessalonians 5:1–11" (Chicago: Moody Press, 1982), 71.

5. F. F. Bruce, "Eschatology" in *Baker's Dictionary of Theology* (Grand Rapids: Baker Book House, 1960), 188.

6. *Zondervan Pictorial Encyclopedia of the Bible* (Grand Rapids: Zondervan Publishing House, 1975, 1976), 46.

7. Kenneth S. Wuest, *Wuest's Word Studies in the Greek New Testament,* Vol. 4, "The Exegesis of 2 Peter" (Grand Rapids: Wm. B. Eerdman's Publishing Company, 1966), 65.

8. R. V. G. Tasker, *The Biblical Doctrine of the Wrath Of God* (London: The Tyndale Press, 1951), 45.

9. J. Dwight Pentecost, *Things to Come* (Findlay, OH: Dunham Publishing Company, 1958), 229.

10. *The New Scofield Reference Bible,* C. I. Scofield, ed. (New York: Oxford University Press, 1967), 1372.

11. D. Edmond Hiebert, *The Thessalonian Epistles* (Chicago: Moody Press, 1971), 211.

12. William Barclay, *The Letter to the Philippians, Colossians and Thessalonians,* rev. ed., "Thessalonians" (Philadelphia: The Westminster Press, 1975), 204–205.

13. Richard Mahue, "The Prophet's Watchword: The Day Of The Lord," unpublished doctrinal thesis (Winona Lake, IN: Grace Theological Seminary, 1981), 93.

14. Pentecost, *Things To Come,* 229–31.

15. *Ryrie Study Bible,* Charles Caldwell Ryrie, ed. (Chicago: Moody Press, 1978), 1258.

16. Robert D. Culver, *Daniel and the Latter Days* (Chicago: Moody Press, 1954), 177–190.

**Chapter 10. Cosmic Disturbance**

1. *The New Scofield Reference Bible,* C. I. Scofield, ed. (New York: Oxford University Press, 1967), 1372.

2. *The Scofield Reference Bible,* C. I. Scofield, ed., (New York: Oxford University Press, 1909), 1349.

3. Louis Sperry Chafer, *Systematic Theology,* Vol. 4, (Dallas: Dallas Seminary Press, 1948), 398.

4. Paul D. Feinberg, *The Rapture: Pre-, Mid-, or Post-Tribulational?* (Grand Rapids: Zondervan Publishing House, 1984), 61.

5. Richard Mahue, "The Prophet's Watchword: The Day of the Lord," unpublished doctrinal thesis (Winona Lake, IN: Grace Theological Seminary, 1981), 93.

6. Charles C. Ryrie, *What You Should Know About the Rapture* (Chicago: Moody Press, 1981), 106.

7. John F. Walvoord, *The Revelation of Jesus Christ* (Findlay, OH: Dunham Publishing Company, 1966), 136.

8. *Tyndale New Testament Commentaries,* Leon Morris, "Revelation" (Grand Rapids: Wm. B. Eerdmans Publishing Co., 1974), 102.

9. William R. Newell, *The Book of Revelation* (Chicago: Moody Press, 1935), 107.

10. Gary G. Cohen, *Understanding Revelation* (Collingsworth, NJ: Christian Beacon Press, 1968), 84–85.

11. David L. Cooper, *An Exposition of the Book of Revelation* (Los Angeles: Biblical Research Society, 1972), 72.

12. John F. Walvoord, *The Rapture Question* (Findlay, OH: Dunham Publishing Company, 1957), 55.

**Chapter 11. Elijah Must Appear First**

1. *Ryrie Study Bible,* Charles Caldwell Ryrie, ed. (Chicago: Moody Press, 1976, 1978), 1800, note on Rev. 11:5–6.

2. J. Dwight Pentecost, *Things to Come* (Findlay, OH: Dunham Publishing Company, 1958), 310.

3. John Sproule, *In Defense of Pretribulationism* (Winona Lake, IN: BMH Books, 1980), 33.

4. John F. Walvoord, *The Rapture Question* (Findlay, OH: Dunham Publishing Company, 1957), 51.

5. *Ibid.,* 148 (This statement appeared in the first edition of *The Rapture Question* but was removed from subsequent editions).

**Chapter 12. The Day of His Wrath**

1. John Sproule, *In Defense of Pretribulationism* (Winona Lake, IN: BMH Books, 1980), 54–55.

2. Paul Feinberg, *The Rapture: Pre-, Mid-, or Post-Tribulational?* (Grand Rapids: Zondervan Publishing House, 1984), 59.

3. D. A. Carson, *Exegetical Fallacies* (Grand Rapids: Baker Book House, 1984), 69–70.

4. Gary G. Cohen, *Understanding Revelation* (Collingswood, NJ: Christian Beacon Press, 1968), 156.

5. *Ryrie Study Bible,* Charles Caldwell Ryrie, ed. (Chicago: Moody Press, 1976, 1978), 1673.

6. Note that with the opening of the seventh seal, the seven trumpets are immediately referred to in advance of their being individually blown. The seventh seal contains all seven trumpets, and once again they are understood to collectively represent a comprehensive whole—the last trump.

7. David L. Cooper, *An Exposition of the Book of Revelation* (Los Angeles: Biblical Research Society, 1972), 9.

**Chapter 13. The 144,000 and a Great Multitude No Man Could Number**

1. John F. Walvoord, *The Revelation of Jesus Christ* (Findlay, OH: Durham, 1966), 139.

2. The identity of the "great multitude" of Revelation 7 is not crucial to the prewrath rapture. The biblical evidence, however, strongly favors identifying them as the raptured church in heaven before the Day of the Lord commences.

**Chapter 15. The Apostasy and the Man of Sin**

1. John F. Walvoord, *The Rapture Question* (Findlay, OH: Dunham Publishing Company, 1957), 51.

2. W. E. Vine, *Expository Dictionary of New Testament Words,* Four Volumes In One (Grand Rapids: Zondervan Publishing House, 1940), 126.

3. 1 Maccabees 1:54–56; 2 Maccabees 6:1–2; *JPS Popular Judaica Library, Minor and Modern Festivals,* gen. ed., Raphael Posner, ed. by Priscilla Fishman (Jerusalem: Keter Books, 1973), 36–37.

4. This text has frequently been taken out of context, even by gifted expositors, and used to suggest that if the Great Tribulation were not cut short, all men on earth would perish. But the Great Tribulation is uniquely Jewish. It is "the time of Jacob's [Israel's] trouble." It will impact the world but will be centered in Israel and the Middle East.

5. This covenant cannot be restricted to Assyria, as some commentators suggest. The context makes it clear that the ultimate covenant in view is that made between Israel and the Antichrist.

6. William R. Newell, *The Book of The Revelation* (Chicago: Moody Press, 1935), 186–187.

7. Charles Caldwell Ryrie, *Revelation* (Chicago: Moody Press, 1968), 83.

8. The reader is reminded that the Day of the Lord, which includes the trumpets and bowls, has not yet begun to be poured out on the entire world. This is still the "time of Jacob's [Israel's] trouble."

**Chapter 16. The Coming and the End**

1. Lawrence O. Richards, *Expository Dictionary of the Bible* (Grand Rapids: Zondervan, 1985), 66.

2. Paul D. Feinberg, *The Rapture: Pre-, Mid-, or Post-Tribulational?* (Grand Rapids: Zondervan Publishing House, 1984), 80.

3. W. E. Vine, *Expository Dictionary of New Testament Words,* Four Volumes In One (Grand Rapids: Zondervan Publishing House, 1940), 208.

4. Richards, *Expository Dictionary of the Bible,* 68.

5. Some have attempted to diminish the impact of this statement of the Lord by suggesting that this is the opposite of what occurred during the Flood. At the Flood, the wicked were taken and the righteous (Noah and his family) were left. But here the righteous are taken and the wicked are left. Therefore,

the reasoning goes, this cannot refer to the Rapture but refers to the judgment at the end of the seventieth week. Such reasoning misses the whole point of the Lord's teaching—that men did not anticipate the Flood. But once it started, it was too late to get into the ark. And once Christ begins His coming *(parousia)*, it will be too late to escape the Day of the Lord judgment. The Savior was emphasizing one primary fact: the sudden, unanticipated separation of the righteous from the unrighteous at His coming.

6. John F. Walvoord, *The Rapture Question* (Findlay, OH: Dunham Publishing Company, 1957), 53.

7. W. E. Vine, *Expository Dictionary of New Testament Words,* Four Volumes In One (Grand Rapids: Zondervan Publishing House, 1940), 27.

8. Some have attempted to diminish the implications of this text by suggesting that here the wicked are burned first and then the righteous saved. Such attempts cannot be allowed to stand. At the end of the age, the righteous will be raptured and then the wicked judged.

First, it must be remembered that a parable is an earthly story focusing on one primary point. In this case, the point is that the wheat and weed will grow together, only to be separated at the end of the age. Second, the ancient Israelite farmer would gather the tares (weeds) in piles at the side of his field to be burned. Then he would gather up the wheat. When he was done, he would come back to burn the piles of weeds. The facts of the earthly story are accurate, and the sequence of end-time events (first the Rapture and then the Day of the Lord judgment) is not disturbed.

9. *Ryrie Study Bible,* Charles Caldwell Ryrie, ed. (Chicago: Moody Press, 1976, 1978), 1383, footnote on Matthew 24:3.

**Chapter 17. Kept From the Hour**

1. Robert H. Gundry, *The Church and the Tribulation* (Grand Rapids: Zondervan Publishing House, 1973), 54.

2. Douglas J. Moo, *The Rapture: Pre-, Mid-, or Post-Tribulational?* (Grand Rapids: Zondervan Publishing House, 1984), 90.

3. This statement builds on the argument presented in chapter 12 that the seventieth week has three identifiable components: the beginning birth pangs, the Great Tribulation, and the Day of the Lord.

4. It is understood that the mark on the forehead is given to the 144,000 Jews and is here employed figuratively.

5. The concept of partial rapturism is substantially based on the observation that the church of Philadelphia is "kept from the hour of temptation" but the other six churches are not. The church of Philadelphia, according to partial rapturism, is more spiritual and, therefore, worthy of rapture. The remaining churches have to endure part of the Tribulation for cleansing before rapture. The distinction partial rapturists make between the church of Philadelphia and the other churches is correct. However, it is not the Rapture which is in view but the Great Tribulation.

**Chapter 18. Are Pretribulation Rapture Arguments Really Unanswerable?**

1. Some have the church reappearing in Revelation 19:14, based on the fact that Christ is seen returning with an army from heaven. This army is better understood to be referring to angelic beings rather than the church (cf. Matt. 24:31; 25:31; 2 Thess. 1:7–9).

2. Here Walvoord's logic must be challenged. He teaches elsewhere that believers will be given their crowns at the Bema Seat of Christ, in the middle of the seventieth week. The text under discussion is three and one-half years earlier than the Bema Seat Judgment. Therefore, if the elders represent the church, it would not be fitting for them to be wearing gold crowns. They have not yet been given their reward.

3. John F. Walvoord, *The Revelation of Jesus Christ* (Chicago: Moody Press, 1966), 106–107.

4. Henry Alford, *The Greek New Testament*, vol. 4 (Grand Rapids: Baker Book House, 1980), 596–597.

5. Clarence Larkin, *The Book of Revelation* (Philadelphia: Edwin W. Moyer Co., 1919), 38.

6. William R. Newell, *The Book of the Revelation* (Chicago: Moody Press, 1935), 374.

7. Walvoord, *The Revelation of Jesus Christ*, 106.

8. *Ryrie Study Bible*, Charles Caldwell Ryrie, ed. (Chicago: Moody Press, 1976, 1978), commenting on Revelation 5:9–10 notes, "Many manuscripts omit 'us' in v. 9, and read 'them' and 'they' instead of 'us' and 'we' in v. 10," 1794.

9. Walvoord, *The Revelation of Jesus Christ*, 107.

10. J. Dwight Pentecost, *Things to Come* (Findlay, OH: Dunham Publishing Company, 1958), 205.

11. *Ryrie Study Bible*, note on 2 Thessalonians 2:7, 1706.

12. Judah J. Slotki, *Daniel, Ezra, Nehemiah* (London: The Soncino Press, 1978), 101.

13. Ruth Rabbah I.

14. Rashi from Sotah 39a.

15. *Ryrie Study Bible*, note on 2 Thessalonians 2:11, 1706.

16. The identification of the archangel Michael as the restrainer is not crucial to prewrath rapturism. The identification of the restrainer as human government or law (the view of the majority of scholars) would also sustain the thesis of this book.

17. This view is also mentioned in more recent sources such as *De Antichrist*, V. Hepp, 102, and W. Neil, *The Moffat New Testament Commentary: The Epistle of Paul to the Thessalonians* (New York: 1950), 172–73.

18. J. Dwight Pentecost, *Things To Come*, 194.

19. *Ibid.*, 196.

**Chapter 19. The Prewrath Rapture: Why This View Now?**

1. Pretribulation rapturism would not concur. In their view, the church is raptured before the events of Daniel 12 begin.

2. Jewish theology divided history into two major parts, the time that was and the time that would be hereafter (the kingdom age). Between the two ages, they understood there to be a brief period of sorrow and testing. The physical return of the Lord will initiate the kingdom age. At Christ's coming to establish the kingdom, the righteous dead will be resurrected; at its end, the unrighteous dead will be resurrected (cf. Dan. 12:2; John 5:25–29; Rev. 20:4–6). The latter phrase in Revelation 20:5, "This is the first resurrection," modifies v. 4.

3. *The Annotated Study Bible* (Grand Rapids: Baker Book House), note on Daniel 12:2, 1294.

4. *Ryrie Study Bible,* Charles Caldwell Ryrie, ed. (Chicago: Moody Press, 1976, 1978), note on Daniel 12:4, 1243.

5. *The Annotated Study Bible* (Grand Rapids: Baker Book House), note on Daniel 12:4, 1294.

6. *The Expositor's Bible Commentary,* Frank E. Gaebelein, gen. ed. (Grand Rapids: Zondervan Publishing House, 1985), 153.

7. *Tyndale Old Testament Commentaries,* D. J. Wiseman, gen. ed., "Daniel," Joyce C. Baldwin (Downers Grove, IL: InterVarsity Press, 1978), 207.

8. Leon Wood, *A Commentary on Daniel* (Grand Rapids: Zondervan Publishing House, 1978), 324.

9. *Ibid.,* 326.

**Chapter 20. The Prewrath Rapture: Catalyst for Holy Living**

1. John F. Walvoord, *The Rapture Question* (Findlay, OH: Dunham Publishing Company, 1957), 191–199.

2. *Ibid.,* 16.

3. J. Sidlow Baxter, *Explore the Book,* "Thessalonians" (Grand Rapids: Zondervan Publishing House, 1966), 218.

4. *Ryrie Study Bible,* note on Revelation 2:1, 1788.

5. Gary G. Cohen, *Understanding Revelation* (Collingswood, NJ: Christian Beacon Press, 1968), 48.

# SCRIPTURE INDEX

# ABOUT THE AUTHOR

If Marv Rosenthal were asked to present his credentials to justify the writing of this book, he would say that he is "a servant of the Lord." In that statement there would be neither false humility nor inflated pride. There would be a sense of amazement and awe, for no one knows better than he his own inadequacy or the rock from which he is being hewn.

Born and raised in a conservative Jewish family, Marv was born again by following the example of his godly mother while still a teenager. During a period of rebellion against God and things eternal, he served in the United States Marine Corps. This was followed with stints as a salesman and as a professional dancing instructor. Those years of experience sealed to his heart the reality of the solomonic revelation that, without God, "vanity of vanities . . . all is vanity" (Eccles. 12:18).

Repentance and restoration to fellowship led to Bible college and two years of seminary training.

Following his formal education, Marv served five-and-one-half years in an exciting, growing pastorate. For the next sixteen years, he was the executive director of The Friends of Israel Gospel Ministry, Inc., an international faith mission. In that capacity he was the editor of *Israel My Glory,* a leading evangelical magazine.

Marv has been in great demand as a Bible conference speaker throughout North America and abroad. He has traveled to Israel almost fifty times—most of those trips in the capacity of Bible teacher. Literally millions of cassette tapes of his expositional teaching of God's Word have been distributed throughout the world.

Presently, Marv is the executive director of Zion's Hope (a faith mission) and editor of *Zion's Fire,* a monthly Bible-teaching magazine dealing with Israel and the prophetic Word.

For more information on Zion's Hope or for a one-year gift subscription to *Zion's Fire,* write: Zion's Hope, P.O. Box 690909, Orlando, FL 32869; or call 1-800-4-ISRAEL.